"This is a book that leaders of all types of organizations should read. It explains the enormous size of the AI opportunity and the challenges in getting there. From banking to manufacturing and from fashion to mining, the impact of AI systems will be ubiquitous, like electricity and the internet."

—**DOMINIC BARTON,** Chair, Rio Tinto; former Global Managing Partner, McKinsey & Company

"AI may be to the twenty-first century what electricity was to the twentieth. Anyone thinking about our economic future needs to ponder its implications. This is the best book yet that considers what it will mean for all who participate in our economy."

—**LAWRENCE H. SUMMERS,** Charles W. Eliot University Professor and former president, Harvard University; former secretary, US Treasury; and former chief economist, World Bank

"AI will surely displace jobs and disrupt industries in the decades to come, driven by entrepreneurs who are implementing effectual thinking. The system-level changes that are on the horizon are excitingly discussed in this book, laying the bedrock for the oncoming revolution."

—**VINOD KHOSLA,** founder, Khosla Ventures; cofounder, Sun Microsystems

"It takes courage to dive in and a willingness to invest time to reap the rewards embedded in these pages. But it is so worth it. The book is a hugely thought-provoking and inspiring primer on how to shape strategy and design organizations in the age of AI."

—**HEATHER REISMAN,** founder and CEO, Indigo Books and Music

"This book is pretty damn epic. We're often told that AI will be the most important thing humanity ever works on, yet it feels abstract and niche in its current impact on the world. The authors show us how these two sentiments are not in tension. They provide so many unique and rich examples to really help the reader understand why on a limbic level. It's a perfect description of this counterintuitive moment in AI's history—a must-read for anyone who wants to peek around the corner into AI's future."

—**SHIVON ZILIS,** Director of Operations and Special Projects,
Neuralink; board member, OpenAI; former project director, Tesla

"Nobody provides more insight into the fundamental economics of AI and what AI truly enables. It's not just use cases for low-cost prediction—it's better decision systems. That's a much bigger step for business and the economy."

—**TIFF MACKLEM,** governor, Bank of Canada

"Agrawal, Gans, and Goldfarb have done it again! Their new book, *Power and Prediction*, is destined to become the definitive guide to understanding how and why AI is transforming the economy."

—**ERIK BRYNJOLFSSON,** Jerry Yang and Akiko Yamazaki Professor
and Senior Fellow, Stanford Institute for Human-Centered AI;
Director, Stanford Digital Economy Lab; coauthor, *The Second Machine
Age* and *Machine Platform Crowd*

"Whether we like it or not, artificial intelligence is set to influence every aspect of our lives. How can we make sure that individuals, companies, and organizations benefit from it rather than waste time and resources dealing with unintended consequences? This readable book provides an excellent introduction, emphasizing how AI can improve what we do by providing better predictions and helping reorganize systems."

—**DARON ACEMOGLU,** Elizabeth and James Killian
Professor of Economics, MIT; author, *When Nations Fail*

Power and
Prediction

Power and Prediction

The Disruptive Economics of Artificial Intelligence

AJAY
AGRAWAL

JOSHUA
GANS

AVI
GOLDFARB

HARVARD BUSINESS REVIEW PRESS
BOSTON, MASSACHUSETTS

The web addresses referenced in this book were live and correct at the time of the book's publication but may be subject to change.

Cataloging-in-Publication data is forthcoming.

ISBN: 978-1-64782-419-8

eISBN: 978-1-64782-420-4

The paper used in this publication meets the requirements of the American National Standard for Permanence of Paper for Publications and Documents in Libraries and Archives Z39.48-1992.

To our families, colleagues, students, and startups: you inspired us to think clearly and deeply about artificial intelligence. Thank you.

PART FOUR

Power

PART FIVE

How AI Disrupts

PART SIX

Envisaging New Systems

CONTENTS

PREFACE: SUCCESS FROM AWAY?

When we published *Prediction Machines* in 2018, we thought we had said all we needed to on the economics of AI. We were wrong.

Although we fully realized the technology would continue to evolve—AI was still in its infancy—we knew that the underlying economics would not. That's the beauty of economics. Technologies change, but economics doesn't. We laid out a framework for the economics of AI in that book, which remains useful today. However, the *Prediction Machines* framework only told part of the story, the *point solutions* part. In the years since, we discovered that another key part of the AI story had yet to be told, the *systems* part. We tell that story here. How did we miss it in the first place? We wind the tape back to 2017, when we were writing *Prediction Machines*, to explain.

That year, half a decade after Canadian AI pioneers demonstrated the superior performance of deep learning for classifying images, interest was exploding in the new technology. Everyone was talking about AI, and there was speculation it could launch Canada onto the world's technology stage. It was not a matter of if but when.

We founded a science-oriented startup program, the Creative Destruction Lab, with a stream devoted to AI. Everyone was asking, "Where do you expect to see Canada's first AI unicorn—the first AI startup to reach a billion-dollar valuation?" Our bet: "Montreal. Or maybe Toronto. Or possibly Edmonton."

We were not alone. The Canadian government was placing the same bets. On October 26, 2017, we hosted Justin Trudeau, the prime minister of Canada, at our annual conference on AI at the Creative Destruction Lab: Machine Learning and the Market for Intelligence.[1] In his remarks, he emphasized the importance of investing in clusters—geographic regions with diverse industry participants including large enterprises, startups, universities, investors, and talent, where the whole is greater than the sum of the parts, enhancing innovation and creating jobs. The key idea is that colocation matters. A few months later, his government announced significant funding for five new "superclusters," including one focused on AI based in Montreal.[2]

We felt confident in our beliefs about the commercialization of AI. We were, supposedly, world experts on this topic. We had authored a bestselling book on the economics of AI; we had published a swath of scholarly articles and management essays on the topic; we were coediting what would become the primary reference for PhD students in the field, *The Economics of Artificial Intelligence: An Agenda*; we had founded a program for the commercialization of AI that had, to the best of our knowledge, the greatest concentration of AI companies of any program on earth; we were delivering presentations around the world to business and government leaders; and we served on a number of AI-related policy committees, task forces, and roundtables.

Our perspective that AI should be viewed as prediction resonated with practitioners. We were invited to deliver presentations at Google, Netflix, Amazon, Facebook, and Microsoft. Gustav Söderström, head of product, engineering, data, and design at Spotify, one of the world's largest music-streaming service providers, referenced our book in an interview:

> [The authors] put it perfectly in their book *Prediction Machines.* Imagine the prediction accuracy of a machine learning system as a volume knob on a radio. . . . [W]hen you reach a certain point on that knob—when your predictions are accurate enough— something happens. You cross a threshold where you should actually rethink your whole business model and product based on machine learning. . . . With Discover Weekly we switched the paradigm from "shopping then shipping," to "shipping then shopping," the way [*Prediction Machines*] described. We had reached a level of [prediction] accuracy where we could switch from just giving users even better tools to playlist themselves, to just giving them a weekly playlist and let them save the tracks they really liked. We switched our vision from "even better tools to playlist yourself" to "you should never have to playlist again."[3]

Our approach—to design for a world where quality-adjusted prediction is very cheap—was of practical importance and provided valuable insight into AI strategy.

So, why were we so confident that the first AI unicorn would come from Montreal, Toronto, or Edmonton? We were in communication with two recent Turing Award winners (the equivalent of the Nobel Prize for computer science), recognized for their pioneering work on deep learning, who were based in Montreal and Toronto, as well as one of the primary pioneers of reinforcement learning, who was based in Edmonton. Canada's government was about to generously fund three new institutions dedicated to advancing research in machine learning—in Montreal, Toronto, and Edmonton. Many global corporations were rushing to set up AI labs in Montreal (e.g., Ericsson, Facebook, Microsoft, Huawei, Samsung), Toronto (e.g., Nvidia, LG Electronics, Johnson & Johnson, Roche, Thomson Reuters, Uber, Adobe), and Edmonton (e.g., Google/DeepMind, Amazon, Mitsubishi, IBM).

It's fair to say that we thought we knew a lot about the commercialization of AI. Yet, our speculation would have been wrong—a lot wrong. The first Canadian AI unicorn came not from Montreal, Toronto, or Edmonton. It would not even come from our second set of guesses—Vancouver, Calgary, Waterloo, or Halifax. If not from one of these cities—Canada's technology centers—then where?

On November 19, 2020, the *Wall Street Journal* ran the headline "Nasdaq to Buy Anti-Financial Crime Firm Verafin for $2.75 Billion." Verafin is headquartered in St. John's, Newfoundland. Very few people, certainly not us, would have predicted that the first AI unicorn in Canada would be in this town on the northeast tip of North America.

St. Johns, Newfoundland, is as far away from the action as you can get. Newfoundland is the easternmost province of Canada and has a population of only about half a million people. It is not on the technology community radar. In fact, even though the United States is Canada's neighbor, many Americans learned about Newfoundland for the first time when the hit Broadway musical *Come from Away* was nominated for Best Musical and in four other categories in the 2017 Tony Awards. The musical is based on the true story of what happened during the week after the September 11 attack, when thirty-eight planes were ordered to land in Newfoundland and the humorously kind residents took in the seven thousand stranded travelers "from Away." But it was there, in Newfoundland, that Brendan Brothers, Jamie King, and Raymond Pretty founded Verafin, which eventually provided fraud detection software to three thousand financial institutions in North America. How could we have missed this? Was it a pure fluke? Random chance? Even the experts get it wrong once in a while. Hindsight is 20/20. There's always some chance of a low-probability event.

What NASDAQ was buying was AI. Verafin had invested heavily and built tools that could predict fraud and validate the identity of bank customers. These were key functions of financial institutions both in terms of their operation and also in terms of their regulatory compliance. To do this requires big data, and bank and credit union data was the biggest of them all.

Upon reflection, it wasn't so random that a business like Verafin might lead the pack. It was inevitable. Our focus on the *possibilities* of prediction machines had blinded us to the *probability* of actual commercial deployments. While we had been focused on the economic properties of AI itself—lowering the cost of prediction—we underestimated the economics of building the new *systems* in which AIs must be embedded.

Had we better understood that then, instead of assessing the landscape of prowess in the production of state-of-the-art machine learning models, we would have instead surveyed the landscape for applications focused on prediction problems where the *systems* in which they would be embedded were already designed for machine prediction and would not require displacing human predictions. We would have looked for enterprises that already employed large teams of data scientists who had integrated predictive analytics into the organization's workflow. We would have quickly discovered that financial institutions were among the most prevalent, as they employed large teams of data scientists for predicting fraud, money laundering, sanction noncompliance, and other criminal behavior in financial transactions.[4] Then, we would have looked for small companies that were embracing the recent advances in AI to address these problems. We would have discovered that there was only a handful of such companies in Canada at that time. One was called Verafin, headquartered in St. John's, Newfoundland.

We realized it was time to go back and think more about the economics of AI. Verafin's approach followed the playbook of *Prediction Machines*.

There was no surprise there. What was less obvious was why so many other applications were taking so much longer to deploy at scale. We realized that we must consider not only the economics of the technology itself but also the systems in which the technology operates. We must understand the economic forces that led to the *rapid* adoption of AIs for automated fraud detection in banking and product recommendations in e-commerce on the one hand, but the *slow* adoption of AIs for automated underwriting in insurance and drug discovery in pharmaceuticals on the other.

We weren't the only ones who underestimated the challenges with implementing AI in existing organizational designs. Our colleague at the University of Toronto, Geoffrey Hinton, who earned the moniker "the godfather of AI" for his pioneering work on deep learning, also made forecasts that may have underestimated the difficulty in implementation.[5] He had previously quipped, "[I]f you work as a radiologist, you're like the coyote that's already over the edge of the cliff, but hasn't yet looked down so doesn't realize there's no ground underneath him. People should stop training radiologists now. It's just completely obvious that within five years, deep learning is going to do better than radiologists."[6] While he was correct about the pace of technical advancements—AI now outperforms radiologists in a broad range of diagnostic tasks—five years after his remarks, the American College of Radiology reports no decline in the number of new students training in radiology.

It began to dawn on us that we have entered a unique moment in history—The Between Times—*after* witnessing the power of this technology and *before* its widespread adoption. Some implementations are what we call *point solutions*. They are straightforward. For them, adopting AI is just a simple replacement of older machine-generated predictive analytics with newer AI tools (those are happening quickly, like Verafin), whereas other implementations require redesigning the product or service as well as the organization to deliver it in order to fully realize the benefits of AI and justify the cost of adoption. In the latter case, companies and governments are racing to find a profitable pathway for doing so.

We shifted our focus from exploring neural networks to exploring human cognition (how we make decisions), social behavior (why people in some industries are keen to embrace AI quickly while others are resistant), production systems (how some decisions depend on others), and industry structures (how we've hidden certain decisions to shield ourselves from uncertainty).

To explore these phenomena, we met with company leaders, product managers, entrepreneurs, investors, data scientists, and computer scientists implementing AI. We convened workshops and conferences with experts and policymakers, and we examined up close what worked and what didn't with hundreds of VC-funded experiments in the form of AI startups.

Of course, we also returned to first principles in economics as part of a blossoming field of empirical research on the economics of AI that hardly existed only a few years earlier when we wrote *Prediction Machines*. We began to connect the dots and assemble an economic framework that distinguishes between point solutions and system solutions that would not only solve the Verafin puzzle but also provide a forecast for the next wave of AI adoption. By focusing on system solutions rather than point solutions, we could explain how this technology will eventually sweep across industries, entrenching some incumbents and disrupting others. It was time to write another book. This is that book.

Power and
Prediction

PART ONE

The Between Times

1

A Parable of Three Entrepreneurs

Electricity changed our society. It changed the way we live, providing inexpensive and safe light with the flick of a switch and reducing the burden of housework through consumer goods like refrigerators, washing machines, and vacuum cleaners. It also changed the way we work, powering factories and elevators. What did it take to do all of this? Time.

The ubiquity of electricity makes it difficult to imagine that, at the turn of the twentieth century, two decades after Thomas Edison invented the light bulb, it was pretty much nowhere. In 1879, Edison famously demonstrated the electric light bulb and, just a few years later, turned on Pearl Street Station in Manhattan and lit the streets. Yet twenty years later, only 3 percent of US households had electricity. In factories, there was barely more (see figure 1-1). However, after another two decades, that number accelerated to half the population. For electricity, these forty years were The Between Times.

There was plenty of enthusiasm for electricity but not much to show for it. We tend to forget this when new radical technologies emerge today. When the light goes on, rather than everything changing, little does. AI's light is on. But we need to do more. We are now in The Between Times for

FIGURE 1-1

Adoption of electricity in the United States

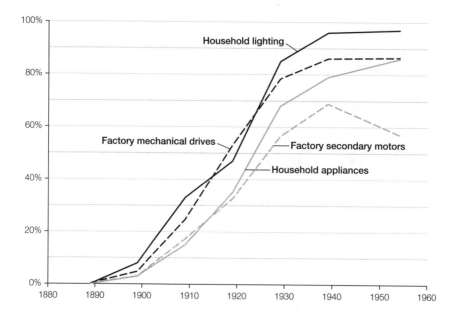

Source: Data from Paul A. David, "Computer and Dynamo: The Modern Productivity Paradox in a Not-Too-Distant Mirror" (working paper #339, Stanford University, Department of Economics, 1989), twerp339.pdf (warwick.ac.uk).

AI—between the demonstration of the technology's capability and the realization of its promise reflected in widespread adoption.

For AI, that future is uncertain. But we have seen the pattern for electricity. Thus, to understand the challenges facing the commercialization of AI, put yourself in the minds of entrepreneurs circa the 1880s. Electricity is the future. How would you envisage making it happen?

The Point Solution Entrepreneur

Steam powered the economy in the second half of the nineteenth century. Coal was used to heat water that generated energy, which was then immediately applied to drive levers, pulleys, and belts that in turn allowed for industrial production. By all accounts, steam was the miracle driving the biggest economic revolution since agriculture. So, an entrepreneur wanting to sell electricity would have to encourage would-be customers to take a closer look at steam and identify its warts.

When placed side by side with electricity, those warts were not hard to see. Steam dissipated heat—which was the point—but much of that heat was wasted. Steam power lost between 30 and 85 percent of its potential from condensation, leaky valves, and friction from using a shaft and belts to carry that power to workbenches.[1] The shaft system can be difficult to imagine. Think of a steam power source at one end turning a long three-inch shaft of iron or steel that then allows belts and pulleys to operate along the line. Some shafts may be horizontal, but many factories had multiple stories with shafts in a vertical configuration. One shaft could power hundreds of looms, for example.

The immediate opportunity for electricity was to provide an alternative source at the same point steam power was used—at the end of the shaft. Frank Sprague, a former Edison employee, saw this in 1886 when he developed one of the first electric motors. While Edison was focused on light, Sprague was among those who realized that daytime electric power would be cheap and electric motors could take advantage of that. Sprague used his insights to power streetcars and building elevators. Others took the motors into factories.

We call these "point solutions" because these inventors were taking steam and swapping it out for the new power source, electricity, at the point of entry to the factories of the time. The point solution entrepreneurs of the late nineteenth century found two types of customers willing to see electricity as a new source of power. One type was large steam-powered mills. A textile mill in Columbia, South Carolina, gave up on steam in favor of electric power in 1893. Hydroelectric power was a simple substitute for a mile-long cable transmission system. The power provided was the cheapest in the country.[2] Another type was clothing and textile manufacturers. The warts of steam were its lack of cleanliness and the potential inconsistencies in the speed generated by power. Electricity improved quality on both these dimensions.

The value the point solution entrepreneurs promised was lower cost and other benefits specific to certain factory types. That it was plug and play made it clear what they were selling. But in many cases, it was still a hard sell. Only so much of a power bill can be sliced off by changing a power source. What a point solution did not offer was *a reason to use more power.*

The Application Solution Entrepreneur

When a steam engine ran, it ran. An electric motor could be turned off and then back on. Thus, while steam power came down the shaft and individual machine operators engaged the power by activating various levers that attached and detached the machine, operators could simply turn on and off an electric engine linked directly to individual machines. This was simpler and required far less maintenance.[3] But, this meant that the amount of power a factory consumed varied depending on use. As economic historian Nathan Rosenberg observed, it brought about an era of "fractionalized power" where "it now became possible to provide power in very small, less costly units and also in a form that did not require the generation of excess amounts in order to provide small or intermittent 'doses' of power."[4]

The entrepreneurial insight here regarding the value of electricity was that it required less power or, more accurately, only power when needed. While this insight began to inform some changes in factory design, such as having separate power sources for different machine types, some engineers began to imagine electric motors available at each machine. But even for groups of machines, there was great value in only paying for power when the machines were being used.

The big change was to mount an electric drive on a single machine. These days we would call this an application solution. Rather than simply swap out a power source, the entire device (i.e., the application) was swapped out. What was more, some machines became far more portable. No longer wedded to a central shaft, the tools could be moved around. The work didn't have to come to the machines, but the machines could move to the work.

That was the promise; the reality was that any individual machine tool—such as a drill, a metal cutter, or a press—had to be totally redesigned to take advantage of having an individual unit electrical engine.[5] Moreover, the engines themselves were generally not off the shelf but had to be tailored to the particular machine or use. Application solution opportunities were abundant, but the devices had to be designed. What's more, if you design one tool in a factory with its own engine, that reduces the value of any engine powering other tools. Finding the right balance was obviously going to require the redesign of many tools. That, however, was going to mean creating a new system, which would take time.

The System Solution Entrepreneur

Throughout the entire Industrial Revolution, factories were designed to leverage steam. As we have seen, a single source of power into the factory was distributed to individual machines through a central shaft upon which belts and pulleys were hung. To modern eyes, this was one big machine with individual people inside as mere cogs. In its large form, it was a contraption where hundreds of moving parts were tied to a single entry point for power. Having a new type of power didn't change that. But having new devices caused some entrepreneurs to rethink the factory. Suppose there were no central shafts or even shafts dedicated to groups of machines. *What would a factory look like if you designed it from scratch, given what you now knew about electricity?*

Factories were built so that the machines were close to the source of power. That meant there were advantages to a vertical design with multistory shop floors. The cramped multifloor factories of the late 1800s had their own costs in terms of work conditions, safety, and machine performance. Electricity removed the need to squish all this stuff into small spaces.

More entrepreneurial managers realized that the true value of electricity would come from providing a system solution—specifically, a system that could take advantage of all electricity had to offer. By system, we mean *a set of procedures that together ensure something is done.*

Just think of the economics of space within a factory. With steam and its central shaft, space near the shaft was more valuable than space elsewhere. So work was done near the shaft, and anything else was stored and moved away. That meant real stuff was moved back and forth according to the demands of power.

Electricity equalized the economic value of space, providing flexibility. Now it was worth organizing production on, say, a line so that you reduced the mileage incurred in moving real stuff back and forth and, instead, from one process to the next. Henry Ford could not have invented the production line for the Model T car with steam power. Only electricity, decades after its commercial promise was shown, could achieve that. Yes, Ford was a car entrepreneur. But he was largely a system solution entrepreneur. These system changes altered the industrial landscape. Only then did electrification finally show up in the productivity statistics, and in a big way.[6]

AI Entrepreneurs

We can draw three lessons from this. First, the path to large productivity increases lies in understanding what a new technology offers. An entrepreneur pitching electricity in 1890 would have focused on "saving fuel costs"' as the key value proposition for the technology. But electricity was not just a cheaper steam engine. Its true value was that it provided a way of decoupling energy use from its source. That freed users from the constraint of distance, leading to a cascade of factory and workflow design improvements. An entrepreneur pitching electricity in 1920 would have figured out that the key value proposition was not "saving fuel costs" but rather "enabling vastly more productive factory design."

The same pattern is what we expect to see with AI. As we already noted, the initial entrepreneurial opportunities involved point solutions such as those of Verafin that swapped out one way of predicting for another that is better, faster, and cheaper.

We also see application solutions that require a redesign of devices or products around AI. All those robots powered by AI are applications, and so is much of the way AI has been implemented to enhance software on your devices. Consider your phone camera, which can identify your face. That requires a special camera as well as specialized hardware to keep that information secure. But perhaps the most apparent push of this type of innovation has been the billions of dollars trying to design and launch vehicles that can be self-driven in existing road conditions. While the cars may externally look the same, their internal hardware had to be reconstituted to enable sensor placement, onboard processing, and then machine handling.

What we have yet to see are the plethora of high-value system solutions for AI that are likely to emerge. This book will lay out the potential as well as the challenges in realizing such opportunities.

Second, once we understand that, we need to ask a fairly straightforward but potentially hard-to-answer question. Given what we now know about AI, how would we design our products or services or factories if we were starting from scratch? The new flat factory architectures did not emerge first in traditional industries but rather in the newly emerging ones in the 1900s such as tobacco, fabricated metals, transportation equipment, and electrical machinery itself. We see echoes of this in the early adoption of AI-centered system designs in the new and digitized industries of today: search, e-commerce, streaming content, and social networks.

For AI, we can ask these same two questions: (1) What is AI really giving us? (2) If we are designing our business from scratch, how would we build our processes and business models? If electricity was not "lower cost of energy" but rather "enable vastly more productive factory design," so too, perhaps, is AI not "lower cost of prediction" but rather "enable vastly more productive products, services, and organizational design." Whereas the primary benefit of electricity was that it decoupled energy use from its source, which facilitated innovation in factory design, the primary benefit of AI is that it decouples prediction from the rest of the decision-making process, which facilitates innovation in organizational design via reimaging how decisions interrelate with one another.

We argue that by decoupling prediction from the other aspects of a decision and transferring prediction from humans to machines, AI enables system-level innovation. Decisions are the key building block for such systems, and AI enhances decision-making.

The third and final lesson: different solution types provide different opportunities to obtain power in markets. Entrepreneurs profit when they both create and capture value. With point solutions, the issue is often that there is relatively little value created in the first place. Electricity was a power substitute for steam, but steam already had an installed base. It was not costless to swap out one for the other, and if you did, the value proposition for your consumer was a reduced power bill. In other words, point solution entrepreneurs can earn sustained profits from being best at providing that point solution—something Verafin demonstrated—but that is the best-case scenario.[7]

As we move to applications and then to systems, the value entrepreneurs create becomes more defensible. New devices can be differentiated from the competition and guarded with patents and other forms of intellectual property protection. For new systems, however, the potential is even greater. In electricity, the new factory designs were provided largely by those who owned those factories. In their own domains, this gave them know-how that allowed them to build market share and insulate themselves from competition. While a factory layout may be easy to see, the procedures, capabilities, and training underlying the new system may be less visible and hard to replicate. What is more, new systems can enable scale.

AI Disruption and Power

Electricity took decades to do what we call "disrupt." During its first two decades, it was used as a point solution in some factories and applications, and for lighting in others. But it only changed the economy when new systems developed. That change was profound and shifted power to those who controlled electricity generation and grids and to those who could use electricity at scale in mass production. You didn't want to be a manufacturer of belts and pulleys after that or a holder of downtown factory real estate.

We see the same processes at work with AI. Real shifts in economic power that move control over scarce resources and assets from one group of people to another are accompanied by an ability to shield businesses from competitive pressures. To be sure, there are opportunities to do that with AI, but the ones that will disrupt—that is, will reshape industries and who has power within them—come from new systems. New systems are hard to develop and also, as we will explore, difficult to copy because they are often complex. That creates opportunities for those who can innovate on systems.

But there is still considerable uncertainty. For AI, who might accumulate power from these new technologies is very much an open question. It will depend on what those new systems look like. Our task here is to light your way to anticipate who may gain and who may lose power as AI systems develop and are adopted.

KEY POINTS

- The parable of the three entrepreneurs, set over a hundred years ago and focused on the market for energy, illustrates how different entrepreneurs exploiting the same technology shift, from steam to electricity, can exploit different value propositions: point solutions (lower cost of power and less loss due to friction—no design change to factory system); application solutions (individual electric drives on each machine—modular machines, so the stoppage of one does not impact others; no design change to factory system); and system solutions (redesigned factories—lightweight construction, single story, workflows optimized in terms of spatial layout and flow of workers and materials).

- Some value propositions are more attractive than others. In the case of electricity, point solutions and application solutions predicated on directly replacing steam with electricity without modifying the system offered limited value, which was reflected in industries' slow initial adoption. Over time, some entrepreneurs saw the opportunity to deliver system-level solutions by exploiting the ability of electricity to decouple the machine from the power source in a manner that was impossible or too expensive with steam. In many cases, the value proposition of system-level solutions far exceeded the value from point solutions.

- Just as electricity enabled decoupling the machine from the power source and thus facilitated shifting the value proposition from "lower fuel costs" to "vastly more productive factory design," AI enables decoupling prediction from the other aspects of a decision and thus facilitates shifting the value proposition from "lower cost of prediction" to "vastly more productive systems."

2

AI's System Future

The year 2017 was awash with AI conferences. That deluge brought together business and governments, and also galvanized academics. Having realized that AI had the potential to transform economies, we wanted some of the best economic researchers in the world to think about AI. We organized a conference in Toronto on AI to set the research agenda for economists.[1]

To our surprise, we had no trouble attracting a crowd. Stanford University's Paul Milgrom, who would go on to win a Nobel Prize for innovations that spanned economics and computer science, recalled a similar invitation he received in 1990 for a conference on the economics of the internet. He had declined that one and regretted it. "I remember vividly when, in 1990, the NSF asked me whether I might be interested in working on the economics of the Internet, and I was too busy working on principal-agent theory, the economics of the firm, and supermodularity. So I declined. Ugh!" he wrote. "No excuses this time. Yes, I'll be there."[2]

Some of the participants were bullish on the impact of AI. Daniel Kahneman, another Nobel laureate, remarked: "I do not think that there is very much that we can do that computers will not eventually be programmed to do."[3] Betsey Stevenson, who served on President Obama's

Council of Economic Advisers, summarized the optimistic sentiment by noting, "It is clear that economists believe that artificial intelligence represents an opportunity for substantial economic gains."[4]

Others were more skeptical. Joseph Stiglitz, another Nobel laureate, was one of several worried about the impact on inequality. Tyler Cowen, an economist and former *New York Times* columnist, worried that AI productivity would increase scarcity in physical resources. Manuel Trajtenberg, who spent part of his career as a politician in Israel, noted that the long-run benefits of a technology are irrelevant if a revolution happens first, foreshadowing increasing resistance to machine automation and the popular perception about the impact on jobs.

One particularly interesting worry was that AI didn't seem to be having much impact on the economy at all. As economists Erik Brynjolfsson, Daniel Rock, and Chad Syverson put it:

> We live in an age of paradox. Systems using artificial intelligence match or surpass human level performance in more and more domains, leveraging rapid advances in other technologies and driving soaring stock prices. Yet measured productivity growth has declined by half over the past decade, and real income has stagnated since the late 1990s for a majority of Americans.[5]

For those who study the history of technology (and as we saw with electricity), this paradox is not unprecedented. In 1987, MIT's Robert Solow famously quipped that "[w]e see the computer age everywhere but in the productivity statistics." Computers were appearing all over the place without measured improvements in productivity. The pattern was familiar, and economists became interested in what happens when "general purpose technologies"—technologies that enable sustained productivity growth in a wide range of sectors—emerge.[6] General purpose technologies include the steam engine and electricity, and the semiconductor and internet as more recent instantiations. To participants at our conference, AI looked like a plausible candidate to add to the list. What should we expect? Yes, historically, such technologies eventually transformed economies, businesses, and work, but what happened during the decades all that was happening? What happened in The Between Times?

System Innovation for AI

Google CEO Sundar Pichai said that "AI is probably the most important thing humanity has ever worked on. I think of it as something more profound than electricity."[7] Google has already seen a benefit from AI. Many companies haven't. A 2020 study by MIT's *Sloan Management Review* and BCG, a global consultancy, found that just 11 percent of organizations reported significant financial benefits from AI.[8] This wasn't for lack of trying. Fifty-nine percent said they had an AI strategy. Fifty-seven percent had deployed or piloted AI solutions.

AI pioneer Andrew Ng, who founded the Google Brain project and was chief scientist at Baidu, proclaimed that "AI is the new electricity. It has the potential to transform every industry and to create huge economic value."[9] We agree. AI has the transformation potential of electricity, but if history is a guide, that transformation is going to be a long and bumpy ride.

The example of electricity shows that there is no inherent inconsistency between optimism about the future of AI and disappointment in the results thus far. Brynjolfsson, Rock, and Syverson highlighted this age of paradox. We should expect optimism about the future to coexist with disappointment about where we stand today. Indeed, there are good conceptual reasons to expect them to simultaneously exist when the economy undergoes the kind of restructuring associated with transformative technologies.

In the first wave of electricity, light bulbs replaced candles and electric motors replaced steam engines. These were point solutions, with no restructuring required. The economy did not transform.

AI is in the same situation. It is applied as a new tool for predictive analytics. A handful of companies like Verafin are seeing a benefit from enhanced prediction. This is the 11 percent of companies that are already seeing a financial benefit.[10] They already did prediction, and AI is making their predictions better, faster, and cheaper. The lowest-hanging fruit for AI are point solutions, and that fruit is being picked.

Just as electricity's true potential was only unleashed when the broader benefits of distributed power generation were understood and exploited,

AI will only reach its true potential when its benefits in providing prediction can be fully leveraged. For us, that points squarely at the role prediction plays in enhancing decision-making. *We will demonstrate that, in many cases, prediction will so change how decisions are made that the entire system of decision-making and its processes in organizations will need to adjust.* Only then will AI adoption really take off.

We sit in The Between Times, after the demonstration of AI's clear promise and before its transformational impact. Verafin is like the 11 percent of large corporations that achieved success in deploying AI because the predictions fit into their existing system. The process and workflow were already primed to utilize those predictions without requiring significant modifications.

For the other 89 percent, the system is not yet primed. The promise is clear, but the path to achieving that promise is not. There needs to be a way to use machine predictions to do things better. That means using predictions to make better decisions.

AI's impact will be all about the things humans can do because they can make better decisions. It is not only about the technical challenge of collecting data, building models, and generating predictions, but also about the organizational challenge of enabling the right humans to make the right decisions at the right time. And it is about the strategic challenge of identifying *what can be done differently* once better information is available.

Setting the Stage

The Between Times are characterized by enthusiasm and success with point solutions, but with AI still seemingly a niche technology. There is already, however, some development and experimentation with application solutions. However, by their nature, these are often highly specific. These application solutions enhance existing products such as phones or automobile safety features.

The US Census Bureau asked over 300,000 companies about their use of AI. The large firms that had adopted it overwhelmingly emphasized the use of AI for automating and improving existing processes. In other words, their AIs are point solutions and application solutions, so there was no change in the system. These AIs had a modest impact on the productivity of the adopters.[11] Looking at existing workflows and identifying where AIs can replace humans can deliver meaningful, albeit incremental benefits. It isn't where the biggest opportunities lie.

In The Between Times, entrepreneurs and business managers struggle to make the adoption of applications economically viable. As Nathan Rosenberg noted, for all technologies, "Many of the numerous instances of entrepreneurial failure can be attributed to the fact that a would-be entrepreneur failed to consider the relevant conditions of interdependence between the component with which he happened to be preoccupied and the rest of the larger system."[12]

The true transformation will only come when innovators turn their attention to creating new system solutions. Those solutions themselves bring AI to an economywide scale, and their momentum spurs further application solutions. This potential for scale and follow-on innovation will make AI systems economically beneficial to pursue.

Given the importance of these solutions, it is critical to explain carefully what we mean. So, let's define our concepts:

- A point solution improves an existing procedure and can be adopted independently, without changing the system in which it is embedded.

- An application solution enables a new procedure that can be adopted independently, without changing the system in which it is embedded.

- A system solution improves existing procedures or enables new procedures by changing dependent procedures.

The heavy lifting in these definitions is being done by the term *independently*, which appears in the point and application solution definitions but not the system solution definition. Imagine that we have an existing or new procedure that we can make more valuable by adopting a new technology. If the increase in value is greater than the costs of developing and adopting that solution, then the solution is economically viable. Moreover, it is economically viable independent of whether something else changes. However, suppose that the benefits from that new technology are too low and can only be improved by changing other things. Then independent adoption without those changes is not economically possible. Adoption requires changing multiple processes together.

Thus, we saw that some factories found it easy to adopt electricity as a point solution by swapping it out for steam. And some applications could also be built to be integrated with electric engines and used within existing production systems. But in many situations, factories needed to redesign and indeed whole centralized electrical systems and grids had to be provided to make the solution economically feasible. In other words, system solutions transformed electricity from a substitute for existing power into opportunities to use new power.

In the next chapter, we revisit a theme from *Prediction Machines*—that advances in modern AI are, at their essence, an improvement in prediction technology. Moreover, predictions have value only as inputs into decision-making. Thus, we modify the previous definitions for the purposes of this book:

- AI POINT SOLUTION: A prediction is valuable as a point solution if it improves an existing decision and that decision can be made independently.

- AI APPLICATION SOLUTION: A prediction is valuable as an application solution if it enables a new decision or changes how a decision is made and that decision can be made independently.

- AI SYSTEM SOLUTION: A prediction is valuable as a system solution if it improves existing decisions or enables new decisions, but only if changes to how other decisions are made are implemented.

For other technologies, while we have the benefit of hindsight to tell us exactly what was independent and what was dependent, with AI we must still figure out those aspects of the system. This book is about how to find them.

System Change Is Disruptive

The biggest increase in the adoption of AI is, if history is any guide, going to come from changes in systems. But such change will also be disruptive.

By disruptive, we mean that it changes the roles of many people and companies within industries and, alongside those changes, causes shifts in power. That is, there are likely to be economic winners and losers, especially if system change occurs relatively quickly.

To give a sense of that disruption, consider prediction in farming. Farming is an industry where mechanization dramatically reduced employment. But farm management still resides with the farmer. While the farms are large, there are decisions that reside with them, so much so that many farms remain farmer-owned. The farmers used predictions regarding the weather to assist in those decisions, but the nature of the land they owned was something uniquely tied to their own skills in prediction and in decision-making more generally.

Things are changing. Farmers are exposed to weather conditions, but critically, how they are exposed differs depending on the crops and local field conditions. This additional risk was something that David Friedberg, who provided the first internet-accessible weather predictions, realized when he tried to sell insurance to US farmers. Like the weather data, the US government had data—in the form of infrared satellite images and data on soil composition of 29 million fields—that would enable Friedberg to calculate weather-related risk at the field or crop level.[13]

Friedberg started The Climate Corporation to sell insurance to the farmers, but soon found that they were as interested in the data he had regarding their own fields:

> He'd [Friedberg] show the farmer exactly how much moisture the field contained at any given moment—above a certain level, the field would be damaged if worked on. He'd show them the rainfall and temperature every day—which you might think the farmer would know, but then the farmer might be managing twenty or thirty different fields, spread over several counties. He'd show the farmer the precise stage of growth of his crop, the best moments to fertilize, the optimum eight-day window to plant his seeds, and the ideal harvest date.[14]

Prediction was a large driver of farmers' key decisions: fertilization, seeding, and harvesting. The goal of these decisions was nearly universal—to maximize yield: "Farming had always involved judgment calls that turned on the instincts of the farmer. The Climate Corporation had turned farming into decision science, and a matter of probabilities. The farmer was no longer playing roulette but blackjack. And David Friedberg was helping him to count the cards."[15]

Farmers were used to seeing technological change in the form of new tools they could use, but this knowledge was replacing how they made decisions. Indeed, the decisions themselves had not only changed but physically moved. Where? To San Francisco, far from rural America. This urban West Coast corporation was now telling farmers in Kansas that they should no longer be growing corn.

The Climate Corporation does not currently deal with all farming decisions. The farmer still makes some critical decisions. However, as Friedberg notes, "over time that'll go to zero. Everything will be observed. Everything will be predicted."[16] Farmers are embracing this bit by bit. Author Michael Lewis recounts, "[N]o one ever asked Friedberg the question: If my knowledge is no longer useful, who needs me?"[17] In other words, the portends are toward disruption and centralizing farm management. We don't know how long it will take and whether some decisions cannot be automated. We do know that the industry sees high potential in these tools. Monsanto acquired the Climate Corporation in 2013 for $1.1 billion.

Step by step, as prediction machines improve, farmers are not simply taking those predictions and making decisions but ceding those decisions to others. This likely makes farm management better, as people with the right information, skills, incentives, and ability to coordinate increasingly make the decisions. But at the same time, what will the farmer's role be? They are the landowners, but how long before that too changes?

The Plan for the Book

Our purpose here is to motivate the development of AI system solutions. Our focus is squarely on the decision and the role prediction plays in it.

In part 1, we discussed the parable of the three entrepreneurs and introduced the challenges in developing and deploying AI in The Between

Times, which likely mirror those of electricity and other past general purpose technologies. As a bridge to understanding these challenges and opportunities, in chapter 3, we revisit the thesis of our earlier book, *Prediction Machines*, and describe how AI involves prediction at its heart.

In part 2, to build our case that more than just point solutions for prediction will be required to yield high value, we delve into the decision-making process. We explore three broad themes. First, making decisions is hard. It involves cognitive costs relative to simply following a rule. The upside of a decision is the ability to change what you do in response to new information. When there is no prediction, those benefits are muted. Second, AI prediction may tip the balance from rules toward decisions, and how rules and consequent actions taken to shelter an organization from their adverse consequences can hide uncertainty. Thus, it may be hard to find where to apply AI because the uncertainty is buried. At the same time, this is where disruption could be most strongly felt. If that uncertainty surfaces, businesses devoted to keeping it hidden will be in peril. Third are the relationships between decisions. When decisions interact with one another, moving away from a rule to a decision driven by prediction actually adds a measure of unreliability to the system. Overcoming this often requires systemwide change. The problem is that rules glue the existing system together, often in subtle and nonobvious ways. Thus, it can be easier to build a new system from scratch than to change an existing system. So, historically, new entrants and startups often outperform established businesses when a total system redesign is required for optimization. Thus, system-level change is a path to disruption of incumbent firms.

In part 3, we examine the process of creating new systems, which involves more than just changing one decision to respond to prediction but to have that occur for all decisions that interact with one another. We describe the value of adopting a system mindset and seeing the subtle relationships between decisions, especially if much was previously governed by rules. We show that AI prediction is already having a system change effect in the innovation process. This gives a glimpse into what changes may be required elsewhere.

In part 4, we surface a key consequence of systemwide change: its implications for power. Disruption as a process involves a redistribution of economic power—that is, under the new system, those who create the most economic value will change. We revisit more recent history to explain how disruption that has transformed industry has always been associated with systemwide change. We then look at one aspect of fear regarding power that arises when discussing AI: whether the machines will have power. We explain that when you understand that AI is all about prediction and is an input into decision-making, power comes not from machines—even though they might look powerful—but from those behind the machines, guiding how they react to predictions, what we call judgment. We then explore the advantages that better predictions—and the data that fuels them—can give to businesses in competition with one another. In other words, how prediction might drive the accumulation of power.

In part 5, we dig into the mechanism by which prediction can change who holds power, that is, how AI disrupts. We explain how AI adoption involves the decoupling of prediction and judgment that were previously bundled together in how decision-makers without a prediction machine at their disposal made decisions. This raises the question whether the current decision-maker is actually best positioned to supply that judgment. We then turn to who those judges might be following decoupling. In particular, we explore how judgment can move from being decentralized to being at scale with a consequent concentration of power. Similarly, when prediction involves a change from a rule to a decision and then to a new system, new people have a role in decision-making and therefore become the new locus of power.

Finally, in part 6, we consider system design—especially for reliable systems that build on the new AI developments—and provide a tool you can use to understand your business and industry as a system of decisions (or potential decisions). This involves taking a blank-slate approach to map your mission to a small set of the most foundational decisions when you have access to powerful prediction machines. We explain how the home insurance industry might do this. We then look at how health care might achieve this, given that it is already facing challenges at a system level from the application of AI.

We end the book with the example of AI bias, which concerns many. We argue that when seen as a point solution, AI bias is a problem and may create justified resistance to adopting prediction machines. But bias is more properly viewed from a system mindset. Once we understand how the system could adjust to accommodate AI prediction, it becomes easier to see that the elimination of bias is an opportunity afforded by AI rather than one subverted by it.

Overall, we emphasize that AI-driven industry transformation takes time. It's not obvious how to do it at first. Many will likely experiment and fail because they misunderstand demand, or they can't get the unit economics to work. Eventually, someone will succeed and establish a pathway to profitability. Others will try to imitate. The industry leader will attempt to create moats to protect its advantage. Sometimes it will succeed. Regardless, the industry will transform, and as always, there will be winners and losers.

KEY POINTS

- Despite the awesome predictive powers of AI, measured productivity growth has declined by half over the past decade and real income has stagnated since the late 1990s for a majority of Americans. This productivity paradox is not novel. We experienced something similar in the 1980s with computers. We call this The Between Times: *after* witnessing the power of AI and *before* its widespread adoption. Although point solutions and application solutions can be designed and implemented reasonably quickly, system solutions that will unlock AI's vast potential take much more time.

- The key concept in the definitions of the three types of AI solutions— *point solutions, application solutions,* and *system solutions*—is independence. If an AI prediction creates value by enhancing the focal decision and that value creation is independent of any other changes to the system, then a point solution (enhanced existing decision) or application solution (new decision) is feasible. However, if the value of the enhanced decision is not independent but rather requires other substantive changes to the system in order to create value, then a system solution is required.

- System solutions are typically harder to implement than point solutions or application solutions because the AI-enhanced decision impacts other decisions in the system. Whereas point solutions and application solutions often reinforce existing systems, system solutions, by definition, upend existing solutions and therefore often result in disruption. However, in many cases, system solutions are likely to generate the greatest overall return to investments in AI. Furthermore, system solutions are likely to cause disruption in some industries, creating winners and losers.

3

AI Is Prediction Technology

In our first book, *Prediction Machines*, we examined the simple economics of AI. We took all the potential complexity and hype regarding AI and reduced it to a single factor: prediction. Reducing an exciting new thing to its less sensational essence is a key tool in an economist's playbook.

When people think about AI, they think about the intelligent machines littered throughout popular culture. They think of helpful robots such as R2-D2 or WALL-E. They think of brilliant teammates such as Data from *Star Trek* or J.A.R.V.I.S. from *Iron Man*. They also think of those that turned rogue like HAL 9000 from *2001* or Ultron from *The Avengers*. Whatever their quirks or intentions, these representations of AI have one thing in common: no one disputes that they can think, reason, and have agency, just as we do.

We may develop technology that does all of that, but that isn't what we have today. What we have is an advance in statistical techniques rather than something that thinks. But the advance in statistical techniques is very significant. As that advance reaches its potential, it will dramatically reduce the cost of prediction. And prediction is something we do everywhere.

The signature event in recent developments in AI was the demonstration of the superiority of new techniques in machine learning called "deep learning." In 2012, a team from the University of Toronto, led by Geoffrey Hinton, used deep learning to dramatically improve the ability of machines to identify what was going on in images. Using a data set of millions of images called ImageNet, teams had, for the better part of a decade, tried to devise algorithms that would accurately identify what an image was showing. That data set had already labeled each image with a human classification of what was in it. The idea was to take that data set, use it to develop an algorithm, and then feed the algorithm new images. There would then be a horse race between those algorithms and with humans who would identify what was in the images. The humans weren't perfect at this task, but before 2012, they were far superior to any algorithm. In 2012, that began to change.

The deep learning approach conceived of the task—identifying the subjects in images—as a prediction problem. The goal was to be able to predict, when given a new image, what a human would say was in the image. When presented with an image of a puppy, the task was not to understand what really made an image of a puppy. Instead, it was to guess what the thing in the picture was most likely to be among all the labels that existed. The goal, therefore, was to guess the most likely correct label, which became the prediction. By allowing for a large number of attributes and their combinations—a computationally difficult exercise—what the Toronto team showed is that deep learning could outguess any other algorithm and, eventually, most people.

This description can make it seem like what a machine was doing was "winging it" rather than working through a problem. But it is winging it on steroids. Machine prediction is useful by being more accurate than anything else. The reason is that predictions are a key input into our decision-making.

Complementing Prediction

Predictions are not the only input into decision-making. To understand how prediction matters, it is necessary to understand two other key inputs into decisions: judgment and data. Judgment is best explained with an example.

In the movie *I, Robot*, homicide detective Del Spooner lives in a future where robots serve humans. The detective hates robots, and that hatred drives much of the plot. The movie provides the backstory behind Spooner's animosity toward robots.

Spooner's car is in an accident with another car carrying a twelve-year-old girl; the cars veer off a bridge, and both the detective and the girl are clearly about to drown. A robot saves the detective, not the girl. He thinks the robot should have saved the girl, so he carries a grudge against robots.

Because it was a robot, Spooner could audit its decision. He learns that the robot predicted that he had a 45 percent chance of survival and that the girl only had an 11 percent chance. Therefore, given the robot had time to save only one person, the robot saved him. Spooner thinks that 11 percent was more than enough chance to try to save the girl instead, and a human being would have known that.

Maybe. That is a statement about judgment—the process of determining the reward to a particular action in a particular environment. If saving the girl is the right decision, then we can infer he believes the girl's life is worth more than four times his. If she had an 11 percent chance of survival and he had a 45 percent chance, a human with that information who was forced to make the choice would have to specify the relative value of their lives. The robot was apparently programmed to judge all human lives to be of equal value. When using a prediction machine, we need to be explicit about judgment.

Correlation and Causation

Data provides the information that enables a prediction. As AIs acquire more high-quality data, the predictions improve. By quality, we mean that you have data about the context in which you are trying to predict. Statisticians call this the need to predict something on the "support" of your data. Extrapolate too much from the data you have, and the prediction may be inaccurate.

Predicting on the support of your data is not as simple as collecting data from a wider variety of settings to ensure you aren't extrapolating too much or avoiding predicting too far into the future. Sometimes the data you need doesn't exist. This underlies the refrain repeated in every statistics course worldwide: correlation is not necessarily causation.

In the US toy industry, there is a strong correlation between advertising and revenue. Advertising spending increases sharply toward the end of November and stays high for about a month. During this time when advertising is high, toys fly off the shelves. Looking at the data alone, it might be tempting to increase advertising during the rest of the year. Surely it would be possible to increase revenue in April if only the industry advertised in the early spring as it does in the month before Christmas.

The industry hasn't done that. Toy advertising in April is much lower than toy advertising in December. That means that any prediction for what would happen if advertising were increased in April is off the support of the data. From the month-by-month correlation between advertising and revenue, you can't tell if advertising caused revenue or if Christmas caused both. It is possible that the correlation is causal, so increasing ad spending in April will lead to a sharp increase in toy sales. Of course, it is also possible that it isn't advertising that is causing most of the sales in December. Instead, it might be the anticipation of Christmas that causes both the advertising and the sales. It is also possible that advertising does cause sales in December, but since far fewer Americans buy toys in April, there won't be much effect at that time of year.

In other words, prediction machines alone won't provide information on what would happen to April's toy sales if the industry's advertising strategy changed.[1] To discover that relationship, you'd need to use a different branch of statistics called "causal inference." Like AI, this branch has also seen major progress in the past few years (with the 2021 Nobel Prize in economics awarded for advances in the analysis of causal relationships), and it is becoming increasingly clear that these tools are themselves a complement to AI, providing AI with the data necessary to enable effective predictions in many settings. The top AI companies in the world recognize this. For example, of the three 2021 Nobel Prize winners, two worked for Amazon. In addition to their academic positions, Guido

Imbens is a scientist on the Core AI team and David Card is an Amazon Scholar.[2]

Causal inference challenges limit the usefulness of AI to places where it is possible to collect the relevant data. AIs have been very effective at playing games, including chess, Go, and *Super Mario Brothers*. The setting of a game is the same each time you play, so there is no need to extrapolate much from past data to current games. Furthermore, for situations that are not in the data, because games are software, it is possible to run simulated experiments. These experiments allow the AI to fill in the rest of the data, to explore what would happen if a different button is pushed or a new strategy tried. That is how DeepMind's *AlphaGo* and *AlphaGoZero* discovered winning strategies in the game Go that had not been successfully used in high-level competition games. DeepMind ran millions of simulated experiments, and the machine learned to predict winning strategies by simulating what would happen if it tried several different approaches.[3]

In many business situations, the data is available. When not on hand, it is often possible to collect it through experimentation. Experimentation in business takes longer than in games because it occurs at human speed rather than the speed at which a computer can run a simulation. Still, it can be a powerful tool for collecting the relevant data that can be useful input to AI.

Randomized experiments are the main tool for statisticians to discover what causes what. They are the gold standard for approval of new medical treatments. One group is randomly assigned to receive a treatment. The other receives a placebo. While the groups are not identical—they consist of different people—the differences are a result of chance. With enough people assigned to each group, you can conclude whether the treatment caused the outcome. By running the right kind of experiment, it is often possible to fill in the data required to draw conclusions that are causal, not just correlations.

Sometimes such simulated, randomized, or even quasi-randomized data will prove difficult or impossible to collect. At the extreme is the application of AI in military contexts. At first, war might seem the ideal place to apply AI tools. As military theorist Carl von Clausewitz wrote in the nineteenth century, "War is the realm of uncertainty." Prediction could reduce uncertainty and so generate substantial military advantage. The challenge, however, is that wars involve adversaries. In war, "if AI becomes good at optimizing the solution for any given problem, then an intelligent enemy has incentives to change the problem."[4] The enemy will go beyond the training set, and peacetime data will be of little use.

This idea applies in business contexts, too. Predictions will work when there isn't a competitor with incentives to undermine your predictions or a customer with incentives to find a way around them. If a customer could do better by reverse engineering the key aspects of your AI and feeding it false information, then the AI will only serve your goals for as long as customers don't discover how it works. When predictions don't support your data and causal inference issues arise, what might seem like a point solution often requires system-level change. Still, for the 11 percent of companies that have already seen value from AI, the prediction is often on the support of the data they have on hand, so an AI point solution works just fine.

Prediction at the Heart

Consider the decision to accept or reject a financial transaction. Key to this decision is the prediction of fraud, the heart of Verafin's business. A transaction is proposed that involves a request for payment, which is a transfer from one account to another. If the transaction is approved, the money changes hands, which itself triggers the exchange of real goods and services. If the transaction is not approved, no money is moved, which may impede the underlying real obligations. The fact that the transaction requires payment approval at all is because mistakes are costly. Approve a transaction that comes from someone who does not own an account, and a string of liabilities and problems arise. Decline a transaction that would have no such issues, and you disrupt the real-world activities underlying the whole process.

You might think that this would make you want a system that avoids mistakes entirely. The challenge there is not that avoiding mistakes isn't possible. With time and careful review, a bank could likely do that. The problem is that avoiding mistakes entirely is very costly. It would slow down the process, raise transaction fees, and otherwise take away the very convenience that is desired in transacting in the first place. After all, if it is going to cost too much to transact by sending digital messages for approval of changes in account entries, maybe it would be better to use good old cash and show the money right then and there.

Instead, to make the system work, banks engage in a guessing game. They have to balance the possible guessing errors they could make. If they are stringent on what transactions they approve, then they risk declining many legitimate transactions and end up with disgruntled customers. If they are too lenient on approvals, they end up creating an opening for fraudsters to transact illegitimately and make it hard to collect misplaced money, which directly harms the bank's bottom line. Thus, they guess and set thresholds on stringency to balance the two errors they inevitably will make.

AI is the means by which banks become better at the guessing game and reduce errors. As economists studying the new developments in AI over the last decade, we have come to see our role as one of cutting through the hype. AI attracts the attention of philosophers, moviemakers, futurists, doomsayers, and a raft of others who can enliven your dinner party conversation. We play the opposite role. Taking our cue from where the successes in computer science have really been, all the developments in AI with fancy names such as neural networks, machine learning, deep learning, or adversarial optimization, we boil down to an advance—albeit a big advance—in statistics, namely, the statistics of prediction. Thus, rather than AI engaged in a crime-fighting crusade against fraud, what AI is actually doing is improving banks' ability to sort legitimate from fraudulent transactions at a much lower cost—that is, prediction.

AI these days is a prediction machine, and that is all it is. For Verafin, that turns out to be exactly what it wanted. To make the modern payments system work requires a high degree of automation. You want to have high confidence in those approvals. That is where AI slots in. It takes the wealth of information that banks have regarding their customers, patterns of behavior, when and where transactions are taking place, and translates that into a prediction regarding whether a transaction is legitimate or not. Over the past two decades, the accuracy has improved. There is now widespread adoption of AI tools for fraud detection in banking and financial services, and these institutes claim substantial benefits in terms of accuracy.[5]

Prediction is Verafin's business, and as AI is a massive advance in predictive technology, companies like Verafin will surely be the early beneficiaries of it. Banks and other financial institutions used to conduct their own prediction functions. Approval is what their business is. The better those decisions are made, the better they are at their job. And they can use all the information they can get. As it turned out, Verafin was able to supply that information by leveraging its ability to learn and refine its algorithms from the transactions thousands of financial institutions and their clients processed. This is not to say that achieving market leadership in prediction was a piece of cake. Verafin had almost two decades of experience. But the point here is that prediction is and always was its job, and AI created a new opportunity for it to raise its game.

Beyond Prediction

This book is not about companies like Verafin, but Verafin is top of mind because it illustrates an exception rather than a rule for the adoption and impact of AI. Everything fell into place for Verafin. First, prediction—the primary output of AI—was at the heart of its business. Second, very little had to change for its customers—financial institutions—to adopt Verafin's products because prediction was at the heart of those businesses as well. Third, those businesses were already making decisions based on predictions, they knew what to do with those predictions, and they were already accustomed to dealing with the consequences of predictive errors so that AI could be safely deployed. Banks were ripe for point solution innovations.

The bottom line was that Verafin already operated in a system that was primed to adopt AI. The system did not have to change to use prediction. A new way of how to make decisions did not have to be created. Verafin was already supplying predictions to businesses that knew what they needed predictions for, had set themselves up to take advantage of those predictions, and most critically, were able to orient themselves in different directions based on those predictions.

Verafin is an example of the final step in what will be a more challenging process for most businesses that can benefit from AI adoption now and in the future. If your business wants to adopt AI, it will likely have to clear the brush and maybe an entire forest before being in a position to implement it. This book is about that clearing process—identifying what needs to change and the dilemmas and challenges that will face you in implementing such change. We are referring to system-level change, rather than a point solution or application solution that you can implement while leaving the existing system intact. Knowing what you are getting into is a critical step in working out whether it is all worth it.

Illustrating the Challenge

One of the most referenced parts of our earlier book came from a thought experiment. Amazon uses AI to predict what particular consumers might want to buy. When you are shopping on Amazon's site, those predictions inform the decision of what items to recommend from a catalog of tens of millions of options. You sort through its recommendations and order some; those are shipped to you. It is a couple of days between the time you start shopping and the arrival of the goods.

In this context, we wondered, what might change if Amazon's predictions of what you wanted to buy got much better? Amazon might want to give those couple of days back to you by predicting what you want, shipping it to you, and inviting you to accept it or not at your door. In other words, Amazon ships to you based on its predictions and then you shop from the boxes delivered to your doorstep. We called this a move from shop-then-ship to ship-then-shop. While some might find it creepy to have products appear at their house, it wasn't hard to imagine how convenient it might be.

Moving to ship-then-shop was something we envisaged as an application solution. It would take a prediction and give Amazon the decision of whether to ship something, rather than letting the customer decide whether to ship an item. Many people consider shopping a burden, so by being able to provide that cheaply, better prediction offered a solution for that application.

We have yet to see Amazon do this. That has not stopped it from putting its toe in the water. It has already patented the idea of "anticipatory shipping," but its implementation is somewhat muted.[6] For instance, it routinely offers options to consumers to subscribe to a product rather than actively order it. How? It notices how much toilet paper your household uses and promises to provide the product at regular intervals. This gives Amazon certainty in demand; it passes on the savings to consumers as discounts for subscribing.

Once you move beyond the thought experiment, however, you can see why implementing ship-then-shop is a significant challenge. If predictions are perfect, this doesn't seem like a difficult application solution. But predictions aren't perfect and may never be so. For that, Amazon needs to have a way of collecting products you choose to reject. It is hard enough to deliver products safely, let alone having them put out on porches for return. Returns can also be a pain for consumers. Thus, without having a system for virtually costless returns, Amazon's ship-then-shop is unlikely to emerge from the starting gate. Indeed, Amazon already struggles with returns so much that it never resells many returned items but sends them directly to trash.[7] With its existing system, it is cheaper for Amazon to throw away returns than put those products back into its own logistics systems. The lesson here is that ship-then-shop, while it might appear to be an application solution, is one that requires changes elsewhere in the system to be made economic.[8] While we didn't appreciate it when we wrote *Prediction Machines*, ship-then-shop is a system solution because it impacts other key decisions and requires a redesign of Amazon's system to facilitate a much more cost-effective way of handling returns.

Now What?

"OK, now what?" That's the question many businesses and organizations beginning to implement AI technologies were asking us. These companies had heard the hype about AI, and using the playbook we set out in *Prediction Machines*, they had begun their AI journey. They had set up teams to look at their tasks and identify opportunities for leveraging what AI had to offer: prediction. Prediction is the process by which you convert information that you have into information that you need. And as we documented in that book, the recent innovations in AI were all advances in making prediction better, faster, and cheaper.

The results of those advances are so ubiquitous that we don't even think about them anymore. Your phone is packed with AI technologies. When you unlock the phone, it easily recognizes your face. You don't even feel as if the phone is behind a secure barrier that lets you, and only you, in through the front door. You come to a screen where apps are laid out for you based on the phone's prediction of what you might want at that precise moment. Are you near your favorite coffee place and want to order? Are you in your car and want directions? The phone knows, but it feels like it is just being convenient. The point is that the low-hanging fruit for the uses of AI prediction was all being picked. The question businesses were asking was "Is that it?"

This book is the answer to that question: no. Even though AI seems everywhere, like many other breakthrough technologies before, it is only just getting started. Significant technological revolutions such as electricity, the internal combustion engine, and the semiconductor all started slowly, taking decades to hit their stride. AI prediction is not going to be any different, despite the hype that it represents some distinct pattern of acceleration of technological change.

Rather than being on a roller-coaster ride where we are at the whim of forces beyond our control, we are sitting on the edge of opportunity—in The Between Times. People and businesses that are able to find answers to "now what?" will set the path for AI.

As economists, we look to economic forces to guide us in answering such questions. However, we move beyond simple economics where observations of falling prediction costs indicate more applications of prediction. Instead, we dive into the obvious fact that how people and businesses decide what to do is not a magical exercise of arriving quickly at the optimal answer but, instead, involves deliberation, process, and its own costs.

To take advantage of prediction, you need to consider what to use that prediction for and the fact that decision-makers have made do without that prediction previously. When you don't have something, you don't just give up. You compensate for it. If you don't have the information you need to make an informed choice, you insulate yourself from the consequences of having to do things blindly. Thus, when AI prediction comes along, it shouldn't be a surprise that the opportunities for its use are not immediately obvious. Would-be decision-makers have built up a scaffolding based on not having that information.

This all means that determining what's next will require a closer examination of not only what prediction might do but also the walls that have been built up to prevent even asking that question. We will deconstruct decisions to provide a toolkit for you to see beyond the obvious opportunities for AI prediction to the nonobvious but potentially more significant opportunities that AI prediction can bring.

KEY POINTS

- Recent advances in AI have caused a drop in the cost of prediction. We use prediction to take information we have (e.g., data on whether past financial transactions were fraudulent) and generate data we need but don't have (e.g., whether a current financial transaction is fraudulent). Prediction is an input to decision-making. When the cost of an input falls, we use more of it. So, as prediction becomes cheaper, we will use more AI. As the cost of prediction falls, the value of substitutes for machine prediction (e.g., human prediction) will fall. At the same time, the value of complements to machine prediction will rise. Two of the main complements to machine prediction are data and judgment. We use data to train AI models. We use judgment along with predictions to make decisions. While prediction is an expression of likelihood, judgment is an expression of desire—what we want. So, when we make a decision, we contemplate the likelihood of each possible outcome that could arise from that decision (prediction) and how much we value each outcome (judgment).

- Perhaps the greatest misuse of AI predictions is treating the correlations they identify as causal. Often, correlations are good enough for an application. However, if we need AI to inform a causal relationship, then we use randomized experiments to collect the relevant data. These experiments are the best tool for statisticians to discover what causes what.

- In *Prediction Machines,* we introduced a thought experiment regarding Amazon's recommendation engine. We imagined what would happen if it became increasingly accurate. At first, the tool does a better job of recommending items to customers. However, at some point it crosses a threshold where it becomes so good that the folks at Amazon could ask: "If we're so good at predicting what our customers want, then why are we waiting for them to order it? Let's just ship it." Although Amazon filed a patent in the area of "anticipatory shipping," it has not yet adopted this new business model. Why not? The original point solution—AI that provides better recommendations on the existing platform—leverages the Amazon system as is. The new model would require Amazon to redesign its system, especially regarding how it handles returns. At present, its system for returns is so costly that it often finds it more economical to throw away returned items than to restock them for sale to other customers. The threshold in our thought experiment required shifting from a point solution to a system solution. In *Prediction Machines,* we underappreciated the difference.

PART TWO

Rules

4

To Decide or Not to Decide

Psst. Wanna know a secret? Economists don't really believe people are perfectly rational. You know, the caricature of a calculating agent who carefully lays out all the options before them—millions of choices in time and space—knows precisely what their objectives are, whether profit, happiness, or something else, and then makes a choice and sticks to the plan of action. That perfectly rational agent is often what's portrayed in economists' models, if you take them literally. And economists do take the predictions of those models seriously. But they know, if only from their own experience, that real people don't come close to that picture of rationality. Economists roll their eyes when tagged with the phrase "economists believe that everyone is rational." They don't. It would be profoundly irrational to believe that.

Still, treating people as if they are calculating, consistent, and acting according to a set of interests is useful for understanding the behavior of thousands or millions of people. Want to understand whether taxes on cigarettes will reduce smoking? One impact is that if it costs more, people will do less of it. Just how much less and whether it will be enough is another matter. You'll need to understand people's history, stress, social groups, and what marketing techniques tobacco companies deploy. But an excellent starting point for much in social science is the recognition that someone is deciding something in a deliberate manner.

People make decisions about what to wear every day. Steve Jobs famously wore a signature black turtleneck and jeans, regardless of the occasion or weather. Mark Zuckerberg kept the jeans but chose a gray T-shirt. Barack Obama, who, as president, wore only gray or blue suits, explained why to Michael Lewis of *Vanity Fair*:

> "You'll see I wear only gray or blue suits," he said. "I'm trying to pare down decisions. I don't want to make decisions about what I'm eating or wearing. Because I have too many other decisions to make." He mentioned research that shows the simple act of making decisions degrades one's ability to make further decisions. It's why shopping is so exhausting. "You need to focus your decision-making energy. You need to routinize yourself. You can't be going through the day distracted by trivia."[1]

One of us (Joshua) once bought out the global supply of a pair of shoes he liked (a total of six pairs, if you must know) because he didn't want to face shoe shopping for another decade. All these choices were designed precisely to avoid making decisions. When people form habits or keep to rules, they are acknowledging that the costs of trying to optimize are too high. So they, in effect, decide not to decide. This is happening all over the place. Think about yourself for a bit, and you realize that most of what you decide are not actual decisions but latent ones, things you could choose but choose not to.

For our purposes, that represents a considerable challenge in a book about AI. AI prediction is only useful if you are making a decision. But it is more than that. Often our way of building systems of interdependent components is to invest in reliability. What you don't want is one part doing something that other parts do not expect or anticipate. You want reliability. Rules are how reliability is backed into systems. However, if AI prediction is going to break rules and turn them into decisions, then one consequence will be a lack of reliability for existing systems. That consequence may render it not worthwhile to use AI unless you can redesign the system to accommodate the decisions AI is enabling.

That's why we are going to start with the decisions we have decided not to make. We want to understand why we do that, with the goal of evaluating whether adopting AI can change our minds and turn those latent decisions into actual ones. As you will see in this chapter, we believe that AI can, with potentially great benefits and implications for how organizations might have to adjust in response.

Set It and Forget It

It is easier not to have to make a decision than to make one. That is, it is easier to avoid gathering information, processing it, weighing all the options, and then reaching a decision. The economy pretty much runs on this premise, where other people are allocated decisions even if we don't fully trust them to do what we would do.

No one understood this more than Herbert Simon, who not only won a Nobel Prize in economics for his work on bounded rationality but also received the Turing Award for his work as one of the pioneers of AI. He had previously observed, during his first job at the Milwaukee parks department, that funds for activities weren't allocated optimally; that people didn't optimize in the way economists modeled was brought home with the arrival of computers.[2] In the 1950s, as Simon tried to program newfangled computers to be intelligent decision-makers, he saw the costs of optimization. Even if we understood the advanced dynamic calculus required in complex environments, which we surely do not, we don't have the attention to devote to solving the consequent decision problem. Forced to use only limited computing resources, people would do what Simon had to do with the primitive computers of his time: make do.

What "making do" looked like, a term of art Simon cleverly called "satisficing," was to not make the perfect the enemy of the good. Rather than look for solutions they knew might be better, they would take actions that were good enough. Rather than deal with a complex environment, people would narrow the range of options considered. Rather than continually updating their choices based on new information received, they would adopt rules, routines, and habits that would be impervious to new information and, hence, allow them to ignore information entirely.

However, just to note that sometimes people default to rules rather than make decisions, while interesting, isn't enough for our purposes. We need to understand when decisions are made. What determines when a particular problem will be placed in the default rule rather than the active decision basket?

Low Consequences

Two broad considerations drive decisions: high versus low consequences and cheap versus expensive information. We will come to information shortly. For the moment, consider a decision's consequences. The notion that we shouldn't tax ourselves when the consequences are limited is a staple of philosophy. The quintessential parable comes from the French philosopher Jean Buridan, who posited that an ass placed exactly between a haystack and a pail of water would want whichever was closer. Faced with no ability to break the tie and make a choice, the ass starves to death. One can imagine a similar conundrum driving a computer to be locked in a loop.[3] But, for our purposes, the issue is that the time spent making a decision should not be proportionately large relative to its consequences.

Let's return to the Jobs, Zuckerberg, Obama clothing rules designed to limit their cognitive loads. What each realized was that the consequences of choosing one outfit over another were not large. Faced with a wardrobe of options, they would be forced to confront choices every day that were of little consequence. They could have just closed their eyes and taken the first item they touched. But they didn't trust themselves. So, they consciously limited their options.

For most of us, the consequences are not so low. Sure, Jobs and Zuckerberg could turn up to work in whatever they wanted. Sure, Obama had to wear a suit most days, and no one really cared about its color—well, so long as the color was not tan.[4] But the rest of us do not have that luxury. Do you really look through your whole wardrobe every day, or have your clothes sorted themselves into a smaller set you regularly draw from? On reflection, don't many of us limit our choices to make those choices easier? In the end, we try to make these things less consequential to match our desire to reduce the complexity of our decisions.

The clothing choice example resonates as a decision with potentially low consequences and a relatively high cognitive load if you try to optimize. However, both consequence and cognitive load go hand in hand. Think about committing to a life partner or having a child. The consequences of making the wrong choice are large, so the need to spend time and effort deliberating is called for. Thus, if we think of potential decisions as things that we consider with time and effort before launching into them versus setting them aside by delaying them or opting for a default rule, as more important consequences are anticipated, so will our desire to engage in deliberation rather than an alternative of not deciding.

Costly Information

The second driver of whether you choose to actively decide is whether you have information or, specifically, the cost of the information you need to make a decision. Costly information can mean that a decision looks precisely like a decision with low consequences and so drives you to adopt default rules rather than deliberate.

Should you carry an umbrella today? While not earth-shattering in terms of its interest to others, this choice can carry large consequences. If you choose not to carry an umbrella and you are caught in the rain, that constitutes a bad day. You could ensure this didn't happen by carrying an umbrella, but that has its own costs. Of course, if you had the right information (specifically, whether it was going to rain and whether that rain was likely to be on you), you would take an umbrella if that was highly likely and leave it if it was not. But what if it's fifty-fifty?

To help calibrate what is essentially a coin toss, let's suppose that if you get wet, you suffer $10 in personal cost, but if you carry an umbrella and it does not rain, you also suffer $10 due to the unnecessary encumbrance.[5] In terms of the cost you expect, either way you might suffer $10 times one-half, or $5. That makes you indifferent to carrying and not.

Before you make an ass of yourself standing at the door to resolve all this, you could look at the forecast. If the forecast says the probability of rain is greater than 50 percent, then you take an umbrella that day, and if it is less than 50 percent, you don't. But here we have simplified the problem and taken away context that could make even that information insufficient. If the forecast says that it will be dry with 90 percent confidence, then things are clear, but weather forecasts are not always clear. We rarely have the nuanced information to adjudicate this decision if there is a 40 or 30 percent chance of rain any differently than a 50 percent chance. Moreover, by the time you work out all of that, say, by looking at the prevailing winds or barometric pressure, you are back in a situation where the cognitive costs of making this decision are exceeding what you might gain from it—in this case, reducing your cost by at most $5.

We can represent this decision in the form of a decision tree, a staple of MBA courses in economics and decision analysis. The idea is that the branches of a tree represent choices. For instance, in figure 4-1, the choice (at the solid black node) is whether to take or leave an umbrella. This decision is made under conditions of uncertainty, and the outcome of that uncertainty is also represented by branches for rain or clear (at the circular node "chosen" by nature). If you didn't have a prediction, the probabilities associated with both those branches might be 50 percent. Here, however, a prediction is available that says that the chance of rain is 90 percent. The final tips of the final branches are the outcome. Associated with each outcome (there are four: take + rain, take + clear, leave + rain, and leave + clear) is a payoff that we have already described as the monetary equivalent of each outcome.

Here we have represented these outcomes as a cost if bad things happen. The amounts there are what someone (in this case, you) have judged them to be. This is why we refer to the amounts as *judgment*. Judgment is an important concept that will play a critical role throughout this book. In particular, who holds the judgment in many respects controls a decision, and moreover, what prediction machines enable is prediction to be decoupled from judgment as, without a machine, a decision-maker often does both together. Here we chose to make the costs of bad outcomes equivalent, that is, both are $10. This means that with this prediction of rain, if you take an umbrella, you expect costs to be $1, and if you don't, you expect them to be $9. A sensible person would choose to take an umbrella with that prediction.

FIGURE 4-1

Umbrella decision tree

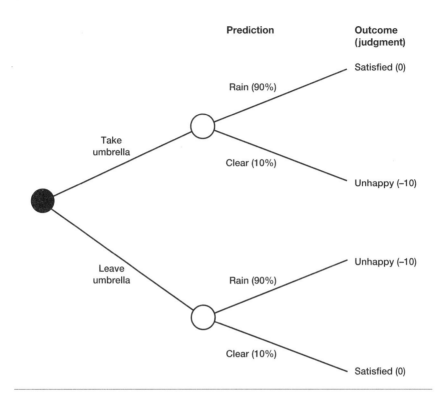

What many do is not decide, especially if they don't have a prediction available. For instance, you might build enough flexibility into your day whereby you can adjust your outdoor time if it happens to be raining. In this case, your default might be to never carry an umbrella. Alternatively, you might buy one of those small retractable umbrellas that are kind of costly because they don't last that long, but they are easier to carry. Then your default would be to always carry an umbrella and never even think about whether or not it's going to rain.

The point here is that, in lieu of gathering information to make an optimal choice, when doing that is costly, we pick up habits or rules to obviate the need to consider information at all. We just do the same thing each time without having to think about it.

What Decisions Buy

If you are refraining from decision-making and are wedded to rules, at first glance, it would appear that AI prediction is not going to be useful to you. AI's job is to serve up information for decision-making. If you are not making a decision, then that information is of no value.

The function of AI is to provide better prediction, which essentially means that you have the information you need to make better decisions. The umbrella-carrying decision is enabled if we have a weather forecast that we can be confident in rather than one that leaves us with a measure of uncertainty. With better information, you may discard your rules and find it worthwhile to spend time making an actual decision.

In the umbrella example, great information frees you from cost. Whether the cost of getting wet or the cost of needlessly carrying an umbrella, if you know what is going to happen, you incur neither cost. To do that, you would have to break your habit, say, of always carrying an umbrella. Instead, you'd need to look at an app—the repository of your rainfall prediction machines—and then decide whether to take an umbrella or not. You could also conceivably just have the app tell you whether to take the umbrella and not even think about why. That still counts as moving from a rule to a decision, even though the app's programmers have determined the thresholds for umbrella-taking. We might not have gotten there with regard to umbrellas, but many of us pay attention to suggested song playlists or the news served up by social media. There's a decision at the heart of that. Choosing to follow the suggestions means not relying on rules (e.g., reading newspapers from front to back) and allowing decisions to be made.

What you might obtain from a move to decision-making based on AI prediction could be quite valuable. We have an inkling of that from past accounts of "forced experimentation," something familiar to anyone who had to work from home during Covid-19. Previously, we didn't really know how productive we might be at home, but being forced to do something different gave us that lesson. We learned something new that came from breaking our past habits. If post-Covid, we don't return to work as we did before, this suggests that the decision of where to work is now meaningful for us.[6]

A similar account was measured during the 2014 two-day strike that impacted the operation of the London tube railway network. Over 60 percent of stations were closed, altering the usual patterns for many people. Given the way stations were closed, for most people the next most convenient station was almost the same distance for them. Also, as it was England, it rained during those days, which likely discouraged people from walking or using bicycles. A study of this event showed that, despite the short duration of the strike, more than 5 percent of commuters changed their commuting patterns following that experience.[7] The people most likely to switch were those for whom the underground map (traditionally a stylized representation) was at its most distorted; that is, where seeming distances between stations were different from what you would perceive if taking the map as a literal representation. Estimates showed that those who switched saved over six minutes daily. With average commuting times of thirty or so minutes, that was a 20 percent time saving, the sort of time you could use deciding what to wear.

While this shows how rules may fail to adapt and be suboptimal, when a three-week price war in retail gasoline broke out in Perth, Australia, in May 2015, the publicity and price fluctuations became apparent to many. Interestingly, a platform (and then app) that showed the prices at different gas stations had existed in the city since 2001. The price war immediately raised the value of using the app. Interestingly, researchers established that the app was used 70 percent more both during and in the year following the end of the price war. In effect, the price war gave rise to sufficient incentives for people to alter their previous habits of not searching for the lowest price and to start doing so as part of their decision-making.[8]

The point is that when you are following a rule, you may be unaware of the value of gathering information and making a decision. These examples provide evidence that there are latent and untapped benefits to decision-making. As such, we can anticipate that some forms of AI prediction may similarly unlock those possibilities.

Investments in Not Deciding

Were Jobs, Zuckerberg, or Obama really avoiding decisions with their daily clothing routine? Yes, if you look at the day, but not if you look at the whole picture. If you are going to wear the same thing every day, you better choose something suitable for the purpose. You can't afford to have something that is uncomfortable in different conditions or is inappropriate for a wide range of situations. It is not easy to find that outfit. The chances are that each spent considerable time arriving at their final choice.

Seen in this light, rules are not really a lack of making a decision but, instead, making a preemptive decision. We do that all the time when we plan. Few people travel without first booking accommodations, selecting return flights, and taking considerable effort packing. Those who travel frequently reduce the cognitive load associated with packing by having preprepared items—toiletries and chargers—that they only use for that purpose. This is an entire exercise in managing when and how often to decide that, in effect, allows you to save time by spending time up front.

When you make such investments in not deciding, the resulting habits are hard to break. If they work well, the whole idea is to be unaware that you have a habit that could be improved by decisions. If you are in the business of developing AI whose value is enabling decisions that are not being made, you will face an uphill battle in gaining adoption.

Any investments public figures make with regard to their clothing routines pale in comparison to the investments most businesses and organizations make in not deciding. Despite maintaining reputations for the opposite, most organizations are not-deciding machines. At the heart of this are standard operating procedures (or SOPs). These are detailed documents describing procedures for doing things all over an organization. Obviously, they differ from business to business, but no business does without them.

While an SOP might economize on the need to revisit the wheel in terms of making decisions and, thus, play the role of an investment in reducing cognitive load similar to the personal choices we have described thus far, they bring with them another benefit: reliability. When people in an organization are following rules, they are doing things that make it easier for other people to do their things without having to engage in costly communication such as meetings.

The construction industry often breaks down the whole process into simpler tasks. There is a construction schedule with a line-by-line and day-by-day listing of every task to accomplish and in what order.[9] The outcomes of those tasks are planned in advance. No one person on site has to think about more than their task. Their only role on completion is to report that they are done, by indication of a check mark, and then move on. There are exceptions that require changes and review, but for the most part, everything proceeds according to a plan. Each person does their part and notes when they have completed their assigned task.

Such rules generate reliability that reduces uncertainty and the need to do anything active to coordinate tasks. In effect, decisions are made up front and put in the plan. But the plan itself means that it is costly to change direction. So long as the issues that arise are small, things can proceed. However, a big issue can derail a plan. And a fixed set of SOPs can make it hard to change and adapt. As we will see later in the book, if you want to throw AI into the mix of this finely tuned system of rules, there will be an immediate challenge. The point of AI is to allow for decisions, but when decisions are made, coordination becomes difficult.

New Decisions

AI prediction may be significant enough that it will provide the requisite information so that making a decision that relies on the prediction rather than sticking to a rule is warranted.

New decisions replace old rules. But old rules don't just exist in isolation. Instead, edifices and scaffolds are put up to insulate those rules from the uncertainty that still exists. There are entire businesses and industries devoted to providing that insulation. Thus, the opportunities for new decisions may be hidden from view. The challenge is to recognize that, find those hidden decisions, and make new decisions that can replace existing rules. We will examine that challenge next.

KEY POINTS

- Rules are decisions that we make preemptively. Making a decision, unlike following a rule, allows us to take into account information available at the time and place of the decision. Therefore, actions resulting from decisions are often better than those resulting from rules because they can respond to the situation. So, why would we ever use rules rather than make decisions? Decisions incur a higher cognitive cost. When is the cost worth it? When the consequences are significant and when the cost of information is small. Introducing AI does not change the consequences, but it lowers the cost of information.

- The trade-off between rules and decision-making is critical in the context of AI systems because the primary benefit of AI is to enhance decision-making. AIs provide little value for rules. AIs generate predictions, and predictions are a key information input to decision-making. So, as AIs become more powerful, they lower the cost of information (prediction) and increase the relative returns to decision-making compared to using rules. Thus, advances in AI will liberate some decision-making from rule-following.

- However, rules not only incur lower cognitive costs but also enable higher reliability. One decision often impacts others. In the context of a *system* with interdependent decisions, reliability can be very important. For example, most organizations rely on standard operating procedures (SOPs), which are rules. SOPs reduce cognitive load and enhance reliability. If you are going to use AI prediction to turn rules into decisions, then you may need to redesign the system to account for the reduced reliability.

5

Hidden Uncertainty

Economist George Stigler once remarked, "If you never miss the plane, you're spending too much time in airports."[1] He said that decades ago, but would he have made the same statement today?

The architects who designed the new Terminal 2 of South Korea's Incheon Airport would hope not. Arrive early for a flight there and you have plenty to do rather than simply wait. You can visit a spa, gamble at a casino, take in an art exhibition, watch a dance performance, or go ice skating. You can also simply shop to your heart's content, grab a meal, or catch some sleep at the "NAP zone." For new airport terminals, this isn't the exception, but the norm. Singapore recently installed a garden with a five-story waterfall. Doha will give you a swimming pool and kids' entertainment center. Vancouver has an aquarium. Amsterdam regularly features art collections moved from its famous museums.[2]

To Incheon's architects, Gensler, the goal was to make the airport the "destination":

> A new generation of airports treats the terminal as more than a threshold. In fact, we are recognizing a new reality: because of security, passengers spend more time in the terminal, making them vital to revenue growth and reputation and creating new

possibilities for what airports can be. This awareness sees airports increasingly treating terminals as destinations, where passengers also spend money.[3]

Take that, Stigler. You can't spend too much time at an airport if you want to spend time there. And that is what people are doing:

> "Passengers are spending up to an hour longer inside the airport than they did just a decade or so earlier," says Tom Theobald, architect and principal at Fentress Architects, which specializes in airport design. He noted that even as air travel has changed dramatically, too often that added time is spent in airports built in the '60s and '70s.[4]

But what came first? Airports are only now being designed as a "destination." Despite airports being what they previously were, people were spending more time there. It was a choice. Why? Because getting to their flight had become more uncertain. There's traffic, parking, and security lines to contend with. The flights themselves have change fees, overbooking, connections, and overhead bin races. Getting to a flight on time is harder, and the consequences of failing to do so have risen. Even without a nine-hole golf course (fly to Bangkok and see), you might want to arrive a little earlier and just read a book.[5] With each new amenity, however, you forget why you arrive at the airport an extra hour before your flight. It becomes your new rule.

Reflect on just how strange this state of affairs is. Since 1992, Incheon has spent $10 billion expanding its airport. Much of that cost has been to build architecturally challenging and expansive terminal spaces beyond the security lines. But look at the mission statement of Incheon Airport; its goal is to "ensure smooth air transportation."[6] You won't find an airport that claims to be doing anything other than moving people through it. And yet those designing airports are thinking about ways of keeping people at airports. What's more, around 40 percent of airport revenues now come from nonaeronautical charges, the biggest component of which are rents from retailers.[7] The designers are doing their job—ensuring that the airports can generate more revenue and, at the same time, causing everyone not to think about the extra time they are spending at airports.

Modern airports are a monument to what we call "hidden uncertainty." When people do not have the information they need to make optimal decisions—say, regarding when to leave for the airport—they will adopt rules. Changes in air travel and getting to and through airports have made it desirable to select rules that leave you waiting at airports longer. Airports know that if waiting is unpleasant, travel will be unpleasant, and you'll do less of it. So, when taking on big new investments in infrastructure, they aren't just thinking about getting people through. They are thinking about making waiting more pleasant and, in the process, making money from that. Once you have arrived earlier at the airport, you are more willing to pay for a meal or other activities in much the same way that popcorn, even highly priced tubs, looks better as you are about to go into a movie. If you don't feel the cost of a rule and rarely miss a flight to boot, you won't reflect on your rules and habits. The uncertainty moves to the background, while the consequences of that entire system of choices can be seen in the form of gleaming new buildings with amazing five-story waterfalls.

In looking for opportunities to use AI to make new decisions, the previous chapter showed that you should take a hard look at rules and see if they can be turned into decisions that utilize AI to embrace rather than tolerate uncertainty. In this chapter, we will show that it is not simply the rules themselves that represent the target of opportunity for AI-enabled new decisions but the edifices and scaffolding that have built up to hide the uncertainty that leads to feelings of waste and inefficiency in the rules we have adopted. Not only are they a sign that there is an opportunity for AI; they also represent the magnitude of that opportunity. Indeed, for airports, some very simple applications of AI represent a threat to all they currently stand for.

The Alternative Airport Universe

Before considering the threat AI prediction may pose to airports, as with everything, there is an alternative system that can show us what the other side looks like. One example is the alternative universe of the very, very wealthy. They don't fly commercial and so have no occasion to deal with either the old or newly designed public airport terminals. Instead, they fly privately and go through private terminals. Normally, glitz, glamour, nice restaurants, and art galleries are going to be where the very rich are. But in the world of airports, private terminals are positively spartan.

The reason there is no investment in making private terminals better places is that the very uncertainty that plagues the rest of us doesn't plague the rich. With a commercial plane, you are tied to a schedule, and those planes will leave late passengers behind. With a private plane, the schedule is more flexible or even nonexistent. If the passengers aren't there, the plane doesn't leave until they arrive. If the passengers are there earlier, the plane leaves then. The whole system is designed so there is no waiting—at least, on the part of the passengers. No waiting means no need to invest in making waiting more pleasant. At the same time, the rich don't have rules about when they need to leave for the airport. They leave when they want. If more people could have that experience, then surely the optimal terminal would be more spartan than cathedral.

You don't have to be rich, however, to see this alternative universe. Instead, just compare the world on the other side of the arrival gates to those at departure. When arrival areas are separated from departure areas, they are spartan. You might find some light food outlets, but everything else is designed to get you out of the airport. The critical issue is how close the taxi and parking facilities are, even though you may not be in a stressful rush. Do you even remember any details of arrivals at your regular airport, other than how best to get out?

The AI Airport Threat

Airports are no strangers to AI. Air traffic control has adopted AI-based systems to better predict aircraft arrivals and congestion.[8] At Eindhoven Airport, a new AI baggage-handling system is being piloted whereby passengers simply photograph their bags, drop them off, and pick them up at their destination—no labels required.[9] Subject to privacy requirements, it hopes to do the same with people.[10] All this will help you get to your flight more quickly.

None of these things, however, hit at the key drivers of uncertainty in your travel to your flight—traffic and security. Change, however, is already here with regard to traffic. Navigational apps such as Waze account for traffic conditions and can reasonably estimate how long it takes to get to any airport based on the time of day. The apps aren't perfect, but they keep getting better.

The apps free passengers from having rules that tell them how early they need to leave for the airport. Instead, they can add that flight time to their calendar, and an app tells them the best time to depart and schedule their time accordingly. Even better, in the near future, the uncertainty in the actual time a flight leaves will be taken into account. Rather than just telling you when you need to leave based on a scheduled departure, the app will tell you when to leave depending on the flight's predicted actual departure. Again, there is residual uncertainty, but the leap from having no information to having more precise information could save hours of waiting time. Similarly, many Uber riders who previously thought they wouldn't care about knowing the predicted arrival time of their taxi now cite that information as one of the most valuable features of the service. Uber uses AI to make that prediction.[11]

AI could also predict security line wait times. Put it all together, and you can use the AI to decide when to leave for the airport rather than rely on rules. As with everything, there will be some who leap at this possibility ahead of others. At Incheon and many other airports, waiting isn't bad anymore, so maybe you don't need to make an informed decision.

Those developing an AI-driven navigation app or flight departure predictor have no direct interest in the earnings of in-terminal airport activities. However, the value of their AI applications depends critically on how many people do not want to wait at airports. Thus, if airports are currently less costly to wait in, the value of those apps is diminished.

The security line prediction is another matter. Airports claim that they want to improve security times and reduce uncertainty. But as economists, we don't think their incentives are aligned with passengers. Yes, improving security times leaves more time to spend at the facilities past security. But, at the same time, it will reduce uncertainty and cause people to tighten their airport arrival times. Combined with AI that solves the other uncertainty for passengers in getting to the terminal, will the airports want to eliminate the uncertainty under their own control?

Accommodating Rules

Our broader point is not about airports but about rules. Rules arise because it is costly to embrace uncertainty, but they create their own set of problems.

The so-called Shirky Principle, put forth by technology writer Clay Shirky, states that "institutions will try to preserve the problem to which they are the solution." The same can be said of businesses. If your business is to provide a way to help people when they wait for a plane, what's the chance you are going to ensure they don't have to wait for planes?

If you want to find opportunities by creating new AI-enabled decisions, you need to look beyond the guardrails that protect rules from the consequences of uncertainty and target activities that make bearing those costs easier or to reduce the likelihood of bad outcomes that the rules would otherwise have to tolerate.

We can see this in the long-standing protection farmers employ in England—building hedgerows. A hedgerow is a carefully planned set of robust trees and plants that serve as a wall between fields. It is extremely useful if your field is full of farm animals, and you do not want to employ a person to ensure they do not wander off. It is also useful if you do not want heavy rainfall to erode soil too quickly or if you want to protect crops from strong winds. Given all this protection against risky events, we are not surprised that this practice was the origin of the term "hedging," which evolved to have a broader insurance meaning.

But hedgerows come at a cost. By dividing farmland, they make it impossible to use certain farming techniques—including mechanization—that are only efficient for large swathes of land. After World War II, the British government actually subsidized the removal of hedgerows, although in some cases, that removal was excessive, given their role in risk management. Today, there is a movement to restore hedgerows, led most prominently by the Prince of Wales.[12]

In many situations, costly investments are made to cover or shelter a would-be decision-maker from risk. Miles of highways are cocooned with guardrails to prevent cars from going down embankments, hills, or into oncoming traffic. Most are, fortunately, never used, but each allows a road to be built in a way that might have otherwise not been sufficiently safe, given the fallibility of human drivers.

More generally, building codes precisely specify various measures to protect those inside buildings from uncertain events. These include fire but also damage from weather, weak building foundations, and other natural phenomena like earthquakes.

What these protection measures have in common is that they typically generate what looks like overengineered solutions. They are designed for a certain set of events—the once-in-a-lifetime storm or the once-in-a-century flood. When those events occur, the engineering seems worthwhile. But, in their absence, there is cause to wonder. For many years, *Freakonomics* authors Steven Levitt and Stephen Dubner pointed out how life vests and rafts on aircraft—not to mention the safety demonstrations of each—appeared wasteful, given how few aircraft had successfully landed on water.[13] Then, in 2009, Captain Sullenberger landed a US Airways plane with no working engines on the Hudson River. Does that one example of a low-probability event make the precautionary life vests worth it? It is hard to know. But we cannot conclude that the absence of a possible outcome causes us to assess the probability of that outcome at zero.

Levitt and Dubner's main point, however, is that while it is often possible when protection measures are employed to assess the likelihood or change in the likelihood of underlying uncertainty over time, it is not possible to measure whether the investments made to reduce the probability of a consequence are excessive, as the very risk management strategy employed takes away that information. It is entirely possible that too much is wasted on something that, for other reasons, is no longer high risk at all.

Greenhouse Systems

Airports may seem a daunting place in which AI can upend the costs of uncertainty. But the opportunities may be right there in your own activities. Finding hidden uncertainty and creating AI predictions to foster new decisions may lead to dramatic changes in how you do your business.

Growing crops is rife with uncertainty, mostly due to the weather. If conditions are too hot, too cold, too humid, not humid enough, or too windy, then yields may be low. All that might lead you to farm inside so you can control the weather. The problem is that crops also need light. Hence, the greenhouse, a place for growing plants inside that still has the benefits of sunlight. A greenhouse gives the farmer extraordinary control over temperature, humidity, and irrigation.[14] This control doesn't come cheap. Heating, cooling, and supplemental light all require energy. The energy required is predictable and can be managed.

The problem, however, is that crops aren't the only things that like a controlled climate. Pests also thrive there. Aphids, gnats, bloodworms, mites, and others therefore grow and multiply more rapidly than outdoors.[15] Massachusetts has a handbook for greenhouse management, a third of which is devoted to pest control.[16] Doing this takes considerable time on the part of farmers. They inspect plants, eliminate standing pools of water, sterilize tools, and use pesticides. Much of the work involved in managing greenhouses involves protecting the greenhouse from the chance that pests enter or reducing the impact of any pests that get through the door.

AI can help. Ecoation is one startup that is using AI to improve pest management in greenhouses.[17] Ecoation is a scouting system. A human operator drives the machine around in a greenhouse. The machine vision systems generate predictions of possible infestations and areas of risk. This enables prediction of the present: telling the farmer where pesticides or other pest-control tools are needed today. This data also enables AI to predict pest pressures across the entire greenhouse one week in the future. The week of lead time is about how long it can take to order and deploy pest-control tools.[18] The headline advantage is cost saving: AI means the right pest-control tools are ordered at the right time, which is how Ecoation currently markets its services.

But looking at the system as a whole will tell you there are bigger benefits than cost saving. Farmers adhere to a whole lot of rules that minimize pest issues, including planting pest-tolerant crops, keeping greenhouses small so they can be inspected, calibrating climate conditions in certain ways, and so forth. There is real value in being able to relax those rules. If AI for pest prediction gets good enough, then greenhouses can operate differently. Farmers can grow pest-sensitive crops. Larger greenhouses become possible. Alternative strategies to save on energy might arise. If AI companies like Ecoation do a good enough job controlling pests, then we can replace existing rules and build a new system. In agriculture, just like in airports, AI can enable moving from rules to decisions.

KEY POINTS

- It is not simply the rules themselves that represent the target of opportunity for AI-enabled decisions but the edifices and scaffolding that have built up to hide the uncertainty that leads to waste and inefficiency in the rules we have adopted.

- Modern airports are an example of expensive edifices and scaffolding constructed to hide uncertainty. The prime sources of uncertainty are potential delays caused by traffic and security. Lavish new airports are designed to help people forget that they are operating under a rule that forces them to arrive at the airport long before their scheduled departure.

- In greenhouses, AI predictions of pest infestations can be used to enhance the grower's ability to prevent them. This is a point solution. If AI for pest prediction becomes good enough, then instead of being used as a point solution, AI could enable a *system-level change*. The entire structural design and workflow of the greenhouse are influenced by the risk of pest infestation. With better prediction, farmers can grow different (more pest-sensitive) crops, operate larger greenhouses, and pursue novel alternative energy-saving strategies.

6

Rules Are Glue

Surgeon and medical writer Atul Gawande loves checklists. His ode to checklists, *The Checklist Manifesto*, had a single aim: to explain to highly skilled super-specialist experts that ticking off a checklist is far from beneath them. It is an essential part of doing their job in ever more complex environments.

Checklists are a staple of modern organizational living. When the US Army was looking for a new bomber, it initially rejected Boeing's Model 299 over McDonnell Douglas's alternative, despite its ability to carry five times the payload, fly faster, and go twice the distance because, well, it crashed. The crash was not due to a design issue but instead to pilot error. It was a more difficult plane to fly.

The army decided to buy a few planes anyway. But rather than give pilots more training, as Gawande notes, it instead did something simpler: it developed and gave the pilots a checklist of the steps required in various activities such as takeoff and landing:

> Its mere existence indicated how far aeronautics had advanced. In the early years of flight, getting an aircraft into the air might have been nerve-racking, but it was hardly complex. Using a checklist for takeoff would no more have occurred to a pilot than

to a driver backing a car out of the garage. But this new plane was too complicated to be left to the memory of any pilot, however expert.

With the checklist in hand, the pilots went on to fly the Model 299 a total of 1.8 million miles without one accident. The Army ultimately ordered almost thirteen thousand of the aircraft, which it dubbed the B-17.[1]

Gawande argued, convincingly, that modern medicine had grown so complex it could benefit from the same approach. He knew it was a tough sell. After all, top surgeons were still resisting having to wash their hands and scrub down.[2] But checklists were used for complex environments all over the place, from construction sites to the Cheesecake Factory. If they could save lives, doctors should surely suck it up.

We aren't going to argue with Gawande about the value of checklists, but we are going to sympathize with those who use them. The checklist exists because of uncertainty. As there are many interrelated parts to a complex system and many people doing tasks within them to make it all work, checklists are not simply indicators that something has been done. Instead, they are the manifestation of rules and the need to follow them. They are there to ensure reliability and reduce error. The alternative is that experts make decisions based on their own observations, which create problems and uncertainty for other people.

Large businesses have checklists. They also have standard operating procedures (SOPs), which serve a similar role. As discussed in chapter 4, SOPs are large manuals identifying all the steps people need to follow, including checking off whether they have done them. The SOPs make complex organizations function. But we have to recognize them for what they represent. They are rules to follow rather than decisions to make.

SOPs and checklists are the detritus of hidden uncertainty that has generated the myriad rules chiseled into the veins of the organization. For each rule, there is uncertainty that has led to it. And for each, we can ask the question: If we had AI prediction, could we enhance productivity by turning the rule into a decision and removing it from the SOP manual?

Different People Are Different

Rules involve doing the same thing for everyone as if they are all the same. But they aren't all the same. Different people are different. That is perhaps the fundamental lesson of marketing. So marketers try to segment the population into groups and target products to the groups that might find the product attractive.

When marketers treat everyone the same, it is because they lack information. If they had information, they would provide personalized products and personalized services. Marketers could move from rules that treat everyone the same to decisions that allow them to provide the right products to the right people at the right time.

Radio was all about rules. Radio stations hired DJs who would broadcast the same songs to everyone listening. Streaming music services such as Spotify, Apple Music, and Pandora allowed for the creation of personalized playlists.

But what challenges are involved in creating value from personalized playlists? Researchers David Reiley and Hongkai Zhang at Pandora asked this question when they turned their attention to examining other rules at their company. Although playlists were personalized, otherwise the business operated by rules. Pandora has a freemium model. Some customers pay a fee and get an advertising-free listening experience. Everyone else listened for free as long as they sat through a set number of advertisements per hour.

Reiley and Zhang, working with University of Washington professor Ali Goli, realized that they could apply AI to data from an experiment that determined how much people disliked the ads and how much they liked the service. The AI provided personalized predictions so that they could assess not just how much people disliked the ads, on average, but the differences across people. With that information, they no longer needed to stick with a rule on how ads were inserted. Instead, some people could receive more ads, and some fewer.[3] By personalizing the number of ads, they realized they could increase profits substantially. The AI predicted which customers would listen more if the number of ads decreased. It also predicted who might be induced to switch to the paid version.

With this information in hand, they no longer needed the rule of show-ing the same number of ads to everyone. They could decide to show fewer ads to those consumers who would listen more if the number of ads per hour declined. They could show more ads to those consumers who would switch to the paid version. Pandora's research department showed how AI could enable new decisions.

It wasn't straightforward. Expanded advertising capacity requires finding advertisers. Goli, Reiley, and Zhang estimated that just two-thirds of the ad slots would be filled. The challenge was that they needed new advertisers in order to avoid sending the same ad to the same customer over and over again.[4] Successful implementation required a new advertis-ing sales strategy.

It also required an understanding of customer reactions. The most profitable aspect of the AI would be to ratchet up advertising to custom-ers who were on the fence between the free and the paid versions. By degrading the quality of the free version, these customers would switch to the paid version. However, customers might well be upset if this was how Pandora used their data. Thus, this strategy risked having them leave the service altogether.

These constraints have meant that Pandora has not yet implemented this AI. It still uses a rule to determine how many ads to show. Building an AI is the first step in dropping a rule. Processes still need to change in order to enable decisions.

Another Brick in the Wall

Education is filled with rules. Where to sit. How to act. What to do. One of us (Avi) received a fifty-nine-page "parents' guide to policies and prac-tices" from his child's school. It covers health and safety rules related to allergies, lice, injury, and immunization. It also covers the homework pol-icy, how birthdays are celebrated, cell phones, drop-off and pickup, and the class placement policy. That's just for the parents!

These rules serve a purpose. They enable a safe and efficient education system. As Cosmo Kramer put it on *Seinfeld*, "A rule is a rule and let's face it, without rules, there's chaos."[5]

Of course, it is possible to have too many rules. The worry that education creates uniformity has a long history. In 1859, John Stuart Mill wrote in *On Liberty*, a "general State education is a mere contrivance for molding people to be exactly like one another."[6]

Educators are well aware of this tension between rules and flexibility. Education documents describe and try to address it. The New York State Kindergarten Learning Standards emphasize:

> Rather than prescribe a lockstep progression of lessons or curricula for all children in all settings, the standards serve to articulate the expectations of what children can learn and do as a result of instruction that is not standardized, but personalized, differentiated, adapted, culturally and linguistically relevant, and context-based. While we may have the same learning objectives for all children, our means of meeting these objectives are highly responsive to the individual child.[7]

So there are standards for everyone, but the education that each student gets is different. That's a wonderful vision and a challenging one. The best teachers make this happen. They adapt the lessons to the individual children in their classroom. Other teachers find this more challenging. From a global perspective, it is even harder. High-income countries spend thousands of dollars per child. Many low-income countries spend just $50 per child per year. With so few resources, it is difficult to move away from rules.[8]

A place to start is entrepreneurship education. Aid agencies like the World Bank and governments around the world spend more than $1 billion to train about 4 million potential and existing entrepreneurs in developing countries every year.[9] Many of these training programs work to improve business practices and profits, but they are expensive and the return on investment is not always clear. Online training holds promise, but it can't be uniform. One-size-fits-all infomercials make little difference. One of the main lessons is that intensive personalized training works best. The challenge is how to deliver that personalized education at scale.

Economists Yizhou Jin and Zhengyun Sun thought AI could help. They worked with a large e-commerce platform to deliver entrepreneurship training to hundreds of thousands of new sellers. The training program involved dozens of possible modules and focused on setting up a website, marketing strategy, and customer service. For example, the training might provide a checklist for best practices in product descriptions so that customers understood what they were buying. Another aspect of the training focuses on search engine optimization and keyword selection.

Not all modules were relevant to all sellers, and a new seller might not know what kind of training would help. The AI enabled personalization. It took in data about a seller's actual operations and products, and developed a sequence for training. It then recommended modules to the sellers. Sellers then implemented the modules. This meant personalized entrepreneurship education to hundreds of thousands of sellers. Rather than the rule that every seller receives the same information, the AI enabled new decisions on which entrepreneurs received which training.

The program was run using a randomized control trial so that its effectiveness could be measured.[10] Of 8 million new businesses on the platform, 2 million were offered the training. Of these, about 500,000 used it. The businesses that used the training experienced a 6.6 percent increase in revenue. Over the course of a year, the program increased seller revenue by about $6 million. That might not sound like much: $12 per business per year. But that's starting from a base of $200 in total revenue. A personalized training program with human teachers could never be cost-effective. The AI enables decisions on which training to send to which entrepreneur while reaching hundreds of thousands of businesses. AI enabled decisions over rules and created value at scale.

Unsticking the Rules

When rules have existed for a long time, it can be hard to see the system that they are embedded in. Because rules are reliable, a myriad of rules and procedures can stick together. If something moves, they have to all move at once.

On the free version of Pandora, every user receives the same amount of advertising. This is generally true of advertising-supported media. Network television stations used eight minutes every half hour for advertising. This was the rule that drove network revenue. Around this rule a variety of other processes developed. Programs were designed to be twenty-two minutes or forty-four minutes, which meant the writers needed to write every episode of a show at the same length, with natural pauses at the intervals when commercials take place. This rule is affixed to this system.

YouTube provides an example of an alternative system design for content. Unlike network television, YouTube content creators can create content of any length. The system's AI can predict which viewers will be most attracted to which content. The AI driving the search engine and the recommendation engine enables viewers to find suitable content despite a seemingly infinite catalog of options. Furthermore, the AI can predict which users will be most attracted to which advertisements. Importantly, *this prediction capability is much more valuable in a system that allows different users to view different content.* Even if network television had an AI that was able to generate similar predictions, the value would be much less because its system forces every viewer to view the same content. So, the best it could do is to predict which advertisement would be most appealing to the most viewers.

In other words, the same AI that predicts viewer attraction to content and advertising is much more valuable in the YouTube system than in the network television system. And while the AI *directly* enables discovery in a vast catalog of content and enables advertisement matching, it *indirectly* enables flexible content lengths because the solutions for discovery and advertising solve the problem of an infinite number of combinations of content, advertising, and timings that make flexible content lengths intractable for network television.

In school systems, students in the same grade learn the same things. *There is a fixed curriculum.* "Students are educated in batches, according to age, as if the most important thing they have in common is their date of manufacture."[11] For example, in Ontario, where we live, almost all students born in 2009 enter first grade in 2015 and high school in 2023. These rules are in place to manage the uncertainty around which level a given student should be at, for both academic and social reasons. These rules, in turn, glue together in a system: teacher training to manage a limited diversity in learning needs; modest extra help and resources to students who fall behind. And, at the high school level, there are nominal programs for students who do not conform to the standard process for their cohort, including alternative schools, work-study programs, and processes to get high school equivalency certificates.

An AI that predicts the next best learning content for each student would personalize education, allowing students who master a topic quickly to move to something new before they get bored and at the same time allowing students who need more practice on a topic extra time, examples, and exercises to develop competency in that area before moving on. As a point solution, this AI could enhance learning in the existing school system to some extent, although the impact would be limited because once a student completes their grade's age-based curriculum, they would be done for the year or need to continue any further learning with limited teacher support because teachers are often trained for a specific level (e.g., middle-school math). In the existing system, this problem would become increasingly severe in later grades as the spread between faster and slower learners in a subject area grows over time. To support their students, teachers would need teaching mastery over an increasingly large range of topics.

Imagine, instead, a system where students progress through school as a class (their physical and social development is paced by biology), but many different tutors and teachers come and go to support different students, depending on their individual learning needs. The tutors and teachers that students work with are independent of the students' ages but are instead determined by the nature of their questions and ability in a subject area. The impact of the AI would be much greater in this new system compared to the impact of the same AI in the existing system because each student could receive an education personalized to their learning needs and style. Students who learn fast in one subject and slow in others could be accommodated. Students who need to focus on particular skills would have teachers who specialize in those areas. The teacher would not need to select the style that helped the most students. Teachers who are great at helping struggling students to read, and those who excel at helping students shine in mathematics competitions, would spend all their time on what they do best.

Rules such as twenty-two-minute programming and the age-based curriculum were put in place to deal with uncertainty. Then, various forms of scaffolding were developed to optimize the performance of the system. While invisible to the casual observer, the rules became the glue that holds the system together. So, introducing an AI that enables a rule to be transformed into a decision might seem attractive at first glance, but its impact may be limited because the rule it's replacing is tightly coupled with other elements of the system.

Dropping an AI that predicts the next best content into the existing school system would have limited impact because the age-based curriculum rule with a single teacher per class is a cornerstone of the current educational system, especially in elementary school. In contrast, using exactly the same AI, but embedding it in a new system designed to leverage the AI's personalized content and pacing by coupling it with personalized discussion, group projects, and teacher support, which would require much more flexible tutor and teacher allocations and modified educator training, would likely result in a much bigger impact on education and personal growth and development.

In other words, the age-based curriculum rule is the glue that holds together much of the modern education system, and so an AI that personalizes learning content can only provide limited benefit in that system. The primary challenge for unleashing the potential of a personalized education AI is not building the prediction model but unsticking education from the age-based curriculum rule that currently glues the system together.

KEY POINTS

- Like SOPs, checklists are the manifestation of rules and the need to follow them. They are there to ensure reliability and reduce error. The alternative is that people make decisions based on their own observations. While switching from a rule to a decision may improve the quality of that particular action, it may also create problems and uncertainty for other people.

- Rules glue together in a system. That's why it's hard to replace a single rule with an AI-enabled decision. Thus, it's often the case that a very powerful AI only adds marginal value because it is introduced into a system where many parts were designed to accommodate the rule and resist change. They are interdependent—glued together.

- An example is a personalized education AI that predicts the next best content to present to a learner. Dropping this AI into a system designed around the age-based curriculum rule would stifle the benefit. In contrast, embedding the very same AI into a new system that leverages personalized (not age-based) discussion, group projects, and teacher support would likely result in a much bigger impact on overall education and personal growth and development. The primary challenge for unleashing the potential of a personalized education AI is not building the prediction model but rather unsticking education from the age-based curriculum rule that currently glues the system together.

PART THREE

Systems

7

Glued versus Oiled Systems

AI didn't save us from Covid-19, but it could have. It didn't because, in the face of uncertainty, many countries followed public health procedures based on rules rather than decisions. We've already noted that AI prediction has the potential to move away from rules to decisions. Consequently, the pandemic is a salient place to start our discussion of how AI can facilitate such changes.

That AI didn't save us from Covid-19 does not mean that AI wasn't ready but that we weren't ready for it. In many countries, the traditional rules established by public health authorities in the public sector did not accommodate the type of decision-making that would be required to preserve the economy in the face of an unexpected pandemic. However, there were some exceptions. We describe one where a small group of large companies created an innovation platform precisely to oil the system. This would allow for decision-making under uncertainty in order to prevent a shutdown due to the harsh rules-based system that ignored information.

The Most Costly Rule

We are now all familiar with the health risks that arise during a pandemic. In January 2021, about 9 million Americans had Covid-19.[1] For them, Covid-19 was a severe health problem. For most of the other 320 million Americans, however, Covid-19 was not a health problem. They were not sick. They were not infectious. Yet many were still severely affected in their ability to work, study, and play. The majority of people were impacted by Covid-19 not because of a health problem but because of a prediction problem. We lacked the information to predict who was infectious and could spread the virus to others.

The message from public health authorities was that you can be safe by treating everyone else as equally infectious and dangerous. With infectious diseases that spread from person to person, contact with others becomes more dangerous if you don't know who is infectious. This is why we distance ourselves from others during a pandemic. It is the simplest way to protect ourselves.

Let's consider this in a decision tree context. The action being taken is whether to isolate or interact with others (depicted in figure 7-1). If you isolate, you do not spread the disease, but you have to distance, which is personally costly. If you interact, then the outcome depends on whether you are infectious. If you are, you may spread the virus. If not, your life goes on as normal.

The decision tree highlights the issue that arises because most people are not infectious. If you are currently infected with Covid-19, you are much more dangerous than if you are not. In other words, if we *knew* who was infected and who was not infected, we could do something different. We could keep away from the infected and act more normally around those who aren't infected. This is the core prediction problem at the heart of a pandemic: we could avoid many of the costs of the pandemic if we just knew who was infectious and kept them away from others.[2] Others could then safely go about their business while keeping infectious people quarantined. Do that and not only do you keep things more normal, but you bring the pandemic to heel as you break chains of transmission. The problem was that information was needed to turn social distancing from a

FIGURE 7-1

Isolate or interact decision tree

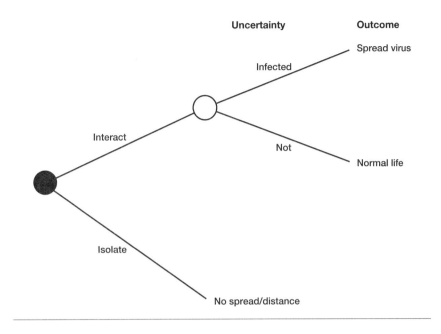

rule to a decision. And the need for information to resolve uncertainty meant we had a prediction problem.

Covid-19 as a Prediction Problem

The first step in identifying a prediction problem is to ask where the uncertainty is. From that perspective, pandemics are laden with uncertainty. The big unknown is when a pathogen with pandemic potential might strike. That may, indeed, be a problem that AI might solve. However, what we want to focus on is something closer to home: pandemic management. That is, when a pathogen on the brink of becoming a pandemic or one that has become one has already emerged, what is the key uncertainty in bringing it quickly to heel?

This is perhaps a strange way to formulate the problem of pandemic management. After all, we are used to thinking of it as a public health challenge. How do we find vaccines to bring it to an end, treatments that can save lives, or mitigations to minimize spread? But when we unpack what is really making a pandemic a pandemic, with all its human costs in terms of not only health but also economic livelihoods and social life, we realize that those very mitigations that stop people from infecting one another are taking our normal lives with them.

Over the first months of the pandemic, a wide variety of tools were developed to predict who might be infected. One of the oldest ways that public health officials separate who is or is not likely to be infected is by tracing exposure. If you are near an infectious person, you are more likely to be infected yourself. Such contact tracing can help officials predict who might have been infected recently. In many countries, this was a labor-intensive and uncertain process, with officials calling the infected and asking them where they had been. In South Korea, public health authorities developed new procedures by combining data from closed-circuit cameras, credit card swipes, and mobile phones to support the contact tracing efforts.[3]

Innovation wasn't limited to contact tracing. AI experts also developed tools for predicting infectiousness. One team developed tools to detect asymptomatic infections by having people cough into their phones.[4] At the Greek border, an AI tool that took into account factors such as mode of travel, departure points, and demographic information and was updated weekly could detect 1.85 times as many asymptomatic people as random surveillance, thus helping to identify which travelers could enter the country without need for further testing.[5] Non-AI prediction tools were also developed. Many places used thermal cameras and thermometers to detect fevers, assuming that people with elevated temperatures were more likely to have Covid-19. In Thailand, dogs were trained to sniff out the disease in people.[6]

By fall 2020, it was clear to many that rapid antigen tests were the most efficient tool for predicting infectiousness. While polymerase chain reaction (PCR) tests could detect very low quantities of the virus, they were slower and more expensive than antigen tests.[7]

Prediction is the process of filling in missing information, and Covid-19 tests helped fill in the information of whether someone was infectious. Like other predictions, rapid antigen tests are not 100 percent accurate.

Still, false positives are rare with antigen tests, meaning it is unlikely for someone to test positive and not be infectious.[8] So if you could test people and require those with positive antigen tests to stay home, then the spread of the disease could be kept in check. The same is not true of PCR tests, where it is possible to test positive for weeks or months after the infectious period. In other words, by fall 2020 we had an inexpensive Covid-19 prediction tool that could be mass-produced. It wasn't an AI tool but a different type of prediction device.

Armed with this knowledge, we partnered with epidemiologist Laura Rosella, political scientist Janice Stein, and Creative Destruction Lab executive director Sonia Sennik to design, and help corporations implement, a rapid testing program to enable workplaces to open safely.[9]

The idea was to test workers regularly, keep Covid-positive workers at home, and allow everyone else to go to work, comforted by the knowledge their colleagues had recently tested negative. The prediction tool was available and the plan seemed straightforward to implement. It would make the essential workplaces that hadn't closed safer, and over time, allow the economy to begin to reopen.

However, we soon learned that the prediction tool was the easy part. The system was glued together by many rules that did not lend themselves to information-based decision-making. There were privacy rules around collecting people's health information, union rules around limiting access to workplaces, data security rules around storing and processing personal information, hazardous waste disposal rules for discarding buffer solution after tests were administered, workers' compensation rules about who would bear the cost of time off when someone tested positive, and the list goes on.

Despite the urgency of solving the information problem that threatened to shut down the economy, the extent to which the system was glued together with rules rendered an information-based decision-making solution nearly impossible. We needed to find a way to oil the system to make it more responsive to information—specifically, to predictions of infectiousness.

We discussed the problem with a group of CEOs and thought leaders, including Mark Carney, the former governor of the Bank of England and the Bank of Canada; Brenda Fitzgerald, the former director of the Centers for Disease Control and Prevention in Atlanta; and author Margaret Atwood. By October 2020, twelve CEOs emerged who agreed to provide the setting for an oiled system.[10] Each committed to appointing one of their direct reports to work firsthand on this project and remove rule-based barriers wherever possible. Our goal was to design a system in this oiled environment that was sufficiently compelling to inspire other companies as well as public health officials to trade in some of their rule-based, glued system for information-based, oiled decisions.

These twelve large companies—the founding partners of the CDL Rapid Screening Consortium—represented manufacturing, transportation, financial services, utilities, entertainment, and retail. Together, they employed over half a million workers. The CEOs were eager to get the testing regime started, open their workplaces up, and keep their employees safe. Soon after we started, the employees surveyed reported feeling comforted that they and their coworkers would be tested before entering the workplace.[11]

One of our founding members launched the first pilot on January 11, 2021, at a site in downtown Toronto. Over the next few months, the system proved to work well. The small fraction of people who were infected were identified so they never came near their colleagues at work, workers reported feeling safer, and managers were able to keep facilities open that they likely would otherwise have needed to shut down. We then created a playbook to share with other companies and eventually other types of organizations, including not-for-profits, camps, day cares, and schools. The playbook included guidance on how to set up a data reporting process, administer the rapid antigen tests, set up a physical testing kiosk, train the staff that managed the process, communicate the program to employees and their unions, manage the data flows, discard used tests, handle the logistics associated with employees who test positive, order rapid antigen tests from the government, and so on.

Over time, the glue at other companies began to unstick. In Canada, both nationally and province by province, workers could initially test themselves at work under supervision, and eventually at home, without the need for a health-care professional.

It was also necessary to keep track of the tests. People feared that some participants who had been exposed to Covid-19 would misinterpret a negative test as a signal that they would not develop the disease for several weeks when, at best, it would be days. Frequent testing mitigated this risk, so we needed a data system to keep track of who tested and when. The companies, however, would only accept the data system if it protected worker privacy. We developed a data tracking system that satisfied both employee concerns around privacy and public health requirements for ensuring compliance.

Company policies evolved to support rapid testing. In the absence of sick pay and other workplace protections, workers were wary to participate, so the employers needed to determine who would test and when. Companies needed to decide whether testing counted as part of the workday, where the testing would take place, and what to do when someone tested positive. They also needed to assign responsibility for these health and safety decisions. Initially, there was no existing process to determine the responsibilities of workers, managers, and health professionals. The glue began to unstick as companies gained confidence in our playbook, which included standard operating procedures that were freely shared and constantly updated.

Eventually, our workplace rapid antigen testing system was used in more than 2,000 organizations in Canada, keeping thousands of Covid-19 cases out of workplaces and schools when people tested positive and stayed home. Nonetheless, the challenges were substantial. It took six months for most of the initial participants to deploy testing at scale and a year before tens of thousands of workers were tested regularly. The prediction tool was the easy part. However, it was just one small piece of the change needed to help solve the Covid-19 information problem and allow people to get back to work and school.

Oiled Systems

The message from this chapter is that in order to take advantage of prediction machines, we want to turn rules into decisions. However, the system—the set of procedures according to which something is done—has to be able to accommodate that change. If one rule is glued to another in order for the system to be reliable, putting a decision within that system may be fruitless.

Here we have highlighted the rule that many of us followed in the spring of 2020: stay home. We didn't know who was infectious, and that uncertainty meant the rule was to stay away from people.

That rule, in turn, created all sorts of difficulties. First, many people work outside the home, and the customers for their businesses need to be able to leave their homes. Restaurants, retail, and theaters can't operate during a lockdown. If people aren't allowed to go out, then many people will be unemployed. Governments worldwide added wage subsidies and business support, an expensive solution developed to compensate for the challenges the rule created.

Second, isolation generates its own challenges. It affected people's mental state. It made it difficult to check whether children were safe and whether the elderly had what they needed. Doctor visits moved online or were canceled completely. These issues generated their own new rules. Family members checked on each other. Many schools had policies of calling home. Doctors were asked to proactively check on their patients. In some parts of the world, in-home monitors were added to ensure the elderly were safe.

The pandemic reminds us that we often gravitate to rules and that rules carry their own inefficiencies. For Covid-19, not having a prediction solution to the problem of infectiousness meant we had to quickly shut down entire economies, causing mass unemployment and disruption to social life and schooling. Prediction, if it were available and integrated into a well-functioning, oiled system, would have allowed decisions to be used for pandemic management without sacrificing health outcomes and while minimizing the costs incurred on the whole society. We discuss this issue in chapter 6. Rules that mean we give everyone the same product or the same education limit the decisions we make and the value we create.

Rules are our primary target when looking for new opportunities for decision-making that AI prediction might unlock. For the pandemic, there were tools to generate the predictions needed. Rapid antigen tests helped fill in the missing information of whether someone was infectious. There was also innovation in dependent procedures, like sick pay and isolation. When decisions interact, moving from rules to decisions requires an oiled system of coordination. Decision-makers need to know what others are doing, align their goals, and enable change. However, a new system may be so disruptive that you may need to start using it in a new organization, where it can grow organically, rather than trying to adapt to it in existing organizations.

More broadly, uncovering uncertainty provides a first step to opening up new decisions through prediction. Doing so effectively requires changes to dependent procedures, which, as noted in chapter 2, defines a system solution.

KEY POINTS

- We used a rule—social distancing—to manage the pandemic. This rule was expensive. It led to shutting down a significant fraction of education systems, health-care systems, and the world economy. The resultant isolation had mental health impacts that will take decades to fully comprehend. Many other rules were built around the social distancing rule, such as restaurant capacity limits, public transit protocols, school teaching methods, sporting event restrictions, wage subsidies, and emergency care procedures.

- While most people thought of Covid-19 as a health problem, we reframed it as an information problem.[12] For those who were infected, Covid-19 was indeed a health problem. However, for the vast majority who were not infected, Covid-19 was not a health problem—it was an information problem. That's because without the information on who was infected, we had to follow the rule and treat *everyone* as if they could be infected. That led to shutting down the economy. If, instead, we could have made a reasonably accurate prediction, then we could have solved the information problem and only quarantined people who had a high likelihood of being infectious. Rules are our primary target when looking for new opportunities for decision-making that AI prediction might unlock.

- In order to take advantage of prediction machines, we must often turn rules into decisions. However, the system has to be able to accommodate that change. If one rule is glued to another in order for the system to be reliable, putting a decision within that system may be fruitless. We describe a Covid-19-related example where we developed a small but oiled system, initially consisting of twelve large companies, where the CEOs directed their senior leadership teams to make information-based decisions based on predictions of employee infectiousness from rapid antigen testing. This enabled these twelve companies to keep their businesses running in an environment where the prevailing system would have likely other-wise forced a shutdown. The demonstration of this success subse-quently motivated over 2,000 more organizations to adopt this system and shift from rules to decisions.

8

The System Mindset

Every year contestants assemble at Bletchley Park—where Alan Turing once worked to crack German codes in World War II—to outcompete computer programs in being human. The contest is based on the famous imitation game (now known as the Turing test) whereby a person has a message conversation over a computer with an unseen entity. The entity may be a computer program or a person. Each is trying to convince their counterpart that they are, in fact, human. If you are a person competing, effectively you are, as author Brian Christian put it, trying to be "the most human human."[1] Usually, a human wins, but many people have trouble convincing their counterparts that they are a person.

Horse races like this, where a person is pitted against some machine intelligence, are a mainstay of AI research. How much better is an algorithm in identifying what's in a picture? Are self-driving cars less likely to get into accidents than those driven by people? Will AI be able to select better candidates for interviews and hiring than your HR department? Can a computer beat the world champion at Go?

The contests invite comparison and are the source of angst about whether machines will replace people. Interestingly, cars were better than horses, but horses still race. And when machines were faster than people over any distance, the Olympics continued on without trouble. Why would it be different even if a machine were better at playing Go? The metrics captured something, but replacement didn't necessarily follow.

But when the person is choosing who does a particular task, sentiment or sport won't cut it. The metrics are chosen in order to evaluate performance based on pure efficiency and to invite substitution based on cost. If a machine can do that task and is cheaper, replacement surely will follow. The horses may still race, but they don't move people around anymore. Just as machines replaced people in physical tasks, maybe they will do the same for cognition.

A whole industry has popped up trying to examine people's jobs, task by task, in order to evaluate whether machines might do those tasks in the age of AI. There are thirty distinct tasks associated with the occupation of radiologist (see figure 8-1).[2] Just one of these tasks relates directly to machine prediction: task three on interpreting the outcomes of diagnostic imaging procedures.

Every job can be unpacked this way and assessed for vulnerability to AI. In 2013, a study from the Oxford Martin School declared that nearly half of US jobs are vulnerable to automation.[3] This is the headline fear about AI. Erik Brynjolfsson, Tom Mitchell, and Daniel Rock measured the "suitability for machine learning" of 964 occupations, 18,156 tasks, and 2,069 work activities. The at-risk occupations included workers who make many of the predictions we've already highlighted, including concierges (who make recommendations) and credit authorizers. Massage therapists, animal scientists, and archaeologist jobs remain safe. Not surprisingly, the world's leading labor and macroeconomists have expressed worry that as AI takes over certain tasks, little could be left for human workers, particularly those who are not already at the top of the earnings distribution.[4]

A decade into the current AI wave, machines have replaced humans in very few tasks. Chatbots are playing a bigger role in customer service, and machine translation is gaining an increased share of that activity. But technological unemployment is not on the horizon quite yet, and there are lots of jobs for people to do. While there are AIs that can outperform people, in many instances, those people—warts and all—are still cheaper than their machine replacements. So while economists such as Daron Acemoglu and Pascual Restrepo might argue that due to capital costs

FIGURE 8-1

Thirty tasks associated with the occupation of radiologist

1. Obtain patients' histories from electronic records, patient interviews, dictated reports, or by communicating with referring clinicians.
2. Prepare comprehensive interpretive reports of findings.
3. Perform or interpret the outcomes of diagnostic imaging procedures including magnetic resonance imaging (MRI), computer tomography (CT), positron emission tomography (PET), nuclear cardiology treadmill studies, mammography, or ultrasound.
4. Review or transmit images and information using picture archiving or communications systems.
5. Communicate examination results or diagnostic information to referring physicians, patients, or families.
6. Provide counseling to radiologic patients to explain the processes, risks, benefits, or alternative treatments.
7. Instruct radiologic staff in desired techniques, positions, or projections.
8. Confer with medical professionals regarding image-based diagnoses.
9. Coordinate radiological services with other medical activities.
10. Document the performance, interpretation, or outcomes of all procedures performed.
11. Establish or enforce standards for protection of patients or personnel.
12. Develop or monitor procedures to ensure adequate quality control of images.
13. Recognize or treat complications during and after procedures, including blood pressure problems, pain, oversedation, or bleeding.
14. Participate in continuing education activities to maintain and develop expertise.
15. Participate in quality improvement activities including discussions of areas where risk of error is high.
16. Perform interventional procedures such as image-guided biopsy, percutaneous transluminal angioplasty, transhepatic biliary drainage, or nephrostomy catheter placement.
17. Develop treatment plans for radiology patients.
18. Administer radioisotopes to clinical patients or research subjects.
19. Advise other physicians of the clinical indications, limitations, assessments, or risks of diagnostic and therapeutic applications of radioactive materials.
20. Calculate, measure, or prepare radioisotope dosages.
21. Check and approve the quality of diagnostic images before patients are discharged.
22. Compare nuclear medicine procedures with other types of procedures, such as computed tomography, ultrasonography, nuclear magnetic resonance imaging, and angiography.
23. Direct nuclear medicine technologists or technicians regarding desired dosages, techniques, positions, and projections.
24. Establish and enforce radiation protection standards for patients and staff.
25. Formulate plans and procedures for nuclear medicine departments.
26. Monitor handling of radioactive materials to ensure that established procedures are followed.
27. Prescribe radionuclides and dosages to be administered to individual patients.
28. Review procedure requests and patients' medical histories to determine applicability of procedures and radioisotopes to be used.
29. Teach nuclear medicine, diagnostic radiology, or other specialties at graduate educational level.
30. Test dosage evaluation instruments and survey meters to ensure they are operating properly.

Source: O*NET, https://www.onetonline.org/link/summary/29-1224.00. From "29-1224.00—Radiologists," by the National Center for O*NET Development. Used under the CC BY 4.0 license.

being subsidized relative to labor it is only a matter of time, for now we can all take a breath.

There is, however, another perspective on how AI might change our work lives and how things are produced. Stanford professor Tim Bresnahan has argued that the whole exercise of deconstructing the potential for AI into the tasks AI might perform ignores what has driven radical adoption of new technologies in the past: systemwide change.

Bresnahan argues that we already see this in places that have aggressively adopted AI: Amazon, Google, Facebook, and Netflix:

> Task level substitution plays no role in these applications of AI technology. These very valuable early applications are not ones in which labor was undertaking a task and was replaced by capital. Observers focus on task level substitution, not because it occurs, but because the definition of general AI includes "tasks usually done by humans." Until general AI is commercialized, which is not likely in the foreseeable future, analysis should focus on the capabilities and applications of actual AI technologies. While there may be some task level substitution in the future, it is unrelated to the value proposition of AI technologies.[5]

The AI at the leading technology companies is not a demonstration project. It includes full-scale production systems that generate billions of dollars of revenue. It wasn't built task by task, with AI involved in some of them. Instead, the large tech firms built completely new systems.

The successful adoption of AI presents what we will term here the *system mindset*. It stands in contrast to a task mindset in that it sees the bigger potential of AI and recognizes that to generate real value, systems of decisions, including both machine prediction and humans, will need to be reconstituted and built. This is already happening in some places, but history tells us that it is easier for those new to an industry than for established businesses to implement systemwide change to take advantage of new general purpose technologies like AI prediction. Cars were able to be better than horses, but cars needed gas stations, good roads, and a whole new set of laws.

Value versus Cost

Economists tend to focus on cost, and, as economists, we are as guilty of that as anyone. The entire premise of our first book, *Prediction Machines*, was that AI advances were going to dramatically reduce the cost of prediction, leading to a scale-up of its use. However, while that book suggested that the initial uses of AI would be where prediction was already occurring, either explicitly in, say, forecasting sales or the weather, or implicitly in classifying photos and language, we were mindful that the real opportunity would be the new applications and uses that were enabled when prediction costs fell low enough.

At the same time, through our work with AI startups at the Creative Destruction Lab, we noticed that the initial pitch by entrepreneurs was all about how such and such an AI system would be of value to businesses because it would save them the costs of employing people. In pricing those AI products, they were taking a cost mindset and calculating the saved wage and other costs and pricing their own replacement machine based on that.

More often than not, that was a tough sell. If you go to a business and tell it you can save it $50,000 per year in labor costs if it eliminates this one job, then your AI product better eliminate that entire job. Instead, what entrepreneurs found was that their product was perhaps eliminating one task in a person's job, and that wasn't going to be enough to save their would-be customer any meaningful labor costs.

The better pitches were ones that were not focused on replacement but on *value*. These pitches demonstrated how an AI product could allow businesses to generate more profits by, say, supplying higher quality products to their own customers. This had the benefit of not having to demonstrate that their AI could perform a particular task at a lower cost than a person. And if that also reduced internal resistance to adopting AI, then that only made their sales task easier. The point here is that a value-enhancing approach to AI, rather than a cost-savings approach, is more likely to find real traction for AI adoption.[6]

We have seen the same dichotomy in previous technological revolutions. For electricity, which we discussed in chapter 1, replacement of steam in manufacturing was slow and took decades. It was only worth-while for existing factories to adopt electricity if it cost less than steam. That was a hard sell to factories that were already designed to run on steam. By contrast, once manufacturers realized that electricity afforded them the opportunity to redesign factories into large flat installations out-side of expensive city rents, there was much greater interest in investing in new factories that promised significantly higher productivity due to their new design. Indeed, electric cars were once thought to be a more promising technology than gasoline-powered ones. As it turned out, gas-oline allowed cars to travel longer distances, and that ended up winning out, at least until battery technology advanced at the beginning of the twenty-first century. In the case of redesigned factories, electricity enhanced value, while in the other, transportation, it did not. Value won out.

Critically, adopting a new system requires replacing an existing one. A pure cost calculus will rarely drive such replacement. There are transi-tional costs in building new systems, and if the best you are going to do is save a fraction of the costs of the existing system, it is unlikely to prove worthwhile. Instead, if the new system does something new—that is, leads to new value creation opportunities—then that is what will drive adoption.

The Challenge of System-Wide Change

Plenty has been written about the potential for AI in medicine.[7] Eric Topol's book *Deep Medicine: How Artificial Intelligence Can Make Health-Care Human Again* explains how AI could improve diagnosis, freeing up doctors to spend time with their patients and understand their needs. AI applications in medicine include disease diagnosis, automated surgery, at-home patient monitoring, personalized treatments, and drug discovery and repurposing.[8] These opportunities have created worries about a "dark side to AI in health care" where AIs compete with MDs for diagnosis.[9]

Perhaps the reason *Deep Medicine* is such an influential book is because Topol understands the health-care system (he's a cardiologist and a pro-fessor of molecular medicine at Scripps Research), he understands AI (he invested significantly in learning the capabilities and limitations of this technology as it relates to health care), and he is a master communicator and translator of complicated things (he's the founder and director of the Scripps Research Translational Institute).[10] There's only one problem. He's not an economist. So, he doesn't write about human behavior in terms of incentives. Or perhaps he believes that doctors are above such primal instincts. Our concern is that if we simply drop new AI technologies into the existing health-care system, doctors may not have the incentive to use them, depending on whether they will increase or decrease their compensation, which is driven by fee-for-service or volume-based reimbursement.

Topol believes that if AIs save doctors time, then doctors will spend that extra time talking and connecting with their patients. The evidence is not at all clear that past productivity-enhancing tools for doctors have increased the time they spend connecting with their patients. It might be the opposite. If AIs increase the productivity of doctors, they may be able to spend less time with each individual patient without diminishing their income. In order to achieve the worthy goals that Topol aspires to, we need more than new AI technologies. We need a *new system*, including new incentives, training, methodologies, and culture for doctors to utilize their technological tools in the manner aspired to in Topol's book.

So, not surprisingly, despite the many opportunities for enhancing medicine with AI, as described in *Deep Medicine* and elsewhere, health care is not at the forefront of AI adoption. In a study of AI and machine learning jobs across industries, health care ranked near the bottom. At the end of 2019, health care had a smaller fraction of jobs involving AI than every other industry except construction, and arts and entertainment. Even accommodation and food services, and transportation and warehousing, involved more workers with AI-related skills.[11] One reason might be that the health-care system is particularly complicated. Figure 8-2 shows an image of the US health-care system that Congress created in 2010 to map Obamacare.[12]

With so many coordinated decisions, point solutions and application solutions have limited value unless other changes are made. It might be easy to imagine how AI enables personalized treatments, but too many different people need to change what they do in order to make it happen

FIGURE 8-2

Diagram of the US health-care system, 2010

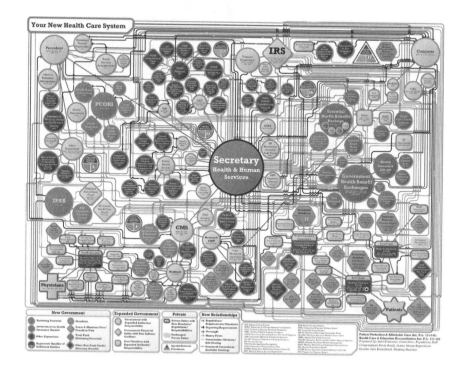

Source: Joint Economic Committee, Republican Staff, "Understanding the Obamacare Chart," July 2010, https://www.jec.senate.gov/public/_cache/files/96b779aa-6d2e-4c41-a719-24e865cacf66/understanding-the-obamacare-chart.pdf.

(e.g., collect more personal data, provide more personalized care, create more care-centric reimbursements). AI point solutions in health care too often provide predictions that nobody can use (e.g., because treatment options aren't available). AI application solutions too often enable actions that nobody can take (e.g., because liability rules make adoption difficult) or wants to take (e.g., because they are misaligned with the compensation system). The challenge isn't so much that the predictions aren't good enough or that the actions are useless; it is that getting all the moving parts working together isn't easy.

To make this happen, system change is needed. And there is no shortage of visions for a new AI-enabled health-care system. If AI provides diagnosis, the rules about who is allowed to do what in health care should change.[13] With machines doing diagnosis, the primary role of the physician might be in the human side of health care. This would require all sorts of other changes. Medical school would no longer require memorization of facts and would no longer select students based on their ability to understand enough biology to score well on tests. These skills might not improve much with a decade of postsecondary schooling, so instead patient-facing doctors might only need something like an undergraduate degree. That, in turn, would require major regulatory changes to who is allowed to provide which health-care services. Perhaps patient care becomes the primary role of the pharmacist. Perhaps social workers move into what used to be the domain of the doctor. In chapter 18, we provide a process for developing an AI system solution in health care and present one vision for what such a system in emergency medicine might involve. Perhaps none of this will happen, because too much needs to change.

AI might also change the global health system. The World Bank has highlighted how technologies like AI can level the playing field across countries.[14] The combination of remote patient monitoring and machine diagnosis could improve health care in difficult-to-reach locations.

Cameroon's cardiologists are based in hospitals in urban areas, yet many of its 25 million inhabitants live far from these hospitals. Most people with cardiovascular disease never get diagnosed. Cameroonian inventor Arthur Zang developed the Cardiopad to solve this problem. Cardiopad is a tool to allow remote cardiograms. There is no need for a local cardiologist to perform the test. The tool has enabled remote diagnosis for thousands of patients, but it still requires a cardiologist to make the final diagnosis. The twenty cardiologists who worked with Cardiopad in 2020 were overwhelmed. The entire country had just sixty cardiologists. Cardiopad solved the problem of access to the cardiograms, but it did not solve the issue of scaling diagnosis, which requires machines that can conduct diagnosis and humans that will accept the diagnosis. Furthermore, once thousands of people are diagnosed, it requires an infrastructure for treating the disease.

Currently, diagnosis and treatment quantities are glued together. By rationing diagnosis, the existing system creates little uncertainty in how many patients need to be treated. Cardiopad is one piece of that system.

It addresses the issue of distance between cardiologists and patients. Large-scale improvements in cardiovascular care in Cameroon require changes to how diagnosis works and the development of new treatment paths that, in turn, take advantage of the changes to diagnosis. Those system solutions still need to be developed.[15] Until then, Cardiopad will continue to improve health care for thousands of patients in Cameroon, but it will not enable population-level improvements in cardiovascular health.

IBM is a much bigger company than Cardiopad. Its Watson was to be the company's moon shot, with an outsized impact on health care. But it didn't live up to its promise. There were data problems and real risks of getting the predictions wrong. As one IBM partner put it, "We thought it would be easy, but it turned out to be really, really hard."[16] It's easy enough to identify the tasks that lend themselves to AI point solutions and AI application solutions. IBM figured that out. It proved too difficult to embed those solutions productively in the existing system, and a new system hasn't yet emerged.

Flip It Around

At the beginning of The Between Times, AI adoption opportunities are often reactive. A vendor approaches you with a new AI to predict something of relevance to your organization. Or you may have asked your internal teams to conduct an analysis of their workflows to see if there is some opportunity to use AI to assist in one or more of the tasks.[17] This is a good approach, but it is a good approach to do one thing: find point solutions for AI.

By now we hope we have convinced you that there is value in looking for opportunities to adopt AI that are transformational. This requires examining entire systems and understanding how AI might facilitate a change in those systems for the better. It is there that the most significant opportunities for AI lie.

But it is easy to say you should have a systems mindset. What is harder is actually developing one. Hidden uncertainties are, by definition, hard to find. The rules that glue the existing system together are difficult to remove. A first step is recognizing that system change is necessary. That recognition is already happening in one sector of the economy. We turn to it next.

KEY POINTS

- Task-level thinking is currently the dominant approach to planning for the introduction of AI into all sectors of the economy. The main idea is to identify specific tasks in an occupation that rely on predictions that AI, rather than a human, can generate more accurately, faster, or cheaper. Corporate leaders, management consultants, and academics have largely all converged on this approach.

- The dominance of task-level thinking is surprising because the most dramatic implementations of AI to date are not task-level replacements of human labor, but rather new system-level designs that are only possible because of the prediction capabilities now afforded by AI (e.g., Amazon, Google, Netflix, Meta, Apple). Task-level thinking leads to point solutions that are often motivated by cost savings based on labor replacement. In contrast, system-level thinking leads to system solutions that are usually motivated by value creation, not cost savings.

- There are many applications for AI in health care: disease diagnosis, automated surgery, at-home patient monitoring, personalized treatments, and drug discovery and repurposing. However, the health-care system has seen only a marginal benefit from AI to date. Some of that is due to the time required for regulatory approval, but much is due to the muted benefits from using AI point solutions in the existing health-care system. A system solutions approach is required to fully leverage the power of AI in health care. We must begin with a blank slate and imagine how people's health can best be served in a freshly designed system that has access to newly powerful prediction technology. That means rethinking training, delivery procedures, compensation, privacy, and liability. That means adopting a system mindset.

9

The Greatest System of All

"AlphaFold Is the Most Important Achievement in AI—Ever," declared an article in *Forbes*. Admittedly, that outlet is driven to hyperbole. Not so for the staid academic journal *Nature*, but it similarly declared that "[i]t will change everything."[1]

AlphaFold predicts protein structures. Proteins are the building blocks of life, responsible for most of what happens inside cells. How a protein works and what it does are determined by its three-dimensional shape. In molecular biology, "structure is function."

Scientists have long wondered where this structure comes from, how a protein's constituent parts map out of the many twists and folds of its eventual shape. For decades, laboratory experiments have been the main way to get good protein structures.

With AlphaFold as a tool to predict protein structures from their amino-acid sequence, scientists can discover new facts about the building blocks of life.[2] Researchers at the University of California, San Francisco, used AlphaFold to uncover previously unknown details about a key SARS-CoV-2 protein, which advanced the development of Covid-19 therapeutics. Scientists at the University of Colorado, Boulder, had spent years trying to determine the structure of a particular bacterial protein in order to help combat antibiotic resistance. They used AlphaFold to learn the structure in fifteen minutes.[3] Another lab noted that AlphaFold gave it a protein structure in thirty minutes, after trying other tools for a decade.[4] The head of that lab, Andrei Lupas, noted, "This will change medicine. It will change research. It will change bioengineering."

The Invention of a Method of Invention

If we had to point to an area where AI has the most potential for transforming the economy, it is well upstream from most ordinary business activities: in the system of innovation and invention. The good news is that this is also where practitioners of AI appear to recognize the need for a systems mindset in their adoption of AI. If AlphaFold is to change medicine, research, and bioengineering, it must be more than a point solution.

At the first NBER Economics of Artificial Intelligence Conference that we hosted in 2017, economists Iain Cockburn, Rebecca Henderson, and Scott Stern argued that AI "has the potential to change the innovation process itself." Data science was already a component of the scientific process. AI would make that data science better, faster, and cheaper. It would enable new types of predictions. This opens up new avenues of inquiry and improves productivity within the lab.[5] As a new way to create products, rather than an improvement on a specific product, the economic impact of research tools is not limited to their ability to reduce the cost of innovation.[6] Instead, they alter the playbook for innovation.

The microscope was also a new method of invention. From the microscope came the germ theory of disease. From this theory came much of modern medicine. The germ theory of disease made battling viruses and bacteria feasible. It also changed other aspects of medicine. Surgery became medically useful. Childbirth became safer. Hospitals became places where people got better rather than where people went to die.[7]

AI is, however, not just a method of invention. It also appears likely to be a general purpose technology. This is why AI requires system change, and why AI's potential suggests a paradox.

New Innovation Systems

Innovation involves a structured process of trial and error. Figure 9-1 shows how this process works in many contexts. The research organization specifies an objective and generates hypotheses about how to achieve that object. It then designs and runs an experiment to test the leading hypothesis. Often that experiment fails. Hopefully, that failure generates learning and new hypotheses, one of which leads to a successful experiment. The organization then runs a pilot, and if that pilot succeeds, the innovation can be deployed at scale.

This process applies to relatively simple innovation systems like content recommendation engines and more complex systems like those for drug development. We consider each in turn.

FIGURE 9-1

Innovation process

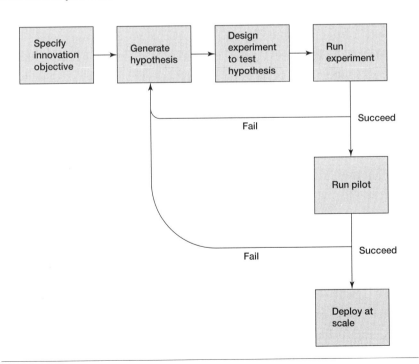

A recommendation system, as occurs on Amazon and Spotify, might have the objective to maximize user engagement or to increase sales. Business school professors Dokyun Lee and Kartik Hosanagar worked with a large online retailer to examine how the details of the recommender engine affected sales. They compared "collaborative filter" recommender engines based on "people who bought this also bought this" suggestions with engines based on fit with the keyword string entered. The company they worked with had a hypothesis or theory that the recommender engine would increase sales. They then ran an experiment and randomly showed some users the new recommender engine and others the older keyword-based search engine. In most product categories, purchases were higher under the new engine. The intervention worked, so the company decided to deploy it.

The recommender engine also suggested some new opportunities. It changed the distribution of products, with more people buying the same popular products and fewer purchases of less popular, or long-tail, products. The distribution changes because a recommendation that "people who bought this also bought this" increases sales of the most popular products. At the time, in books, everyone also bought *The Da Vinci Code*, so it would have been recommended to everyone. The company decided against further improvements that would increase profits throughout the distribution and especially in the long tail. The recommender engine was an AI point solution that fit into the existing workflow. Reversing the decline in purchases in the long tail would require coordination with other divisions. The engineers worried that it would be a lot of work to implement. They were afraid that the new algorithm would have unintended consequences. And, most importantly, "the engineers did not want to break the existing system." The system-level change was too much, given the anticipated benefits.[8]

An innovation-focused AI could change this process. Instead of hypothesizing about the best type of recommendation engine, the AI could use the existing data to generate thousands of possible recommendation engines (see figure 9-2). Once this hypothesis generation step is faster, it will then enable innovation on more impactful measures than short-term purchasing such as churn or long-term sales. With better hypotheses, it might be possible to run more experiments with a higher yield and greater

FIGURE 9-2

Simple: AB testing for engine recommendation

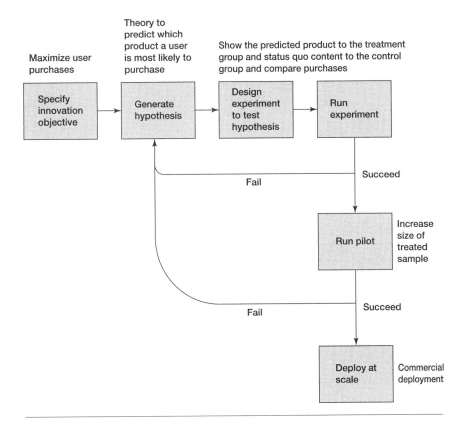

return on investment. Furthermore, if the predictions are good enough, it might be possible to skip the experiment or pilot phases. One of us (Ajay), along with economists John McHale and Alex Oettl, modeled this idea in the field of new materials discovery.[9] Better prediction at the hypothesis development stage could lead to an entirely new system.

The same system change could occur for the more complex R&D system in drug development. The objective is to design new drugs. The process is similar: hypothesize, experiment, pilot, and deploy.

These opportunities depend, of course, on a significant advance in AI prediction. AlphaFold might be exactly that advance. AlphaFold's prediction alone won't change medicine, research, or bioengineering.

Researchers already looking for a prediction will now be able to operate more efficiently. Just like financial fraud detection company Verafin discussed earlier in this book, a much better prediction is a point solution that can be slotted into an existing system and make it work a little better.

The hyperbole around AlphaFold is driven by a vision for a new medical research system. That system will "require more thinking and less pipetting."[10] Once it is easy to predict the structure of any protein, the approach to research changes. Those working to take advantage of the opportunity that AlphaFold offers recognize that there is more opportunity to develop treatments for relatively obscure diseases because discovering the protein structures is now straightforward. Labs that specialized in determining protein structures no longer serve much purpose. The future requires more labs that convert known protein structures into useful treatments.

The prediction AlphaFold provides changes how research can be done. By changing the process of innovation, AlphaFold could change medicine. More generally, the impact of AI on innovation may ultimately outweigh the impact of all other applications of AI. Because innovation is central to productivity, economic growth, and human well-being, through its impact on innovation, AI could have a bigger effect than previous generations of general purpose technologies, from the steam engine to the internet.

With AlphaFold, predicting the target protein structure is no longer an onerous process of iteration between theory and experiment. That stage is now given. With that, the innovation objectives can be more ambitious. More drug protein reactions can be tested. AI can affect the productivity of the discovery pipeline by allowing improved prioritization of innovations that flow through that pipeline. AI can increase the expected value of innovation, and it can increase or decrease downstream testing, depending on the innovation. AI can reduce costs associated with well-defined bottlenecks in the discovery pipeline (see figure 9-3).

Even though it is widely recognized that a new system is necessary, such a system does not appear without a great deal of time, effort, and resources.

FIGURE 9-3

Complex: R&D for drug development

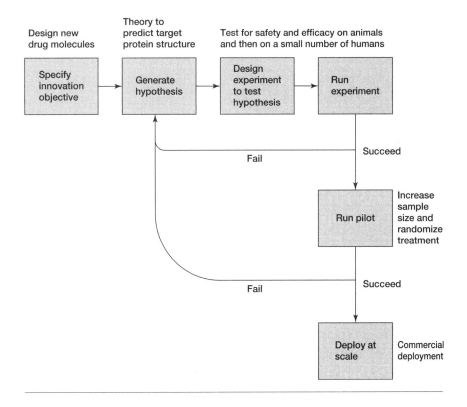

Recognizing Systems

Our point is that even recognizing the opportunity for system change is difficult. We are starting to see progress with respect to AI's impact on the innovation system. A number of AI systems are appearing in the innovation process. For example, University of Toronto professor Alán Aspuru-Guzik is using AI for chemistry. An AI that predicts which hypotheses to test is integrated as part of a system solution involving AI-controlled robotic arms and a fully stocked portable lab for running automated experiments. He calls the system a "self-driving chemistry lab."[11]

Many other parts of the economy, however, have not seen the need for change. And recognizing the need for system change is just the first step. The right kind of change needs to happen, and that takes plenty of investment and a little luck. Large companies rarely find it worth it to transform the way their industry operates, especially if their industry is currently profitable. The risk of getting it wrong is too high.

This is why technological change can lead to disruption. The technology unleashes new opportunities to build businesses and serve customers, but it isn't clear exactly how. When startups and smaller firms have incentives to innovate and larger firms don't, then innovation incubates in small markets served by small companies until their products mature into viable alternatives for large markets, and ultimately incumbents collapse and new ways of doing business arise from these surprising places. We turn to this kind of change next.

KEY POINTS

- Innovations in the innovation system itself can have cascading effects downstream on many other systems. Advances in lens-grinding technology led to innovations in the personal optics market (e.g., eyeglasses) but also in the research tools market (e.g., microscopes), which enabled further innovations in the innovation system. From the microscope came the germ theory of disease, which made battling viruses and bacteria feasible and changed other aspects of medicine.

- One of the core roles for AI in the innovation system is to predict the consequence of new combinations. Where we previously relied on scientific theory or trial and error, we can now sometimes (if we have sufficient data to train models) use AI prediction to generate hypotheses.

- Automated hypothesis generation may enhance innovation productivity significantly. However, to fully benefit from this technology, we must reconsider the entire innovation system, not just the single step of hypothesis generation. For example, faster hypothesis generation will have little impact if the next step in the process, hypothesis testing, doesn't change and simply creates a bottleneck downstream.

PART FOUR

Power

10

Disruption and Power

Let's take a moment to recap. AI is a potentially transformative technology. History tells us that transformation does not come easy. While the initial fruits of a new technology are point solutions and applications, real adoption and transformation come when new systems are created that are driven by the technology. AI provides predictions, and hence, value is created by improved decision-making. Point solutions allow prediction to improve existing decisions. Applications can potentially unlock new decisions. Those new decisions don't come out of the blue. Instead, they replace rules. Rules admit errors and often have scaffolding built around them (e.g., airport terminals) to mitigate their consequences. Therefore, the uncertainty that might otherwise be a target for AI prediction can be buried. The resulting system built on rules can be very robust—what we call "glued." That means changing rules to decisions, and using AI may not be worthwhile unless we adopt a system mindset.

There is work to do in order to innovate at a system level so that AI reaches its transformative potential. The remainder of this book outlines that work and the challenges many organizations will face. The most important thing to understand is that this process will be disruptive.

Disruption. Now, there's a problematic word. As economists, we shy away from buzzwords, and there is perhaps no buzzier word in technology circles than *disruption*. However, when considering the adoption of AI in the context of systemwide change, it is apt for three reasons. First, as we have already seen, the opportunities for the application of AI can be hidden from view, and thus existing industries are vulnerable to blind spots. Second, the challenges and trade-offs in taking down existing systems and building new ones are part and parcel of the process of creative destruction that accompanies transformational technological change. Finally, as old systems are displaced with new, there is necessarily a shift in power—specifically, the economic power—that makes the accumulation of power the reward to system innovation and potential disruption something to fear and resist. These three things are associated with what many put under the umbrella term of *disruption*, so it makes sense to use it here.

Prediction Can Disrupt

The remainder of this book is about how AI prediction and its adoption can be disruptive. Of necessity, since it hasn't happened yet, we have built speculation into that exercise. Such speculation is informed by what we know about AI prediction and about the economics of technology. We have also had advances in our ability to predict before—assisted by data gathering and computerization.

Until the 1990s, electricity generation was a highly regulated affair. In most countries, the whole process of producing and delivering electricity to businesses and households was organized within vertically integrated entities. One reason for this was that electricity was costly to generate and virtually impossible to store. If you knew how much electricity you wanted, you could just produce that. But there were millions of separate decisions made to use electricity at every minute of the day. Fail to meet demand, and the entire network could crash.

In actuality, you could produce however much electricity you wanted, but you also had to take care of a variety of other things. You had to ensure that the distribution lines did not reach capacity in different localities. You had to account for unavailable generating plants. And you had to account for the changing costs of fuels used in the first place. The end result was tight control and excess supply at any given time, just in case. Caution ruled the day.

But over time, prediction—weather prediction, engineering prediction, and downtime prediction—all became better. Computerization helped, as well as cumulative experience. On an operational level, this allowed the electricity companies to ease up on caution a little. But these planned systems did not do a great job economizing on fuel costs. It was too easy to run a big coal or nuclear plant, compared to switching on and off a lower-capacity gas plant.

These improvements in prediction eventually enabled a change in the organizational structure of the industry: toward greater modularity and less centralized coordination. Rather than generators being tightly controlled and planned, better prediction of demand and distribution meant that individual plants could bid to sell electricity into local markets. By the late 1980s, economists and electricity experts realized that such electricity pool markets could reduce costs without compromising quality.

The core problem of ensuring that supply exceeded demand did not go away. Instead, high-quality prediction of local electricity needs meant that individual plant production decisions could be decentralized. Bids could be received a day ahead, and the quantity supplied met the quantity demanded with little risk of extraordinarily high prices. To be sure, some price spikes did occur, and the owners of the generating plants no doubt liked that. Across the system, better prediction meant less central planning and more competition. Overall electricity costs plummeted.[1] Not surprisingly, almost all leading economies now have previously inconceivable electricity pool markets, all enabled by better prediction.

Prediction opened up a new way of organizing the electricity industry, with decentralized electricity generation. Better prediction meant that those events where demand greatly exceeded what was expected became rarer in real time. Thus, the information from the prediction could then be sent out to the various generating plants, transmission line operators, and distributors more than a day in advance, and each could then communicate their supply intentions to the centralized system operator. This meant that they had far greater discretion, which in turn opened up opportunities for investing in different plants and other efficiency-generating options. There did not have to be a central plan for everything.

The transformation of the electricity industry involved a move from centralization to decentralization. But what is critical to remember is the implications of that with regard to who held power, not the electric kind but the economic kind.

You have economic power if what you own or control is both valuable and scarce in a market. This is why owning Picasso's portrait of his spouse is different from owning your five-year-old's drawing of your spouse. Both are unique and, hence, scarce, and both are equally inaccurate representations of how the person looks, but one is more valuable. This is also why owning an original Picasso is different from owning a print of the same painting. Both are aesthetically equivalent, but one is scarce while the other is not.

Scarcity, which underlies economic power, is something that can be ameliorated by competition, so economists sometimes treat economic power and monopoly power as equivalent. When something that was previously scarce is subject to competition, power shifts.

The changes in electricity were very disruptive to producers that had relied on their vertically integrated structure to shield them from the competition. In effect, for power plants in particular, competition meant lower profits, as they now had to bid in order to be dispatched rather than relying on long-term contracts and other arrangements. Similarly, there were opportunities for more distributors to interconnect local systems into broader regional markets. In the mainland United States, there were just ten markets that crossed numerous states.

We often see this with disruption. An industry where traditional providers have economic power suddenly becomes subject to competition and their power is diminished. But power doesn't just disappear; it shifts. In the case of electricity, power shifted from vertically integrated providers to some others, but most significantly to electricity consumers.

In other instances, disruption in the form of competition can shift power from traditional to new producers. In other words, monopoly power continues; just the names of the monopolists change. Thus, economic power is not threatened by new innovation per se; it is the prize from that innovation. As we will see, when disruption takes the form of system innovation, this passing of the torch between powerful actors emerges. However, those who do not have a stake in the current system are often best poised to reap the reward from creating a new one.

Disruptive Threats

Why does disruption—particularly coming from system innovation—pose such a threat for incumbents in removing their economic power and, in turn, pose such an opportunity for new entrants?

The term *disruption* emerged from the work of Clayton Christensen.[2] Christensen noted that incumbent firms can find themselves "asking the wrong questions" regarding new technologies and their value to customers. Thus, they shy away from certain technologies that offer few advantages to their own customers. By contrast, those very same technologies appeal to customers who are either not served or underserved by existing market leaders. For instance, incumbent hard-disk-drive manufacturers emphasized performance and storage, but there were customers willing to trade these off for smaller size or power efficiency. Entrants can seize on those opportunities and, if those technologies improve, end up becoming strong competitors in the industry.[3]

The really challenging disruption arises when radical technological change does not improve performance along traditional metrics but, in some cases, can improve performance on metrics that are not the focus of the existing industry. This can create blind spots for incumbents. As historian Jill Lepore describes the theory:

> In his 1997 book, "The Innovator's Dilemma," [Christensen] argued that, very often, it isn't because their executives made bad decisions but because they made good decisions, the same kind of good decisions that had made those companies successful for decades. (The "innovator's dilemma" is that "doing the right thing is the wrong thing.") As Christensen saw it, the problem was the velocity of history, and it wasn't so much a problem as a missed opportunity, like a plane that takes off without you, except that

you didn't even know there was a plane, and had wandered onto the airfield, which you thought was a meadow, and the plane ran you over during takeoff.[4]

We have already seen that the ingredients for such blind spots with respect to AI lie in rules and hidden uncertainty. When this happens, managing disruption is not simply about targeting a different set of customers but instead about reformulating the organization of businesses and the problems that need to be their priorities. Not surprisingly, a quick path to being disrupted is to miss that a technology requires organizational change.

A case in point was the tank—introduced by the British at the end of World War I. Tanks were relatively fast and could cause chaos in an enemy's army. At least that was the idea coming from Britain's chief of tanks at the time, J. F. C. Fuller. But in the interwar period, Britain ignored Fuller's plans. Instead, tanks were put in the cavalry. When Germany remilitarized, "[t]he top man in the British army, Field Marshal Sir Archibald Montgomery-Massingberd, responded . . . by increasing the amount spent on forage for horses by a factor of 10. Cavalry officers would be provided with a second horse; tank officers would get a horse too."[5] By contrast, the Germans, whose army organization had been decimated, didn't try to slot the new technology into their existing organization. They understood that the new technology meant new army organization and tactics. They called it "blitzkrieg," and they invited Fuller to the launch.

While British military shenanigans make it easy to dismiss such stories as hubris or idiocy, similar tales turn up again and again in the annals of business history. This did not go unnoticed in academia. When Clay Christensen was developing his disruption theories at Harvard in 1990, down the hall were Rebecca Henderson and Kim Clark looking at the same phenomenon.[6] Rather than focus on the demand side (i.e., missing customer values) as Christensen had, Henderson and Clark looked at the supply side (i.e., the lack of organizational fit). They identified many situations where technological change was architectural, changing the priorities of organizations, and because organizations are hard to change, giving an opportunity to greenfield organizations that could start from scratch.[7]

A more recent example of this is the iPhone. In 2007, the mobile phone industry was in the throes of domination by a Canadian business, Research In Motion (or RIM or BlackBerry), that developed the BlackBerry communication device. This was a mobile phone, but more critically, with its embedded keyboard, it was an email and texting machine. Businesspeople were glued to it. One US secretary of state so loved it that she set up her own private server to continue to use it while in office. The reason it worked is that the keyboard hardware was immaculately engineered, the hardware network that sent messages was efficient and secure, and the device was built to be knocked around.

The iPhone was fragile by contrast. It did not have the keyboard that BlackBerry users loved. It relied on interfacing with a slower internet mobile infrastructure. It chewed up battery life. And it had an awful phone. No small wonder that the entire industry including RIM, Nokia, and Microsoft dismissed it. They told Apple to get out of the industry and leave it to the experts.

It might be easy to again consider this as hubris. But the incumbents were right in all their critiques. What they didn't understand was that Apple had chosen a new architecture for smartphones. It integrated hardware and software. To achieve a device that was put together differently, it had to sacrifice performance on all the component parts. Look at those components separately, and it all looked awful. But if you understood the system, the picture was different. No small wonder that a tech player that saw the iPhone opportunity was one without a traditional industry development organization: Google.

Herein lies what is challenging about dealing with architectural or, as we have termed it here, systemwide change. First, to implement it, you need products that do not initially look competitive because they have to make choices that sacrifice performance on what customers appear to care about. Second, as a result, existing organizations that are created to focus on that performance are not equipped to quickly understand all the trade-offs that the new technology is making. In other words, they miss the forest for the trees. Finally, there is no quick feedback regarding that mistake. The iPhone took four years to make a dent in incumbent handset maker's sales. BlackBerry had its biggest sales post-2007. Only after both Apple and Google had devices was the new phone design preferred.

By that time, it was too late for all of the incumbents to reorganize and catch up, even though they did try.

The System-Change Dilemma

When an AI-driven decision is part of a system, adopting AI can necessitate an organizational redesign with a new system. As we just discussed, one difficulty existing organizations face in creating new systems is that they have been optimized to garner high performance from existing technologies, whereas adopting AI can necessitate a change in focus. In some cases, AI drives the organization to become more modular, while in others, it can drive it to have greater coordination among the parts. The challenge is to recognize that the current focus is the problem, and widespread change is needed.

When top management understands that a new organizational design is needed in order to adopt and integrate an AI prediction to one or more key decision areas, a further challenge arises. This is because organizational design invariably involves a change in the value and, hence, power of the suppliers of different resources within the organization. Those who expect to lose in the resulting reallocation of power will resist change. Organizations rarely operate as a textbook dictatorship where what the CEO says goes and change just happens. Instead, those expecting to have their power diminished resist change. In the process, they can undertake actions that at best reduce the ease by which change can be implemented. At worst, the anticipation of those actions may cause an organizational redesign to be curtailed completely or reversed.[8]

There are many examples of resistance to change in response to the adoption of disruptive technologies. Consider, for example, the experience of Blockbuster Video. Blockbuster was the market leader in videotape rentals throughout the 1990s and 2000s. The commonly known narrative of Blockbuster's demise is that it was felled by Netflix and the rise of on-demand video at the end of the first decade of the twenty-first century. But, in fact, Blockbuster did not passively succumb to the new ways. It understood what was coming but ultimately failed to adjust to it.

When Netflix started, it was to exploit the new DVD technology that was small and more physically robust than the previous videotapes Blockbuster was renting. Netflix experimented and then ultimately made a business from customer subscriptions, which allowed customers to rent three DVDs at the same time without any limit on how long they held on to them. Netflix customers ordered the DVDs online, which were then mailed to them. Thus, this model had two advantages. First, customers did not need to visit a physical store to obtain or return DVDs. Second, there were no late fees that, for a typical Blockbuster franchise, could be upward of 40 percent of its revenue. The disadvantages were that Netflix didn't necessarily have the latest new releases, and its customers had to plan their viewing experience and could not just act on impulse to rent a movie.

Blockbuster noticed that Netflix was able to acquire customers, and in some cases, this impacted its own revenue. In the early 2000s, it saw some of the disadvantages of its own model that Netflix was exploiting, and it experimented with on-demand video; Blockbuster was the first to provide on-demand video service! But broadband speeds then were not what they are today, so that experiment did not succeed. But Blockbuster did realize that it could also have a DVD rental model similar to Netflix's. The difference would be that it could provide the option of selecting and returning the DVDs at a store, not just by mail.

The problem was that this type of subscription service cut into the 40 percent late fee revenue that the franchises earned. Moreover, those customers did not necessarily come into the store to buy other merchandise, such as popcorn and candy. So, while Blockbuster corporate may have benefited from following the Netflix model, the franchises were disadvantaged by it. There was resistance, especially as the new model proved to be more successful. In the end, this caused the Blockbuster board to decide to change top management and revert to the original model in support of retail franchises. To counter Netflix, it tried to beef up what those stores offered beyond simple video rentals. In the end, it did not work, and within a few years Blockbuster was no longer in business.[9]

The Blockbuster case is, of course, a dramatic example of both the failure to change in the face of a new technology and also how internal forces prevented that change before it was too late. But it is a prescient case precisely because the conflict between those that benefited from the new technology and those that did not was so stark. There was simply no role for retail outlets in the new world, but that was enough to prevent the business itself from adapting, even though its senior management understood what the new organization had to entail.

At a broad level, as we will outline in chapters to follow, AI can generate organizational change that can have the effect of decentralizing power or coordination that can centralize it. Either way, those who lose from those changes can be quite clear, and precisely because they hold power based on the current organizational system, they will have a vested interest in maintaining it.

Disruption and Opportunities

System-level change is difficult, but the payoff to success can be enormous. One question that has persistently emerged with respect to AI is whether the machines that embody AI prediction—whether physical robots or software algorithms—themselves have power. When you recognize what AI is, your concerns that the machines will have power are misplaced. Because of the persistence of those arguments, we deal with that next.

KEY POINTS

- Incumbents can often adopt point solutions quite easily because they enable improvements in a specific decision or task without requiring changes to other related decisions or tasks. However, incumbents often struggle to adopt system-level solutions because those require changes to other related tasks and the organization has invested in optimizing those other tasks; furthermore the system solution may be inferior in some of those tasks, particularly in the short run. That sets the stage for disruption.

- We define power as economic power. You have power if what you own or control is scarce, relative to demand. Scarcity, which underlies economic power, is something that can be ameliorated by competition, which is why economists sometimes treat economic power and monopoly power as equivalent. When something that was previously scarce is subject to competition, power shifts.

- Sometimes, a system-level solution is required to fully benefit from AI. The redesign of a system may lead to a shift in power at the industry level (e.g., data-rich industries become more powerful as AI becomes more prevalent), the company level (e.g., discussed in chapter 12), or the job level (e.g., Blockbuster franchises lost power in the shift to online movie rentals and mail delivery DVDs). Those that stand to lose power will resist change. Those resistant to change often currently hold power (that's why they resist) and therefore may be quite effective at preventing system-level change. That creates the context for disruption.

11

Do Machines Have Power?

The headlines read "How Amazon automatically tracks and fires warehouse workers for 'productivity,'" "Amazon used an AI to automatically fire low-productivity workers," "Would you let a robot fire your employees?" "Fired by Bot at Amazon: 'It's You Against the Machine,'" and "For lower-paid workers, the robot overlords have arrived." That last one was from the *Wall Street Journal* in May 2019. There, Greg Ip summarized the key takeaway: It's time to stop worrying that robots will take our jobs—and start worrying that they will decide who gets jobs.

Suffice it to say, that grabbed the attention of many. It tapped into a primal fear: Would the machines hold power over people?

These articles would have you believe that workers were entering a small room as they left work for the day and were scanned and then presented with a bright-green sign saying, "See you tomorrow" or, alternatively, a red sign saying "Terminated" along with an automatically printed pink slip.

In the end, the reality of the situation did not live up to the hype. Yes, Amazon was using AI to predict the performance of workers. And, yes, that could trigger a review. And, yes, following that review, a worker could be terminated. But, no, people were not being shown the door without a human in the loop. Instead, what Amazon was doing was measuring worker performance, using an AI to evaluate whether that performance was a cause for concern, and then having a human manager decide what to do. If that manager was just blindly following the AI prediction, it could certainly appear that AI was in control of the decision, just as a manager might hide behind metrics. In this regard, it is not different from any performance measurement scheme, and it is far from obvious that the scheme was worse than some of the more subjective ones most of us have to deal with.

But what if the headlines were all true and you really could be evaluated and then fired without a human in the process? Are machines deciding who gets jobs? Are machines now the bourgeoisie to our proletariat?

The answer, as we will demonstrate in this chapter, is a definitive no. Robots and machines, in general, do not decide anything and, hence, do not have power. A human or group of humans are making the calls underlying the decisions. To be sure, it is possible to automate things and make it look like a machine is doing the dirty work. But that is an illusion. At our current level of AI, someone makes the real decisions.

We don't say this to make some philosophical point; we leave this debate to others. Instead, accepting that machines don't decide is critical if we are going to properly assess the disruptive potential of AI. *While AI cannot hand a decision to a machine, it can change which human is making the decision.* Machines don't have power, but when deployed, they can change who does.

When machines change who makes decisions, the underlying system must change. The engineers who build the machines need to understand the consequences of the judgment they embed into their products. The people who used to decide in the moment may no longer be needed.

The notion that machines don't decide is not new. Ada Lovelace, who wrote the first computer program in 1842, saw this limitation:

> Ada warns the readers about the computer's inability to do anything about it if the user entered "untrue" information. Today we call this concept "Garbage in, Garbage out." Here is the way she said it: "The Analytical Engine has no pretensions whatever to originate anything. It can do whatever we know how to order it to

perform. It can follow analysis; but it has no power of anticipating any analytical relations or truths."[1]

Machines follow instructions that must come from somewhere.

Consider the hypothetical version of Amazon's termination algorithm, whereby it actually measured performance and terminated people without a human as part of the process. In programming this algorithm, someone, at some point, must have specified the judgment elements—including how to weigh in factors such as the prevailing wage, the availability of substitute employees, training requirements, and other things such as legal rules on workplace practices, as well as how to weigh probabilistic elements such as AI predictions of likely skills, ability, and cultural fit. Some engineer somewhere may have been trying to complete a program, but more likely, if such an automated system is deployed, those judgment elements will come from a more deliberative process. A new system of decision-making is needed.

It is tempting to think that we might give over an entire decision to a machine. However, while the implementation of a decision may become fully automated, the decision of what action to take after a prediction still has to come from one or more people.

Going Global

Machines appear to make decisions because AI allows automation. Prediction machines can change the time and place of decisions, allowing a human to engage in a deliberative process, judge what to do when a situation arises, and then to code that into a machine.

Automation requires codifying judgment. A human must specify judgment when the machine is deployed, rather than upon receiving a prediction. That means that judgment has to be useful for a large number of decisions, and it has to be described in a way that can be coded. That isn't so easy.

It is worth visiting the process that Toronto startup Ada uses to automate customer service.[2] Ada's founders describe it as the automation layer that powers interactions between companies and their customers.

Ada provided the automated layer behind Zoom's customer support as it grew from 10 million daily users to 300 million daily users in the first half of 2020—before and after the arrival of Covid-19.[3] It automated 70 percent of sales calls and 98 percent of customer support interactions with free users and 85 percent of those interactions with paid users. Chances are if you needed to reset your Zoom password or if your camera wasn't working, then you interacted with Ada's automated agent.

The process of building judgment was key. Ada's process starts by *predicting the intent* of a customer when they initiate a service interaction. The intent might be to change a password, update credit card information, or upgrade to a more comprehensive service. Ada might start with just one prediction that it can do confidently: the customer wants to change their password.

Then Ada develops a workflow and judgment. The workflow is the set of actions to help the customer change the password. If the machine is confident that the customer wants to change a password, then Ada initiates the automated workflow on changing passwords. Otherwise, Ada sends it to a human.

Here's where judgment comes in. How confident should Ada be before initiating the automated sequence? It depends. There is a reason why it automated 98 percent of interactions from free customers and only 85 percent from paid customers. And it isn't only because free customers have easier queries. In addition, it judges that making a mistake with a paid customer is a bigger deal. The stakes are higher, so the threshold to allow automation is higher.

As Ada collects data about incoming inquiries and customer intent, it builds more automated workflows. In addition to passwords, it can add credit card updates and various technical issues. It can also identify which inquiries are sales calls, either for purchasing the paid service or for upgrading to a higher tier.

Now judgment becomes particularly important. The consequences of messing up a sales call are higher than the consequences of messing up a password fix. In order to do this well, Ada needs access to data and a decision process for determining which incoming inquiries to automate. Some decision-making power moves from customer service representatives to company management and the engineers at Ada. Better prediction of the customer intent creates an opportunity for automation. But whether that opportunity is worthwhile depends on human judgment to weigh the benefit of automation relative to the cost of mistakes. Doing all this well requires system-level changes to data collection, decision-making, and allocation of responsibility.

Are You Feeling Lucky?

Another fear that arises with respect to machines having power is that prediction machines are now often responsible for the information we see to help our understanding of the world and make decisions, all the way from shopping to whom to vote for. If the machines are serving up information to us, is our power subtly being diminished? As we will see here, our relationship with the prediction machine is not one-way. Yes, it provides us information and that influences us, but we also provide the machine with information that is used to change the machine's predictions. In other words, from an economic perspective, machines (and their owners) do not hold all the cards. They need us to maintain their quality. So, while it might feel like you do not have control, you have more than you think.

Let's consider the closest thing we have to a super AI today: Google Search, which is a prediction machine. You ask it a question or even just a few terms you want more information about, and it examines websites and then gives you a list (sometimes in the tens of thousands) ranked in order of those Google regards as most likely to be the one you want. Previously, these rankings were determined largely by PageRank, a scoring system Larry Page created that presumed that you were more likely to want a site that other sites linked to. Now, based on trillions of searches and clicks, the Google ranking is a deep learning–based prediction that not only takes into account what others have done in the past but continues to update and also utilize what it knows about you to offer a personalized ranking—just for you. How lucky are you?

As it turns out, not necessarily that lucky. You may not have noticed it, because most Google searches are not conducted from Google's home page (at www.google.com), but that home page has two buttons (see figure 11-1). When you enter a search term, you can click "Google Search," which then returns that familiar ranked list of sites, along with ads that fund the

FIGURE 11-1

Google home page, 2021

Source: Google and the Google logo are trademarks of Google LLC.

whole operation. But next to that is another button, "I'm Feeling Lucky." Click on that button instead, and it takes you right to the website ranked first. The fact that we rarely click that button suggests we aren't feeling that lucky. The predictions aren't good enough.

This is not a new button. It appears on the very first Google home page (see figure 11-2), and despite Google's famous desire to guard its home-page real estate for a very minimalist look, it is still there. "I'm Feeling Lucky" was originally placed there by Google cofounder Sergey Brin, who saw it as a way of highlighting how good Google Search was when it was launched. In 2007, Brin stated that Google users were only about 1 percent lucky, as that was the number of searches that used the "I'm Feeling Lucky" button. At the same time, estimates indicated that keeping the button there was costing Google $100 million in lost ad revenue. Google kept that button for pure branding reasons, keeping a human face on the whole, otherwise artificial operation.[4]

Why aren't we feeling lucky? The simple answer is that the first result is usually not what we want. We want to browse that first page and select something. Then we may realize it isn't right. So, we come back and select another link. From Google's perspective, it can't do any better. If someone were to Google "prediction machines" and feel lucky, they would be taken to our first book's website (predictionmachines.ai). But what if they want to buy it from Amazon? In that case, this would not be

FIGURE 11-2

Google home page, 1998

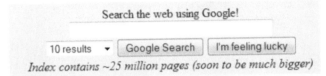

Source: Google and the Google logo are trademarks of Google LLC.

the most efficient path to that information. What if they didn't want the book, but a summary article? You may know, but Google doesn't know what decision you might be making. Without that, it serves you its best guess, but leaves room open for your own judgment to finish the process. Google may aspire to be a decision machine, but without judgment, it cannot be your decision machine. Thus, it is left with a role in prediction and has to leave the rest to you. Of course, that is just as well, as you might choose to click on an ad.

The Google Search example demonstrates how hard it is to automate a decision. Hard, but not impossible. As of this writing, Google is, in fact, feeling luckier. With the advent of voice-assisted search, people are asking more fully formed queries for which Google does have a clearer and likely more confident answer for. Thus, for many queries that are more frequently asked or asked in ways when the intent is clearer, Google will, in both voice and other search, give a clear answer that does not even require visiting another website for further information. For other situations, even with voice search, it refers the person to a screen for them to decide. The same is true for other voice searches such as Alexa or Siri. This process is similar to Ada's. When that happens, Google's machine observes the choices that are made and uses that information to update its predictions. *People are a critical part of the system.*

When the prediction is good enough and the judgment and action are clear, automation is possible. Otherwise, let the human decide. This process is called judgment by exception. As author Janelle Shane comments, AIs work better when there are very narrow contexts and goals.[5] The solution is often to build in judgment for new situations, but given a sufficiently complex set of possible situations, there will always be some in which the AI's recommendations are problematic.

From this, we can conclude that we are likely to have formed appropriate judgment and also be able to describe that judgment for situations that are more common. For those situations, it may be possible to code judgment into an automated process and obtain good outcomes. Outside those situations—in less common ones—this coding is not possible. If we recognize when those situations arise, rather than expect the machine to be automated to deal with all situations, a hybrid solution would be more appropriate. The key is that when a situation is outside the judgment that has been coded into the machine, then that is known and communicated to a human who then decides what to do.

To review, AI predictions are imperfect. To mitigate the risk of being wrong, we embark on two lines of attack. First, before the fact, we work through contingencies and arrive at a conclusion as to what the machine should choose for each of those contingencies. Second, after the fact, we acknowledge that not all contingencies will be covered, so we will rely on humans to step in and make the call. As AI prediction improves, we will need to allocate more human resources to both of these judgment functions. In other words, the exceptions require a system design that includes human-machine collaboration.

Responsibility for Judgment at Scale

Sometimes, it is possible to fully automate a decision process by specifying the judgment in advance. When you swipe your credit card, you set in motion a set of algorithms that determine whether the transaction should be processed or rejected. The decision of what transactions to process happens long before you swipe your card.

No AI can make those judgments; nor can those judgments be feasibly or sensibly done in some decentralized manner. Instead, judgment is applied ahead of millions of accept or reject decisions and then coded to be used at scale. Machines don't make decisions. Instead, machines can change the people who make the decisions, from individuals deciding at the moment a decision is made, to individuals judging what matters before the specific decision arrives.

This brings us back to the reasons why the notion of machines being able to fire employees had such an impact. Machines cannot fire (or hire). Instead, a person (or group) who has exercised judgment in choosing criteria for how a machine might use prediction to arrive at a choice makes the decision. This is more general: nobody ever lost a job to a robot. They lost their job because of the way someone decided to program a robot.

How we arrived at a time when we can so easily blame machines for what are ultimately the actions of humans is an interesting one. Ironically, one of the main traits of capitalism—highlighted by Friedrich von Hayek— is that it allows individual decision-makers to operate and, in our terms, apply their own individual judgment to choices. As historian Lewis Mumford observes: "It was because of certain traits in capitalism that the machine—which was a neutral agent—has often seemed a malicious element in society, careless of human life, indifferent to human interests. The machine has suffered for the sins of capitalism."[6] Indeed, the whole term—*capitalism*—seems to evoke machine power. In reality, *it is the humans who apply judgment as coded in machines that have that power.* Those humans are responsible, and there is a need for the legal and regulatory systems to understand that.

The problem with machine automation is that it obscures the ultimate person who is responsible for a decision. Codifying judgment means that a person's decisions can have extraordinary scale. For various reasons, we like to know who that person is. After all, without responsibility and its identification, how can someone be accountable for a decision? The implications of the need for a new system design are obvious when we consider the possibility of shifting from judgment applied at the time and place of the decision to judgment codified in advance of the decision and possibly far away from the decision location. We will unpack this in detail in chapter 13.

Having debunked the argument that machines have power, we turn to another aspect of AI that tends to run alongside the fear of control by machines, and that is feedback. Prediction machines are learning machines. In some configurations, they can be programmed to continue to learn and update automatically. That is a key part of their value. They can evolve as circumstances change. But at the same time, when it comes to power, a machine that gets ahead can stay ahead. In the process, it is more difficult to compete against. The potential for an accumulation of power to AI adopters is what we consider next.

KEY POINTS

- Machines cannot make decisions. However, AI can fool people into thinking that machines make decisions. Machines can appear to decide when we are able to codify judgment. The AI generates a prediction, and then the machine draws upon codified human judgment in order to execute an action (decision).

- AI predictions are imperfect. To mitigate the risk of being wrong, we embark on two lines of attack. First, before deploying AI, we work through contingencies and arrive at a conclusion as to what action the machine should take for each contingency. Second, after deploying the AI, we rely on humans to step in when the AI is unable to predict with high enough confidence or when the AI predicts a scenario for which we have not codified the judgment (human in the loop).

- Although machines do not have power, they can create power through scale, and they can reallocate power by shifting whose judgment is used where and when for decision-making. Systems predicated on AI can decouple the judgment from the decision such that it can be provided at a different time and place. If judgment shifts from individually deployed by people for each decision to instead codified into software, then this can lead to (1) scaling and consequently a shift in power due to a shift in market share, and (2) a change in who makes the decision and consequently a shift in power from whoever used to apply judgment to whoever provides it for codification or owns the system in which it is embedded.

12

Accumulating Power

System-level innovation is hard. Why not let your competitors go through all the pain and expense of figuring it out and then copy them? Because AI confers an advantage on first movers. AI learns, and the sooner it is deployed, the sooner it can begin to learn. The more it learns, the better it gets in terms of prediction accuracy. The better it gets, the more effective the new system is. The flywheel begins to turn. This flywheel explains why some in the venture capital community are investing so aggressively in seemingly nascent AI projects. Learning comes from data, and so first-mover advantage comes from a feedback loop in that data.

BenchSci is an AI-in-medicine company. Its target is the length of the drug development process. Its challenge is to make it easier for scientists to find needles in haystacks: specific information embedded in the vast wealth of published scientific research and pharma companies' internal databases. To get a new drug candidate into clinical trials, scientists must run experiments. BenchSci realized that scientists could run fewer and more successful experiments if they applied better insights from a vast number of prior experiments.

Using machine learning to read, classify, and then present insights from scientific research, BenchSci found that scientists could run half as many experiments as normally required to advance a drug to clinical trials. By finding the right tools (in this case, biological reagents—essential tools to influence and measure protein expression) in the published literature rather than by rediscovering them from scratch, the time to produce new drug candidates could be cut dramatically. All that added up to potential savings of over $17 billion annually. In an industry where the returns to R&D had become razor-thin, that could transform the market. In addition, many lives could be saved by bringing new drugs to market quicker.

What is most remarkable here is that BenchSci is doing what Google has been doing for the whole of the internet: search. It is simply doing it in a specialized domain. Without machine learning, BenchSci would not be able to process published biomedical research and interpret it in a way that could translate into real cost savings for its customers. In the same way that Google can help you find a way to fix your dishwasher without a long trip to the library, BenchSci helps scientists identify a suitable reagent without running a series of experiments. Before BenchSci, scientists would often use Google or PubMed to search the literature (for days), then read the literature (for days), then order and test three to six reagents before choosing one (for weeks). Now, they search BenchSci (for minutes) and then order and test one to three reagents before choosing one (meaning fewer tests and fewer weeks).

Should BenchSci be worried about competition from Google? That depends on the ability to create a defensible moat around a business, which in turn depends on the nature of the data underlying the AI.[1]

Data and the Business of Prediction

To understand what it takes to compete in a world with AI, we first need to consider what it takes to produce better and cheaper predictions. There isn't some magic wand that you can wave and suddenly have AI. Instead, it requires identifying and managing the elements of generating predictions and the data that is required to link those elements together.

The business of prediction is, therefore, the business of obtaining better and cheaper algorithms and data. So, where do those come from? Consider the algorithms. To build a predictive algorithm, you need to train the model with inputs (say, images) and outputs (say, text descriptions of what is in those images). This requires training data. The better your training data, the better your predictive algorithms will be out of the gate. The key challenge many businesses face is that they either have to create the training data they need (by, say, hiring experts to classify things) or procure it from other sources (say, from health records).

The training data is only the beginning of the story. AI is different from other tools because it learns. The more you use it, the better it gets. The AI learns from feedback. It ingests data and makes a prediction. The AI can then observe if the prediction came to pass. If it did, the AI gains confidence in its algorithm. If the prediction did not occur as expected, the AI learns how to improve its future predictions.

AI models often need to be retrained on new and up-to-date data because the underlying environment changes. This can happen for navigational apps as roads change and the population moves around in a location. It can also happen for targeted advertising as consumer habits change. AI models, therefore, become out of date, and the predictions worsen over time.

While new training data can alleviate this problem, in some cases, by purposefully collecting new data to account for each new circumstance, perhaps the most competitively relevant approach to maintaining the accuracy of predictions in dynamic environments is to continuously update the model with what we term *feedback data*. Feedback data is generated by continually measuring the performance of predictions. To do this, you independently gather information regarding the accuracy of predictions and map that information to the input data that generated those predictions. Combining this data, you have feedback data that you can use to update algorithms.

For instance, when your phone uses your image for security, you initially train the phone to recognize you. But then you don't have to do it again, even though your face can change. You may or may not be wearing glasses. Your facial hair may grow, or you may be wearing makeup. Given these circumstances, the prediction that you are you may start to become less reliable. So, your phone updates its algorithm using the images that you provide it every time you unlock it. This can all happen on the phone because all the training data is about you. In other situations, the training data needs to be updated with input data and prediction outcomes from many users. In that case, privacy issues can loom large and introduce challenges from coordinating information across many sources.

In summary, to compete with prediction, you need to start with good algorithms and access to input data. But in many situations, you will also need access to feedback data. Not surprisingly, your data strategy will drive whether you can compete in a sustainable manner. In some cases, there may be considerable first-mover advantages because higher-quality predictions attract more users who, in turn, generate more feedback data, which improves your predictions and attracts even more users. In that situation, competitors, who do not build feedback data collection into their design, may not be able to catch up. Feedback loops can create first-mover advantages.

Minimum Viable Predictions

These first-mover advantages depend on how good the prediction needs to be to enter the market. In the industrial economy, factories often are built to a minimum size just to be sufficiently cost-competitive to enter the market. That's because, in manufacturing, the average unit cost often decreases with factory size—up to a certain point. That point is called the "minimum efficient scale."

Many AIs also face a minimum efficient scale. However, the scale is not based on factory throughput but rather on training data, and the threshold measure is not unit cost but rather prediction accuracy. The market success of an AI depends on the accuracy of its predictions. In order to be useful, predictions must be good enough to be commercially viable. The threshold prediction accuracy might be set by regulation (e.g., the minimum prediction accuracy required in order to make medical decisions based on an AI for diagnosis), usability (e.g., the minimum prediction accuracy required from an automated email reply service to warrant the cost of the screen real estate), or competition (e.g., the minimum prediction accuracy required to enter an existing market, such as search, to compete with Google and Bing).

Writing an accurate AI program does not require a huge investment in physical assets; software is not a capital-intensive business. The main barrier is data. For an AI to be accurate enough, it needs enough data. Gathering the data to achieve this minimum efficient scale takes time and effort. The advantage to launching first depends on how much effort is required to have a commercially viable prediction.

Sometimes not much effort is needed. In the initial years of internet search, we had a high tolerance for error. Search engines provided multiple links, and the user could scan those links and choose the best one. If the search engine showed an irrelevant link, little harm was done. In the early days of the commercial internet, this led to dozens of different search engines, each with its own method for identifying the best search results. Competition was fierce.

In contrast, in autonomous vehicles, our tolerance for error is low. The AI needs to be measurably better than humans to be trusted with people's lives. The first company to build such an AI will have little initial competition because of the scale of data needed to build that AI. There is some urgency because the sooner AI can reach a minimum efficient scale, the sooner AI can begin generating a return on predictions.

Still, this advantage of reaching a minimum efficient scale early will be short-lived if the market is growing rapidly. All that is needed is for other companies to get enough data to build predictions that cross the minimum threshold to be viable. Minimum efficient scale is not enough to generate a sustained advantage from being a first mover.

The reason is that, in a technical sense, there are decreasing returns to scale in data. You get more information from the tenth observation than the hundredth, and much more from the hundredth than the millionth. As you add observations, each new observation has a smaller impact on the quality of your predictions.

For data to generate a long-term advantage, early movers need to harness a more important economic force to work in their favor: feedback data. Operating in the field, they could collect feedback data that they could then use to directly improve their predictions, making it harder for others to catch up. The advantage isn't in launching when others can't. The advantage is that launching enables the collection of feedback data.

Launching also motivates investment in the computing hardware and talent needed to get the most out of the data. Competition between early entrants accelerates this investment, improving quality and making it harder for others to compete. The phenomenon of early leaders being able to dominate an industry holds for many technology-intensive industries. As the established companies improve their products, the learning and R&D investment required to compete with established companies becomes prohibitive. For example, there were once many commercial airplane manufacturers. Today, starting an airplane manufacturer that can compete with Boeing and Airbus on performance, safety, and cost efficiency might cost tens or hundreds of billions.

In his book, *Technology and Market Structure*, London School of Economics professor John Sutton identified dozens of such examples, from pharmaceuticals to semiconductors to liquid chromatography. The steady improvement in technology means that, in effect, the minimum efficient scale increases over time. This increase (which Sutton called "endogenous sunk costs") can lead to long-term market power and thus a very large prize for early movers.

This has happened in online advertising and in search. Compared to the Yellow Pages or a newspaper, Google makes excellent predictions about who wants what when, which allows targeted advertising. By linking advertising to purchases, Google can benefit from a feedback loop such that the system learns whether each prediction was correct or not—and then updates the model for next time—making it difficult for any new players to catch up. Despite the relatively low minimum efficient scale for launching a search engine in the 1990s, continual improvements by Google—through investments in hardware, talent, and data—have meant that it is very difficult for any new search engine to enter the market today.

Fast Feedback Loops

If you can get your AI into the field early, then the AI can collect data from customers. That data will make the predictions even better, generating a positive feedback loop and a barrier to entry for anyone else who wants to compete. An early lead can accelerate if the feedback loop is fast enough, and this data continues to generate better predictions.

In this way, prediction machines add what has traditionally been the human advantage—they can learn from outcomes. The extent of AI advantage from learning is related to the delay in feedback. In predicting mortality for life insurance, feedback can be delayed for decades. In this case, with such a slow feedback loop, the ability of a company with an early lead in predicting mortality will be limited in terms of its ability to sustain its lead. But if feedback data can be generated quickly after generating the prediction, then an early lead can translate into an even greater lead over time and, hence, a sustained competitive advantage.

When Microsoft launched the Bing search engine in 2009, it had the company's full backing. Microsoft invested billions of dollars in it. Yet, over a decade later, Bing's market share remains far below Google's, in both search volume and search advertising revenue. One reason it proved so hard for Bing to catch up was the feedback loop.[2] In search, the time between the prediction (serving up a page with several suggested links in response to a query) and the feedback (the user clicking on one of the links) is short, usually seconds. In that case, the feedback loop is powerful. Google had been operating an AI-based search engine for many years, with millions of users and billions of searches daily. It collected more data and learned preferences faster. New content was constantly uploaded online, so the search space was constantly expanding. Every time a user made a query, Google served up its prediction of the top ten links, and then the user selected the best of those links. This enabled Google to update its prediction model, allowing for constant learning in light of a constantly expanding search space. With so much more training data based on so many more users, Google could identify new events and new trends more quickly than Bing. In the end, the fast feedback loop, combined with continued investment in complementary assets, like massive data-processing facilities, meant Google maintained its lead and Bing never caught up. It also meant that any other search engines that tried to compete with Google and Bing never even got started. Search engines like DuckDuckGo, which forgoes personalization for privacy, serve important albeit niche markets.

A fast feedback loop creates a race, because if your competitor is already benefiting from such a loop, its predictions are improving rapidly. A fast feedback loop amplifies Sutton's endogenous sunk costs. If you fall too far behind, it might be impossible to catch up. Imagine the first AI that is able to safely navigate a car through New York City. Once that AI achieves regulatory approval, the AI will continue to collect data and get better and better. When a second AI is approved, it won't have the same quantity and quality of data. It is unlikely to be as good. With no real cost advantage and lower prediction quality, consumer value for the second-best AI will be lower.

Fast feedback loops, therefore, lead to racing. There can be large advantages to being early, so companies may invest aggressively in order to get the flywheel running. In this light, massive investments in AI that doesn't quite seem ready make more sense. General Motors paid an estimated $1 billion for autonomous driving startup Cruise, which seemed to have little more than a prototype and a few dozen people.[3] Why would GM pay so much? Once the flywheel starts to spin, where there are fast feedback loops and endogenous sunk costs, it can be difficult for any late entrants to catch up.

Differentiated Prediction

Competing products are usually differentiated. Often, they appeal to different groups of customers. For example, Coca-Cola and PepsiCo sell competing colas that have different tastes and different brand images. Similarly, BMW and Mercedes-Benz sell competing luxury vehicles that have different styles and different features. These brand images and features appeal to different people. In these situations, it is difficult to define "better." Coke isn't inherently better than Pepsi. Just a little different. When products are differentiated, then there is room for competitors rather than a single dominant provider. Since Coke and Pepsi launched over a century ago, many successful new soft drinks, such Red Bull and Honest Tea, have found distinct niches and thrived.

Similarly, some AIs will appeal to different groups. Consider a company looking to replace its call center with a chatbot. Once a chatbot is good enough to be useful, there are many ways to define the best chatbot. Different companies will have different needs. One company might want the chatbot to be efficient, answering customer questions quickly. Another might want a focus on sales, converting incoming queries into new revenue. A third might want the chatbot to be comforting, making people relax and diffusing anger. Perhaps because of these different ways to define "better," there are dozens of chatbot companies, including many smaller players finding distinct and potentially profitable niches.

A related example is melanoma detection.[4] AIs built in Europe disproportionately draw on data from people with lighter skin. The AIs built in Asia, in contrast, use databases of Asian patients. These AIs are differentiated. The European ones are better for Caucasians, and the Asian ones are better for Asians. While "better" usually means "more accurate," the AIs are differentiated because accuracy in one context might not mean accuracy in another.

Unlike soft drinks, chatbots, and melanoma detection, many AIs are only differentiated by quality. It is clear what a better prediction means, and it can be measured. When quality is well defined, as in other industries, the highest-quality products will benefit from higher demand. AI is different from other industries, however, because in most other industries, better quality costs more. Sellers of lower-quality shoes survive by charging lower prices. This will be difficult in the context of AI. AI is software based. This means that, once the model is built, the cost of producing one more high-quality prediction is the same as the cost of producing a low-quality one. If the better prediction costs the same as the worse prediction, then there is no reason to purchase the lower-quality one.

As we noted earlier, Google has more data and benefits from a fast feedback loop. That isn't enough to create an advantage. It also has to be clear to customers what a better search looks like. Google and Bing provide similar results for common searches. Enter the word *weather* into Google or Bing, and the results likely look similar. Where Bing fails is in less common searches. Enter the keyword *disruption*, and (as of the time of writing) Bing's first page only provides dictionary definitions, while Google provides both definitions and links to research on disruptive innovation. While Bing caught up in some dimensions, it did not in others. And there is no category where Bing is widely seen as superior. In search, "better" means finding the link that the user is more likely to click on and stay at. This is true of all users, even though the best links might be different for each person. With a clear definition of prediction and a fast feedback loop, Bing was unable to differentiate enough to gain substantial share.

Feedback Systems

Feedback loops are built deliberately. AIs that anticipate the value of feedback ensure that outcome data can be collected. In chapter 6, we discussed the system solution of an AI that predicts the best learning content for an individual on a particular day. This would personalize education, allowing students to move at the appropriate pace for them, and everyone to learn more. We discussed system-level challenges in terms of teacher allocation and social development. Feedback loops suggest the need for further system-level change. The AI requires data on whether the content improved student performance. The sooner the AI receives that data, the better. The challenge is how to design an academic curriculum to ensure that students deeply understand and remember concepts, while keeping feedback loops fast enough to improve the AI. This will require overcoming regulatory barriers to accessing student data combined with technological advances in protecting student privacy. Like the other parts of this system, the feedback part of the AI system solution for personalized education isn't ready.

While point solution AIs generate a prediction, the power that comes from being an early mover with AI in an industry is a result of feedback. An AI must have access to outcome data in order to learn. An autonomous driving AI needs access to accidents. Every autonomous driving system would ensure that kind of feedback. Accidents, mercifully, are rare. To work well, an autonomous driving system would need access to near accidents. The more such near accidents, the faster it could learn. This requires a system of identifying when a near accident occurs and then building a learning process for avoiding such near accidents in the future. Avoiding accidents isn't enough. Passenger comfort is also important, so an AI system solution that creates an advantage for early movers would also benefit from a way to measure comfort. AIs may, therefore, need to be designed to learn from, and weigh, multiple outcome measures.

Winner Take Most

The potential of prediction machines is immense. Feedback loops mean that early entrants have a real advantage. Early entry means more data. More data means better prediction. Better prediction means more customers, which in turn leads back to more data. Feedback loops create a race to deploy AI at scale.

But remember that predictions are like precisely engineered products, highly adapted for specific purposes and contexts. Companies that differentiate the contexts and purposes, even just a little, can create a defensible space. The devil, or perhaps an angel, lives in the details of the system in which the data is collected and used.

KEY POINTS

- Despite the challenges of doing system-level innovation with AI, there is a good reason for initiating it sooner rather than later: AI confers an advantage on first movers because AI learns. The sooner it is deployed, the sooner it can begin to learn. The more it learns, the better it gets in terms of prediction accuracy. The better it gets, the more effective the new system is.

- AIs are software. So, once an AI model is built, the marginal cost of generating one more prediction is close to zero. Thus, if one AI becomes slightly better than the others early in the development of a market, then more users will move to the system with that AI. With more users, the AI benefits from more feedback data; with more feedback data, the AI generates even better predictions. Better predictions attract more users. And so on. Once the flywheel starts to spin, the AI that had only a small advantage at the beginning can develop a large advantage over time. The significant advantage awarded to first movers leads to racing. Companies will invest more aggressively than seems rational at first glance because the prize for being first is so large.

- Feedback loops can have significant implications for system design. In order for an AI to learn, it must have access to the outcome data.

For example, an educational AI system that employs a prediction of the next best content to show a learner must be designed to collect feedback as frequently as possible, to both determine whether the student has learned the material and to assess their level of engagement. So, this would not be dropping a next-best-content prediction (point solution) into the existing education system. Instead, an educational system redesign would create and collect high-frequency feedback data that is measured in minutes rather than midterms.

PART FIVE

How AI Disrupts

13

A Great Decoupling

Q: "What will your AI do for your customers?"

A: "It will provide them with insights."

If we had a dollar for every time a startup founder gave that answer to mentors at the Creative Destruction Lab, we'd be rich.

Insights is a trigger word for us because it represents precisely the wrong way of thinking about how an AI advance will create value. For a new AI prediction, "insights" is code for "we don't know what to do with that prediction."

The correct response would be to outline the decision that the prediction will improve. AI only has value if it leads to better decision-making. And this means that the new opportunities for value creation from AI are all about how they improve decisions.

The good news is that there are decisions all over the place. Decisions are what put the "general" in AI as a general purpose technology. And there is an increasing need for good decision-making. Estimates show that, in 1960, just 5 percent of jobs required decision-making skills. By 2015, that number was more than 30 percent. And those jobs were higher paid and had more rigorous hiring requirements in education, skills, and experience.[1]

AI prediction has the potential to enhance the value of decision-making skills—that is, the ability to take what one person might call an "insight" and translate it into better decisions. As we will demonstrate in this chapter, however, the critical question is not whether but who will seize the new opportunities for decision-making.

The Key to Decision-Making Is Judgment

"If you had a terrible headache and I gave you a bottle of pills and nine of the pills would cure you and one of the pills would kill you, would you take a pill?"[2]

Chicago Bulls owner Jerry Reinsdorf put this hypothetical question to basketball legend Michael Jordan. Most of us would answer no. The real decision was whether Jordan should return to play as he was recovering from a broken foot. It was his second season in the National Basketball Association, and Jordan wanted to get back out there. But doctors had told him that if he played, there was a 10 percent chance of a career-ending reinjury.[3] Jordan argued that a 90 percent chance that everything would be fine might be good enough. Hence, the question regarding the headache pill.

Jordan's response to Reinsdorf on taking the pill: "It depends how f**king bad the headache is." [4]

In making this statement, Jordan was arguing that it wasn't just the probabilities—that is, the prediction—that mattered. The payoffs mattered, too. In this example, the payoff refers to the person's assessment of the degree of pain associated with the headache relative to being cured or dying. The payoffs are what we refer to as judgment.

To make such distinctions between prediction and judgment concrete, as Michael Jordan did, we show a decision tree for the pill decision in figure 13-1. At the root of the tree are two branches—in one, Jordan takes the pill; in the other, he does not. If he chooses to take the pill, two branches represent the two uncertain outcomes—is he cured of the headache or is he killed by the pill? At the tips of those branches are the outcomes of feeling good or dying. By contrast, if he does not take the pill, there is actually no uncertainty. He will have a headache and have no risk of dying or being headache-free. Thus, the tip of the no-pill branch is the end of the story, with the outcome that Jordan has a headache for sure.

FIGURE 13-1

Michael Jordan's pill decision tree

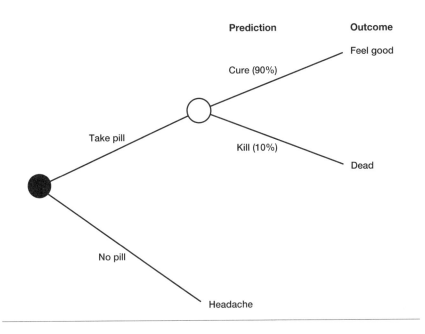

It is easy to rank the outcomes. Feeling good is better than having a headache, which is better than being dead. But is a 10 percent chance of dying enough to rule out feeling good? A descriptive outcome isn't enough. As Jordan noted, some measure of intensity is required to compare what you get from avoiding a headache. That ability to decide how much something matters is judgment.

The hypothetical question was, of course, designed to make the decision stark, as it would be hard to imagine a headache that caused you to take a one-in-ten chance of dying. So let's consider Jordan and Reinsdorf's real decision (depicted in figure 13-2). There we have added numbers to the particular outcomes to reflect their intensity—that is, we have included a representation of judgment. Apart from the labels, the decision tree looks the same as in figure 13-1. But with the numbers that come from judgment added, we now have enough information to work out the decision. Resting gives Jordan –10 for sure, while playing gives a 90 percent chance of 100 and a 10 percent chance of –2,000. Thus, by

FIGURE 13-2

Michael Jordan's play-versus-rest decision tree

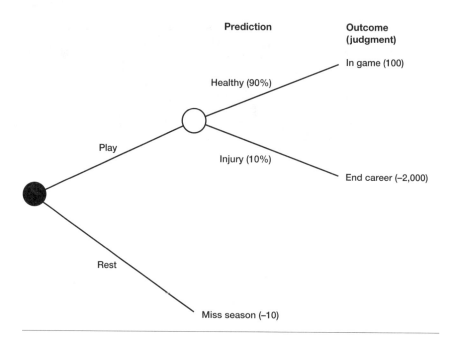

playing, Jordan will get a payoff of –110 (= 0.9 (100) + (0.1) (–2,000)). Jordan shouldn't play, as –10 is better than –110.

But Jordan and Reinsdorf were arguing about judgment. Jordan believed he should be allowed to play and argued that it should be worth, say, 200 to him and the team to have that happen, and that the cost of the career end was –1,000. If that was the correct judgment, then the payoff from playing would become 80 (= 0.9 (200) + (0.1) (–1,000)). Their disagreement was not about the prediction—that had come from medical experts. Their disagreement was about judgment.

In the end, Jordan "took the pill" and got back in the game, albeit with significant time restrictions that Reinsdorf imposed. The Chicago Bulls ended up making it to the playoffs that year, despite losing many games early in the season when Jordan was out. They had the second-worst record (30–52) for a playoff-qualifying team in history. They were rewarded by facing off against Larry Bird's mighty Boston Celtics, who would go on to win the NBA Championship that year. However, in Game 2 of that Eastern Conference First Round, Jordan scored sixty-three points, which, as of this writing, still stands as the NBA Playoff single-game scoring record.

AI Prediction Forces Explicit Judgment

The disagreement between Jordan and Reinsdorf arose because they had already received a diagnosis—in effect, a prediction—from a medical expert, and neither were in a position to challenge that. But consider how many decisions are made without an explicit prediction. What happens then? When a firefighter has to choose in the moment whether to save one person or another in an emergency, they are considering the relative likelihoods that they can successfully rescue one person over another but also who those people are—say, an older person versus a child. The firefighter will make a call, but how precisely they place weights on different outcomes is likely to be implicit rather than explicit. Our evaluation of the efficacy of their decision rests on a combination of factors.

AI prediction, however, takes that part of a decision potentially out of the hands of the decision-maker. Prediction causes decoupling (see figure 13-3).

The decoupling of prediction and judgment isn't a hypothetical concept that applies only in the classroom but not in the real world. This

FIGURE 13-3

AI prediction causes decoupling

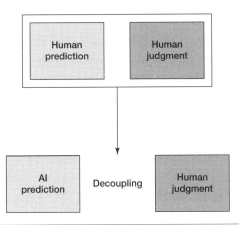

separation of prediction and judgment underlies a recent McKinsey article on the future of insurance.[5] It maps out a vision for car insurance in 2030. A customer gets into their car. The customer's personal digital assistant maps out potential routes. The AI underlying the assistant predicts the likelihood of an accident, and the customer uses their judgment to decide.

This might work as follows. You are visiting Vancouver for work, and you've rented a car. You're staying at the Sutton Hotel on Burrard Street downtown and have a meeting at the University of British Columbia. You can take the scenic route along the water or the dull route along West 4th. The scenic route takes you past Kitsilano Beach, Jericho Park, and Spanish Banks. It's beautiful. The scenic route is a little slower but not much. You'll get to your meeting on time either way.

The real issue is that on the scenic route, lots of other people are looking at the scenery. They are distracted. You have a slightly higher chance of a fender bender. Suppose your rental car is equipped with AI that tells you exactly how much more likely an accident is on the scenic route. You then need to apply judgment and assess whether the scenery is worth that risk. To do that, you draw a decision tree and add payoffs for different outcomes, just as Michael Jordan did in the earlier example. You calculate your expected payoff and decide to take the scenic route.

Who does that? Nobody. It's too complicated. It's academic, in the worst sense of the word. Wonderful in theory and useless in practice.

It doesn't have to be. You can reframe the decision into one you are familiar with and do on a regular basis. After the AI assistant predicts the probabilities, it tells you a price. It says that your insurance premium will increase by a dollar if you choose the scenic route.

This seems like a minor thing. The driver can decide on the route based on the price. The price in turn is determined by the likelihood of an accident and the cost of repair, which is hidden from the customer. The AI is calculating the probability of an accident and assigns costs. The customer just sees a price.

The machine does the prediction. The customer exercises judgment. All the customer has to do is judge whether the price is worth the benefit. Easy.

This is already happening. Companies are pricing insurance based on minute-by-minute driving decisions. Many offer discounts for those who install telematics apps on their phones, assuming that the customers drive well. Tesla, for example, doesn't need to rely on phone data. It can use data from the vehicle itself to measure a safety score based on hard braking, unsafe following distance, and other factors.[6] With insurance pricing based on driver behavior, customers experience lower premiums, and we all might get safer roads.[7]

Prediction and judgment are unbundled. The insurance company prices the risky behavior. The customer judges whether the behavior is worth it.

What the insurance example shows is that judgment can be decoupled from prediction and that we humans are used to making judgments. This is the essence of what economists call "revealed preference." We can understand someone's preferences from their decisions. Marketers have done this for decades.

In 1971, Paul Green and Vithala Rao published a paper describing a radical new tool for assessing what consumers want. The paper, titled "Conjoint Measurement for Quantifying Judgmental Data," begins by noting that "the quantification of managerial or consumer judgment has long posed problems for marketing researchers."[8] They emphasize that "the study of consumer decision making requires ascertaining how buyers trade off conflicting criteria in making decisions." The method asked consumers to rank different options. The choices were hypothetical, but easy enough because they were familiar.

Green and Rao used the example of discount cards. One card might offer a 5 percent discount in ten stores and cost $14. Another card might offer a 10 percent discount in five stores and cost $7. A third card might have a 15 percent discount in ten stores and cost $21. By having consumers rank their preferences, a statistician can figure out the value the consumers place on each card. Choices revealed judgment.

Over time, the method advanced. It was used to assess the value of pepperoni or Hawaiian pizza, Ford trucks or Toyota cars, and even the preferences of Chinese doctoral students at US universities to stay in the United States or return to China. By asking students whether they'd prefer a private-sector research scientist position in Boston for $70,000 or a public-sector management position in Beijing for $50,000, the researchers learned the students' judgment of the relative value of living in the United States or China.[9]

This same revealed preference framework had a parallel research stream in economics, starting with Nobel Prize–winning work by Daniel McFadden in the early 1970s. It is the basis for modern tools for measuring demand using grocery scanner data and online clickstreams.

Fifteen years ago, perhaps the leading economist in the area was Pat Bajari. Bajari is now Amazon's vice president of core AI and chief economist. Before joining Amazon, Bajari was a professor at Harvard, Stanford, Duke, Michigan, and Minnesota universities. He is a fellow of the Econometric Society and wrote papers with obscure titles like "Demand Estimation with Heterogeneous Consumers and Unobserved Product Characteristics: A Hedonic Approach" and "A Simple Estimator for the Distribution of Random Coefficients." (Hint: it's not that simple.) Bajari was one of the leading econometricians of his generation. His papers were abstract. Filled with symbols and equations. We wouldn't have expected that he'd grow Amazon into one of the largest employers of PhD economists in the world.

Yet that is exactly what he did. It had much to do with his skills as a mentor and a leader.[10] It is also directly related to his papers. Demand estimation is central to Amazon's business. It needs to know what consumers value and how much they are willing to pay. If Amazon knows a consumer's judgment on how valuable a product is, it can provide them with the right product at the right time at the right price. The tools for estimating consumer judgment exist in marketing research and in econometrics. Amazon's economics group, under Bajari's leadership, figured out how to determine that judgment at scale.

Once we recognize that we can understand judgment from decisions, then it is clear that we humans make judgments all the time. We are good at judgment. Judgment is only unfamiliar when decoupled from a prediction.

The Judgment Opportunity

Decoupling prediction and judgment creates opportunity. It means that who makes the decision is driven not by who does prediction and judgment best as a bundle but who is best to provide judgment utilizing AI prediction.

Once the AI provides the prediction, then the people with the best judgment can shine. As we've noted, conceptually and increasingly as a matter of practice, AI is able to conduct predictions with a greater degree of precision than many radiologists. While it depends on what precisely is being predicted, in effect, an AI can be trained not by observing the predictions of radiologists but by matching the images to observed, reliable outcomes—for example, did pathology find a malignant tumor? Thus, AI prediction has the potential to become superior to human prediction, so much so that Vinod Khosla, a technology pioneer and well-known investor in AI, suggests that in the future it may be malpractice for radiologists not to rely on AI prediction.

Herein lies the issue—what would AI prediction do to the value of a radiologist's judgment? Given the way radiologists (at least in the United States) operate, they are largely divorced from other information about the patient. Thus, if an AI predicts that a particular patient has a malignant tumor with 30 percent probability, under what imaginable circumstances could a medical system accept the judgment of one radiologist that the patient should be diagnosed and treated for the tumor versus that of another that they should not? Indeed, it is hard to imagine. Instead, one suspects that some committee of medical professionals will deliberate and debate the rules for diagnosis in advance of any machine prediction, and then that committee's judgment would be subsequently applied at scale. The radiologist's decision becomes decoupled into a machine prediction and a committee's judgment.

Once the AI provides the prediction, *new systems* can arise to take advantage of better, faster, and cheaper predictions and more appropriate judgment. In *Prediction Machines*, we highlighted an opportunity for Amazon to change its business model so that it ships items to your door before you even order. That business model now exists. Stitch Fix does it for clothes.[11] As CEO Katrina Lake put it, "We make unique and personal selections by combining data and machine learning with expert human judgment." It doesn't stop there. Inventory is expensive in the fashion industry. The data science team developed algorithms that integrated the rebuy decisions of what to have in inventory with predictions of changes in anticipated demand.

In chapter 11, we showed that machines don't have power because the judgment provided for decisions always comes from a person, even if a machine may end up implementing a decision. In the next chapter, we discuss the skills associated with judgment once it becomes decoupled from prediction. Understanding these skills sets up an explanation of how the decoupling of prediction and judgment changes who the right people are to make decisions. Decoupling creates a new opportunity for AI adoption centered around improving the skills associated with judgment.

KEY POINTS

- Prediction and judgment are the two primary ingredients for decision-making. In a decision tree, prediction generates the probability that each branch in the tree will occur. Judgment generates the payoffs associated with the outcomes at the ends of each branch. Usually, we make decisions without recognizing that the predictions and judgment are two separate inputs as they are both in the mind of the same person (the decision-maker). When we introduce AI, we shift the prediction from a person to a machine, and thus we decouple the prediction from the judgment. That may change who provides the judgment.

- We make decisions all the time and never think about predictions or judgment. We just decide. Even though we don't explicitly think about prediction and judgment every time we make a decision, it is possible to infer judgment via analytical techniques after a decision is made (we call this "revealed preference"). Economists and marketers have long used statistical tools to measure judgment based on choices.

- Decisions are the primary building blocks of a system. Before AI, the distinction between prediction and judgment was irrelevant from a system design perspective because both functions happen inside a single person's mind. However, AI changes that. When we transition the prediction from a person to an AI, we can rethink the system design. If the AI is much faster and cheaper, can we do the prediction more often? Can we do it for less important decisions? Can we codify the judgment and therefore automate and scale the decision? Can we assign the judgment role to a different person or group of people who have significantly better judgment than in the prior system where judgment was constrained to the same mind that generated the prediction? The opportunity for new system design is so great because AI creates new opportunities right down at the most fundamental level: decision composition.

14

Thinking Probabilistically

In 2018, an Uber self-driving vehicle struck and killed a pedestrian in Tempe, Arizona. It was the first fatal accident of a car designed for autonomous driving. The car, it was claimed, saw the pedestrian but did not brake. News reports quoted a Princeton University professor saying that it "should be a warning to all companies testing autonomous vehicles to check their systems to make sure they automatically stop when necessary."[1] On the day of the accident, the Tempe chief of police had a different explanation: "It's very clear it would have been difficult to avoid this collision based on how she came from the shadows."[2]

Did Uber really program its vehicle to kill? Of course not. But it also isn't right that the vehicle didn't see the person. Instead, six seconds before impact, the vehicle predicted the presence of an unknown object. By the time the vehicle predicted that the unknown object was likely a person, it was too late for the emergency brakes to make a difference.[3]

Put differently, both interpretations are wrong because they are deterministic. The vehicle did identify an object, and there was a small probability that the object could be a person. If the vehicle had predicted that the object was likely to be a person earlier, then it would have braked, and the tragedy would have been avoided. Reviewing the accident report suggests that the vehicle sensed a person with a very low probability. Not zero, but extremely small. Furthermore, the vehicle was programmed to proceed as long as the chance that something was a person wasn't too high. That might be 0.01 percent, 0.0001 percent, or 0.000000001 percent, but never zero. That's not how the machines work.

This is a terrible outcome. An autonomous vehicle did not see a pedestrian with a high enough probability to engage the brake. It requires more effort to see that this was a bad decision. After the accident, Uber froze its autonomous vehicle program. When it resumed autonomous driving in December 2018, the program looked different. The cars were limited to twenty-five miles per hour or less, and they had two safety drivers at all times. It implemented a number of other changes, from third-party monitoring of the drivers to different automatic braking procedures. A threshold-based decision was no longer going to cut it.

Thinking in Bets

The distinction between a bad decision and a bad outcome is important. Sometimes good decisions lead to bad outcomes. That's one of the main messages of professional poker player Annie Duke's book, *Thinking in Bets*. As of this writing, Duke is the only woman to win the NBC National Heads-Up Poker Championship. Poker is a game of both luck and skill. It is possible to play your cards perfectly and lose. It is also possible to bet big on a bad hand and get lucky.

When things go badly, Duke argues that it's important to reflect on whether it was a bad decision or bad luck. If it's just bad luck, then classify it as a bad outcome and move on. If it's a bad decision, learn and do better next time.

Too many amateur poker players get a bad outcome and change their strategy. Similarly, too many make a big dumb bet and win. Then, they make their next decisions from past results. This habit, which she labels "resulting," makes these players get worse over time. Without the ability to recognize whether an outcome was a result of luck, uncertainty makes it hard to learn.

Michael Jordan did play toward the end of that 1985–1986 regular season, and he didn't get injured. He landed on a good outcome. That's best, regardless of the probabilities and the relative payoffs of the career-ending injury and sitting out the season. After that season, he won six championships and five Most Valuable Player Awards and became the top-earning athlete of all time, at $2.6 billion. Seems like playing those games was the right decision. Perhaps he should have rejoined the team earlier. Jordan didn't get injured, but that doesn't mean he made the right decision.

Thinking in bets requires you to recognize that predictions are uncertain, and to understand that the outcomes you experience are partly determined by luck. And that isn't easy. For cars, before self-driving, prediction and judgment rested with the driver. If a human driver hit a pedestrian, we never knew whether they made a prediction error (they thought the likelihood of hitting the person was effectively zero, so they did not brake) or a judgment error (they were in a rush and put a higher weight on getting to their destination quickly than avoiding an accident). If they had an accident, we assume their judgment was fine, but they made a mechanical error in generating their prediction of a collision. At present, society seems OK with this.

When you are designing a self-driving car, you can measure prediction error. But then you have to quantify judgment, which involves doing unpleasant things like calculating the cost of life and comparing that with the experience of being a passenger in a car (stopping too frequently from an abundance of caution is unpleasant). People have to trade this off implicitly all the time but demur when asked to be explicit. It will be no less unpleasant for an engineering and, perhaps, ethics team determining what to do regarding a self-driving car.

Embracing Uncertainty

Thinking in bets means embracing uncertainty. We examine the underlying likelihood that something will happen. If it is sufficiently likely, go left; otherwise, go right. In other words, we express our decision rule contingent on the prediction as a cutoff point. This works well if predictions are very precise. Recall Michael Jordan's decision about whether to play and risk further injury. If the doctors said there is zero chance of a career-ending injury, then both Jordan and Reinsdorf would not have hesitated. The decision was difficult because the prediction involved uncertainty. Jordan evaluated that being 90 percent confident was enough. Reinsdorf disagreed.

The idea of basing decisions on thresholds that enumerate confidence is an attractive one. For instance, consider the process by which refugees have been assessed for entry into countries, a decision fraught with uncertainty. Based on the testimony of a refugee claimant, refugee adjudicators need to decide whether they find the person's claim credible and whether the person will come to harm, as covered by the UN Convention on Refugees, if their claim is refused. Furthermore, the supporting documents are necessarily sparse, and the adjudicators receive little feedback on whether their past decisions were correct.

Currently, the adjudicators do their best to weigh the evidence and decide. Adjudicators tend to be quite confident in their decisions. As one scholar put it, "Some people seem to think their gut is a uniquely valid arbiter of truth, and if their gut tells them that somebody's lying, well, they must be lying."[4]

The confidence is misplaced. To make a more considered decision, it would help to have a prediction available that assigned a probability to the likelihood that a given claimant is, say, lying or not. The goal would be to improve decision outcomes rather than, say, increase the rate of accepted claims.

Currently, data is unavailable on outcomes to see if decisions to accept or reject refugees led to the outcomes that adjudicators thought they would. If that data was collected, it would be possible to build a prediction machine that could then assess future claimants. With that machine, we would have a more confident assessment based on the evidence. In one Canadian case, a refugee claimant from Germany asserted that she was being persecuted by the administration at her son's school and that German police could not assist her. There is plenty of data on German police responsiveness to reports of criminality, so it is possible to generate a confident prediction that the police would protect her, at least as required for a refugee claim. Adjudicators can also be confident that the evidence would support a claim about an LGBTQ activist from Yemen or a member of a persecuted minority in Sudan.

Many other cases leave room for doubt. There is often inadequate information about whether a police force will respond to appeals for protection from domestic violence, or whether a claimant's profile is sufficient to draw the attention of the government. In these cases, missing data means uncertainty. Making that uncertainty visible should reduce overconfidence.

The adjudicator needs to apply judgment by comparing the uncertain predictions to an assessment of "[w]hich mistake is worse: to deny a refugee claim that should have been granted, or to grant a claim that should have been denied?"[5] It seems simple enough, but the stakes are high. Refusing a legitimate refugee claim could lead to torture or death. Accepting a false claim means people take advantage of a country's generosity. Under the UN Convention, accepting a false claim is worse. There is a clear "wrong mistake" in refusing a legitimate claim.

By decoupling prediction and judgment, and making it clear that even with the best AIs, the predictions for refugee claims are uncertain, AI could lead to a better process. In the end, if the prediction machine embraced the uncertainty inherent in the prediction, then more claims would be accepted. The costs of saying no would be too high.

The current system doesn't work this way. Adjudicators have little use for a prediction machine that communicates uncertainty. They aren't trained to interpret statistical uncertainty, and the law is ambiguous about how much worse the wrong mistake really is. Even if the adjudicators had training, it couldn't be dropped into the existing process. Accepting all uncertain refugee claims would generate political pressure to make it more difficult for refugees to arrive. It might also create incentives to obscure information. An AI for refugee claims, despite its potential for a fairer process, is not feasible without system change. Part of this new system would be an explicit understanding of judgment, of how to measure the relative risk of a wrong mistake.

Missing Judgment Constrains AI

Judgment is an expression of what you want. But if there is a new context or the information is not something you have dealt with before, do you necessarily know what you want? How should an adjudicator for refugee claims interpret the statement that there is a 40 percent chance that a given claim is legitimate? In the past, adjudicators combined prediction and judgment in their decisions. For many new applications of AI, judgment—decoupled from prediction—may not yet exist. Because there wasn't the ability to predict what was going on, there was no action that could be taken contingent on that prediction and, hence, no reason to find out what the payoff from that action would be.

This means that prediction and judgment are potentially subject to a chicken-and-egg problem, which in turn creates a barrier to adopting prediction machines and building new AI systems. Investing and adopting better predictions are only valuable if you have some use for that information. Working out what you might do if you hypothetically had better prediction is only of use if you anticipate having better prediction. For this reason, not having judgment is itself a constraint on your willingness to invest in better prediction and vice versa.

Finding Judgment

Judgment can be built from working through your anticipated outcomes before the fact. By researching, evaluating, and learning from others, you can establish what outcomes might be likely in different situations. This is how most of us learned not to touch a hot stove. Someone told you that you'd burn yourself if you touched the stove. You learned the judgment without experiencing the burn yourself. Someone else transferred the judgment. The benefit of that is it avoids having to make costly mistakes along the way.

Some of you might have been skeptical. Children are told not to do all sorts of things, and many have few consequences. The more rebellious readers might have touched the hot stove. Then evolution kicked in, and you experienced the pain of touching a hot stove. You learned the other way, from experience.

You make choices and then receive feedback. The outcomes inform you as to the costs and benefits of different paths. The more you experience by making different choices in different contexts, the more your outcomes are mapped out for you. The picture you build from that experience is judgment that allows you to know what to do in the future.

These are the two ways judgment is built. Either it involves planned learning from someone else by reading, instructions, or culture, or it is learned by experience. We now examine each of these ways in turn.

Planning It Out

Having low-cost or quality predictions available makes the task of obtaining judgment through experience easier. But what if those predictions instead require some investment and development? Predictions may be cheap following that development, but the costs involved in acquiring data and training, and then testing the resulting algorithms, may require a clear justification of their use. Undertaking a careful analysis of what choices might be made if predictions were available—that is, prethinking through outcomes in order to obtain the requisite judgment—may be warranted. For instance, many venture capitalists fund startups whose success is predicated on a high degree of uncertainty, but before making that investment, go through the exercise of working out whether it will be better to exit through an IPO or a private acquisition, should that success come.[6]

In undertaking this exercise, it is natural to suppose that outcomes will be investigated for scenarios considered more frequent than for less frequent scenarios. However, when it comes to planning out choices for different scenarios, the issue is not necessarily whether prediction can distinguish between more or less frequent cases, but whether it can distinguish between scenarios when dramatically different actions are warranted.

Let us consider the application of AI in credit card fraud. When you swipe your credit card, this sets in motion a set of algorithms that determine whether to process or reject the transaction. It may be rejected because you have run out of credit or because fraud is suspected. A credit card network does not want to allow transactions it suspects of being fraudulent because it will be liable for the costs associated with that theft. On the other hand, the whole business of credit cards rests on it being easy and painless for customers and merchants alike. Thus, rejecting a legitimate transaction is harmful. Consumers may be frustrated or, worse, switch to using another card.

When a credit card network's algorithm suspects that a transaction may be fraudulent, it assigns a score to that possibility. In effect, that score represents the probability that the transaction is fraudulent. But judgment is required to work out how to react to that information. That judgment does not lie with the merchant or anyone on the ground. Instead, how the information is used is programmed into the system, and the decision of whether to accept or reject a card is automated. How could it be otherwise?

This means that judgment that guides how a score translates into an accept or reject action has to be prethought, which most likely comes from a committee that evaluated the options. If the prediction score was always 100 percent or 0 percent, then you don't need much judgment to decide on the right course of action. However, what you are doing is setting a threshold for the score, above which the transaction is rejected and below which it is accepted. And for the vast majority of transactions, it will be accepted, suggesting that relatively high fraud scores are infrequent occurrences. This perhaps explains why, before any algorithmic scoring, the credit card company left it up to the merchant to decide whether to accept a card or not.

That threshold has to be chosen to balance two errors. The first is that fraudulent transactions may be permitted. The cost of that is simply the cost associated with the card company, rather than the merchant or cardholder bearing the cost of the transaction, which can be calculated from historical data. The second cost is that legitimate transactions may be declined. The cost here is more difficult to calculate, and thus, judgment is harder to come by. The type of cardholder likely plays an important role here. A credit card company might worry about having this sort of error made if the cardholder is a premium customer who may take all transactions to another card if frustrated. Thus, the judgment applied relates to other characteristics of the customer. This can interact with the fraud scoring itself. After all, predicting a fraudulent transaction depends on extrapolating something unusual from the transaction that is under investigation. For premium cardholders who travel often, this might be harder to predict than for ordinary cardholders who have more stable consumption patterns.

It is easy to see how judgment by planning ahead can be a complex exercise with many different dimensions to consider. Those dimensions need to be translated into something describable so that, in the case of credit cards at least, it can be encoded in the automated process. With automation, judgment involves individuals judging what matters before the specific decision arrives. This complexity creates a barrier to adopting AI systems. The people who exercise judgment change. Instead of merchants applying a combined prediction and judgment of whether someone will honor their credit, the credit card company combines moment-by-moment predictions with careful and planned judgment at scale.

The Experience Journey

Experience, by providing judgment—knowing what to do in particular circumstances—can lead to better decisions. However, the journey by which that happens may not be straightforward. After all, whether we experience something depends on (a) what happens and (b) knowing that what happened actually happened. If you accidentally touch a hot oven, you both have had a (hopefully) new experience and can work out what the consequences of that were. But that requires an accident. If you know that an oven may be hot and so never touch it, you don't really find out what the consequences would be. We aren't saying that is a bad strategy. We are just making the point that your choices may guide your experiences.[7]

To make this more precise, consider a situation where you have two actions to choose from. One action, which we will call the status quo action, is the thing you have always done. You know precisely what you get from that, and it has another quality in that what you get is always the same. It is an action with a certain return. The other action, which we will call the risky action, is something you have never done. You just don't know what is going to happen if you take the risky action. For instance, it might be hiring a person who doesn't meet the usual criteria. Or it might be financing a startup that doesn't quite fit your usual investment thesis. Here, even if you receive some signal regarding the risky choice that helps you understand the context for the decision better, you may still not know if it is worth pursuing.

In this situation, you might be stuck. A prediction that gives you information may be available, but if you don't know what you'll do with the information, you might not choose to pay for that prediction. But without that prediction, you will just stick with the status quo anyway and never find out what the risky action has in store for you. Again, the challenges in building judgment are a barrier to building AI systems.

If the payoff of an AI system solution is high enough, it will be worth investing in building judgment, so this chicken-and-egg situation may not be hopeless. The people who are best positioned to build that judgment, through either experience or planning, may be different from those who currently make decisions based on bundled prediction and judgment.

FDAs for Everything

In many cases, we do not know exactly how a person will react to taking a drug to treat an ailment. We often do know that some people will suffer terrible side effects. Different people are different. Pharmaceutical effects are probabilistic. Because even good drugs don't work for everyone, it can sometimes be hard to tell between good drugs and bad drugs.

This problem could have prevented the market for drugs from ever evolving past the snake oil salesmen of the early twentieth century. However, we developed a regulatory process (led by the Food and Drug Administration in the case of pharmaceuticals in the United States) to weigh the overall benefits of each drug for each indication against the costs. The regulatory process recognizes the probabilistic nature of drug effectiveness and uses randomized trials (described in chapter 3) to determine whether a drug works. Furthermore, we consider the benefit-cost ratio in the aggregate as well as for specific narrow groupings throughout the age distribution and other distributions. A recent example is the staged FDA approvals for Covid-19 vaccines, first for adults, then for children.

As we contemplate new system designs that replace deterministic with probabilistic approaches, we may need to consider similar regulatory approaches for domains that were previously not similarly regulated.[8] For example, although we require new drivers to take a simple driving exam but never examine their judgment regarding the costs of potentially harming others, we might need something like the FDA for autonomous-driving AIs that tests whether the vehicles' actions are safe relative to established guidelines.

We similarly might need something like the FDA for AIs that grant bank loans. This regulator would test the AI's loan-granting actions to establish whether those actions meet legal requirements. In addition, we might need something like the FDA for warehouse robot control system AIs, where robots work close to people, to test whether the robots' actions are safe relative to some benchmark.

Just as the hard-to-verify, probabilistic pharmaceutical industry benefited from a regulatory process established to reassure citizens that, despite some risks, the benefits were overall net positive, we might need similar thinking as we design system-level solutions to reap the full benefits of AI. As we move through The Between Times into a new era of ubiquitous AI where most systems transition from deterministic to probabilistic, we might need FDAs for just about everything. These regulatory bodies would become part of the new *system*.

Who Are the Right Judges?

Who has judgment, how it is acquired, and how it is actually implemented in decisions—whether as thresholds or something more complex—are all key choices in the design of systems built around AI prediction. Recall that AI prediction will often mean that you can now choose who is the right judge as opposed to the right combination of predictor and judge, as these functions become decoupled. However, decoupling means you need to choose who is obtaining those predictions and also understand how the predictions will be used. The predictions may go to one place—say, an algorithm that incorporates prespecified judgment to create thresholds for predictions that trigger actions—or to many places, such as predictions for the best navigation route that are available to many drivers.

These changes may be disruptive, creating discord as they are implemented. Nonetheless, the opportunity for rethinking the system is created, starting with decoupling and then based on finding the right judges. These judges might be different from today's decision-makers. They need to understand how to think in bets and have the right planning skills, experience, or opportunity for experience to build their judgment appropriately.

KEY POINTS

- AIs introduce *probabilistic thinking* into a system. When we investigate a car accident, we ask whether the driver saw the pedestrian before they collided. We expect a yes or no answer. We are less accustomed to dealing with "sort of" or "a bit." Yet, that is precisely the response the AI provides. It saw something that it thought was a human approaching the road with, say, a 0.01 percent likelihood. When we introduce an AI into a system, we often transform that system from deterministic to probabilistic. Sometimes the existing system is well designed to accommodate a probabilistic input. Other times, this creates an opportunity for greatly enhanced productivity via system redesign.

- In order to translate a prediction into a decision, we must apply judgment. If people traditionally made the decision, then the judgment may not be codified as distinct from the prediction. So, we need to generate it. Where does it come from? It can come via transfer (learning from others) or via experience. Without existing judgment, we may have less incentive to invest in building the AI for prediction. Similarly, we may be hesitant to invest in developing the judgment associated with a set of decisions if we don't have an AI that can make the necessary predictions. We are faced with a chicken-and-egg problem. This can present an additional challenge for system redesign.

- To fully exploit the power of AI, many applications will require newly designed system-level solutions that include not only prediction and judgment but also a regulatory function designed to assure society when systems transition from deterministic to probabilistic. We don't know in advance how the system will behave in all scenarios because it is not hard-coded. Similar to the hard-to-verify, probabilistic pharmaceutical industry that greatly benefited from a regulatory process to assure citizens that despite risks from side effects, the benefits were overall net positive, we might need an FDA-type regulatory function that examines the machines' decisions against an established testing framework. In many cases, this may be critical to the success of a system redesign that relies on probabilistic information.

15

The New Judges

Lead is a deadly neurotoxin that affects the brain development of children.[1] Lead started being phased out of paint in the 1960s and gasoline in the 1970s. Most lead paint has been replaced. Cars that used leaded gasoline were scrapped long ago. These changes improved the health of millions of people around the world.

The United States banned the use of lead drinking water pipes in 1986, but not for those already installed. As the pipes could last a hundred years, without replacement, they continue to cause harm. A change in water treatment in Flint, Michigan, resulted in a large spike of lead in the drinking water and brought the replacement issue to a head. The problem was city officials didn't know which pipes contained lead and which were harmless. Checking each pipe individually was expensive.

Uncertainty presents an opportunity to deploy a prediction machine. University of Michigan professors Eric Schwartz and Jacob Abernethy took up the challenge. With a team of researchers, they set out to predict which pipes likely contained lead. They successfully built an AI that was deployed in Flint. The city only checked for lead pipes in those homes where predictions suggested they likely had lead. When the prediction machine identified a likely pipe, it was correct 80 percent of the time.[2] Thousands of Flint residents had their lead pipes replaced in 2016 and 2017.

Nonetheless, some residents were unhappy. The prediction might indicate that, say, just one block in a neighborhood was likely to have lead (perhaps because the homes were older), leaving the other residents of the neighborhood anxious about their own pipes. Some neighborhoods, particularly poor ones, were more likely to have their pipes inspected for lead than more affluent areas. Some wealthier residents were angry that their pipes weren't being checked sooner. Flint's mayor brought in a new contractor to manage the lead pipe replacement, requiring that the firm dig across the various city wards and in every house without regard for the likelihood that the drinking water pipes were actually lead.

The success rate plummeted to 15 percent (see figure 15-1). While many residents were now reassured that their homes did not have lead pipes, the process of identifying and replacing the pipes stalled. The AI provided

FIGURE 15-1

Prediction accuracy for finding lead pipes in Flint

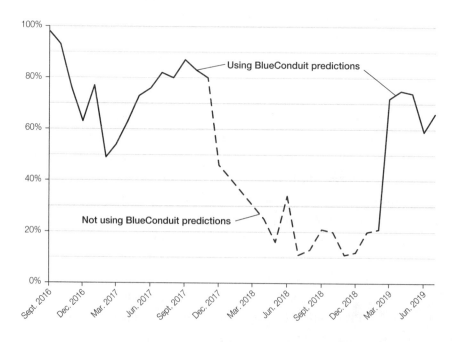

Source: Adapted from data in Jared Webb, Jacob Abernethy, and Eric Schwartz, "Getting the Lead Out: Data Science and Water Service Lines in Flint" (working paper, University of Michigan, 2020), figure 3, accessed online at https://storage.googleapis.com/flint-storage-bucket/d4gx_2019%20(2).pdf on May 10, 2022.

an excellent prediction, but the judgment remained political. As the new project manager put it, the city administration "did not want to have to explain to a councilperson why there was no work in their district" and "the City did not want to leave anybody behind."[3] In the process, while residents of some wards were reassured that their pipes had no lead, residents of the city's Fifth Ward had the fewest excavations, despite the AI prediction that 80 percent of homes in the area would have lead pipes. Following the local politicians' judgment, Flint had decided not to use the prediction machine.

But that wasn't the end of the story. On March 26, 2019, a US court–approved settlement required the city to use Schwartz and Abernethy's predictions. The court removed political discretion. Instead, it prespecified the judgment. Essentially, it judged eliminating lead as equally valuable in every city ward and every neighborhood. What mattered was the likelihood that there was lead. The success rate quickly jumped up to 70 percent, and thousands more Flint residents had their lead pipes identified and replaced. *Time* named Schwartz and Abernethy's AI one of the best inventions of 2021. Now marketed by a for-profit company called BlueConduit, about fifty cities use these predictions to help them save money while identifying and removing lead from millions of homes.[4]

What's interesting here is *how the availability of a new prediction machine caused a struggle for the power to decide.* The predictions were inconvenient to Flint's politicians, so they abandoned the predictions. Others recognized that the predictions could improve lives, as long as each home was judged to be of equal value. After a court case, the decision rights changed. The court settlement prespecified judgment. Local politicians lost discretion, and a centralized system prevailed.

When a prediction machine causes judgment to be decoupled from prediction, there are opportunities to move the locus of judgment to others. And as we already noted, those who hold judgment ultimately decide. Who should and who gets to make decisions may change. This chapter looks at when new judges are likely to emerge and become responsible for decisions.

More critically, in so doing, we highlight an important source of resistance to change in adopting new systems. When we introduced disruption, we noted there are often winners and losers. The losers may be whole parts of organizations—such as Blockbuster's franchises that were against streaming video. The organization was impeded from adopting change internally, resulting from a change in economic power. But economic power also is aligned with who gets to make decisions. In the case of Flint, Michigan, the AI prediction potentially took the decisions away from politicians, and the resulting loss in power caused friction in their adoption. This required decision-making authority to shift again to remove that friction. Thus, when we change who makes decisions, we impact the distribution of power, and that itself can create resistance to the adoption of new systems.

Who Gets to Make Decisions?

Moving judgment from the local politicians to a court-defined priority list likely improved lives. Different people have different incentives, and when prediction machines can change the time and place of decisions, new opportunities arrive to enable better decisions.

In business, when we consider whether, say, an upper-level manager or one of their subordinates should make a particular decision, the primary criterion is "who will make the decision in the best interests of the organization at the lowest cost?"; that is *efficiency*. There are lots of reasons why a person is allocated decision authority in the interests of efficiency. One is that the person has access to important *information* that should guide the decision. This might, for instance, be a field manager making decisions regarding where to deploy local resources. While they could take the information they collect and communicate it up the chain, this can take time and be costly (for all parties); thus, sometimes we keep decisions close to those who have firsthand knowledge of a situation.

Another reason is the *skill level* of the person involved. Decision-making can be hard. In particular, you have to interpret information and then engage in both prediction and judgment to make a choice. All those activities take skill, and those skills may not be widely held. Consequently, you allocate decision authority on the basis of skill.

Related to this are *incentives*. You want a decision made in the interests of the organization. However, when making decisions, people have their own preferences that impact their judgment. This can cause misalignment with organizational interests. While it is possible to align interests by using incentives (so long as the factors driving the misalignment can be measured in some way), in other situations, some people will have more aligned interests with the organization than others, and this will drive the allocation of decision authority.

Finally, decisions do not have contained *impacts* and sometimes have impacts beyond the decision-makers' purview. For example, sales and marketing have to align with production and operations. In this case, someone who understands the relationships between different decisions may be the one to make them all. Thus, decisions can be bundled together so that they can be made in a coordinated fashion—even if this creates some downsides in terms of the availability of information, communication, and even skill.

The whole point of giving someone decision authority is to give them the power that comes with that decision. They need to be able to dictate where resources are deployed, what information to take into consideration, and in whose interests to ultimately make the decision. With this power naturally flows the ability to capture more value. When you are given decision authority, it is because you are able to create value for the organization by making better decisions. Moreover, the reason you, rather than someone else, has that authority is that the information, skills, and interest alignment are not necessarily widely available. It may be that anyone can make decisions. However, the fact that we spend time considering who makes a decision indicates that they bring power along with them.

What happens with AI prediction is that prediction and judgment become decoupled. More critically, AI prediction means that judgment will become the locus for why someone is more efficiently given the power to make a decision. After all, the AI prediction should be the same regardless of who is using it, something that automatically rules it out as a factor in decision allocation.

Decision-Making Talent

Humans with skills are what we generically refer to as *talent*. The issue for talent is that the skills that we value them for are those that generate better decisions, which, until prediction machines came along, meant superior prediction and judgment. The availability of a machine prediction raises the question of what particular skills humans contribute. Whereas before, it was hard to separate good human decision-making from good prediction and judgment, a prediction machine focuses on how skillful human judgment is.

The good news, as we explored in chapter 11, is that judgment has to come from a person. The bad news is that person isn't necessarily the person who was providing it before AI prediction.

When will AI prediction actually change who is the right person to provide judgment? In many cases, AI prediction may reinforce the talent currently making decisions, in which case, they will not be subject to disruption. However, for others, judgment may efficiently reside elsewhere. What factors should you look for to determine the direction of change?

The decoupling of prediction and judgment can change power if the type of person who is most efficient to supply the judgment changes. Someone's judgment becomes more valuable, and someone else's becomes less valuable. This will not happen in all industries and all situations. In many cases, recent advances in AI will have no impact on decision-making. In other cases, better prediction will enable companies to improve existing predictive analytics or incrementally improve existing processes.

Sometimes, however, better prediction means the locus of judgment will change. When this happens, the decision-maker will change, and power will be reallocated. AI will have different impacts on the value of judgment depending on whether or not it is deployed in a situation where, before AI, prediction was relied on for decisions.

All taxi drivers had to predict the fastest route between two points at any particular time. In the city of London in the UK, for example, taxi drivers required three years of schooling to learn "The Knowledge" and at the end were tested on their memory of street names, establishment locations, and their ability to identify the fastest route between any two points, any time, any day of the week. Prediction was, therefore, a core part of the job. So, when a machine could serve up those predictions through an app, nothing changed for existing taxi drivers, but all other drivers now had an opportunity to apply their own judgment, relying on AI prediction rather than their own predictive skill. AI disrupted the taxi industry not because it changed the value of the judgment of taxi drivers, but because it enhanced the value of judgment of others who could now drive for Uber and Lyft. Prediction changed who could make a decision by expanding the set of workers that could drive others.

In the case of Flint's lead pipes, prediction changed the decision-maker from the local politicians to the judge and the parties in the legal case who agreed to the amended decision.

Changing the decision-maker can create resistance and skepticism. Operational meteorologists forecast the weather.[5] They forecast daily temperatures, precipitation, and hazardous weather, like hurricanes, tornadoes, and snowstorms. They communicate the weather, which is particularly important for extreme weather events. Todd Lericos, former president of the US National Weather Association, noted: "What we are doing is making a risk assessment. How at risk is the public and what do we need to communicate to them in order for them to take mitigating actions?"[6]

The forecast is step one, but great forecasts are irrelevant if the communication fails to change behavior. Consider what happened when a tornado hit Joplin, Missouri, in 2011. A tornado watch was issued four hours earlier, and a warning, with sirens blazing, occurred seventeen minutes before the tornado struck. But the majority of surveyed Joplin residents did not head for shelter.[7] Tragically, 158 people died, and many more were injured. Forecasting is part of the process to ensure people make good decisions when the weather turns dangerous.

As forecasts have improved, communication has become more challenging. Suppose the risk of a tornado is 5 percent. Forecasters have to balance the short-term benefits of warning people of a real risk to their lives and property against the long-term cost of alert fatigue if nothing bad happens nineteen out of twenty times. This has changed the day-to-day role of the operational meteorologist. As Lericos put it,

> Traditionally, the weather service's primary customer was the public. Now, the public is becoming more of an indirect customer. Most of the heavy lifting of our services is working with local authorities to make critical decisions. . . . They are influencers. You've probably seen these cases where there is a major winter

snowstorm and the mayor is up there before the snowstorm going, "we need people to stay off the road."[8]

Put differently, the National Weather Service provides decision support. As author Andrew Blum notes, it now spends "more time explaining to emergency managers and public works officials the likelihood of a weather event and the severity of its impacts. In the interim, that has made for more work. In the future, it could well be the only work."[9]

The cause of this is more accurate forecasts. When forecasts were wrong, schools might only close when the snow began to fall. Better forecasts meant actions could take place days in advance:

> Which raises a new challenge: If the weather forecast is nearly perfect, what can you do with it? How do you learn to make decisions using it? In the past, meteorology had been slow to address this reality. "It was always an afterthought for our science, it was somebody else's problem," [meteorologist and Weather Company senior vice president Peter] Neilley explained. "Our science for a long time said, 'We're just going to focus on accuracy and then when we reach utopia in accuracy, society will be in good hands.' But we have realized that that is not entirely true." Their work has expanded. It now includes "the entire value chain, from the production in the forecast starting in the models all the way to an effective decision by an individual," Neilley said.[10]

So far, the meteorologists in local offices have done this best. Take a snowfall warning. Where we live, in Toronto, a forecast of an inch of overnight snow tells you to plan for extra minutes to brush off your car before heading out. That same one-inch forecast might shut down Atlanta. In Las Vegas, it might be even more complicated. The forecast might only be relevant on the west side of the city, where the higher elevation is more likely to have snow. Getting the judgment right is complicated and requires an understanding of how people live.

Lericos described how an AI system solution for weather might operate. He started by describing the point solution: "Better prediction will make communication of impacts and risk a more important part of the meteorologist's job." That then leads to a system-level change:

> There is another frontier for AI in meteorology. Taking more accurate weather prediction as an input and then marrying that information with other societal and personal data to better predict a person's (or a firm's) risk profile and the actions needed to mitigate that risk. Imagine a world where generic Weather Warnings are no longer issued. Rather, personalized weather warnings are automatically delivered to individuals or firms. Goodbye human weather operational meteorologists? It would seem that our human judgment would be better suited to working to create AI that makes the right types of decisions to deliver to a customer.[11]

Doing this would require an understanding of individual behavior to tell them what the forecast means for them. Lericos provided an example. If you live on the east side of Las Vegas, you don't need to change your behavior. Unless your kid's school is on the west side. In that case, you might anticipate that the school will close. If not, you need to figure out a way to get them home. That also depends on your car. In Nevada, plenty of people have rear-wheel-drive sports cars. As the predictions get better, the judgment becomes more nuanced. Lericos emphasized the need for people with the right expertise, "sociologists, transportation experts, and (yes) meteorologists." He admits that "there could be scenarios where meteorologists don't have a seat at the table. . . . [I]t depends on what exact problem you are trying to tackle."[12] If better AI means that the operational meteorologist is no longer central to decisions about the weather, we might expect those meteorologists to be wary of adopting AI at scale.

The examples of Flint's lead pipes, navigational apps, and weather forecasting all show that if the value of a decision-maker's judgment is enhanced by AI, they will retain power, whereas if it is devalued, then they won't. *Ultimately, it depends on decision efficiency.* If having a prediction machine means the people with information, skills, incentives, and ability to coordinate will change, then the power to judge changes, too.[13]

(De)centralization

AI also affects the concentration of power. It can allow judgment to scale, as a direct consequence of AI prediction being software that can be communicated and determined across a wide set of decisions. This scale drives potential efficiencies from formulating judgment and coding it into automated processes.

To see how this might arise, let's consider some cases where AI prediction is already having an impact—radiology and credit card fraud. We introduced the latter in chapter 14. In the former, AI prediction has threatened radiologists' jobs. While AI prediction may be superior to human prediction in this context, in order to assess its impact, we have to determine whether AI prediction will also change who provides judgment.

Recall that judgment is the knowledge of the trade-offs in value generated by different options. When you are making decisions that rely on predictions, it is the weight you place on the consequences of making the wrong decision, because often predictions are imperfect. When AI prediction emerges, who has the knowledge of what to do when predictions are imperfect?

Consider the diagnosis decision for a patient with a suspected malignant tumor. To make a diagnosis, a radiologist examines an image taken of the patient. In the United States, the radiologist typically does not have contact with the patient, so the only data is the image itself.

While, in some cases, the prognosis will be obvious, in others the radiologist formulates a probability that a malignant tumor is present. If they choose to diagnose that a malignant tumor is not present when it turns out it is (that is, a false negative), the patient will be untreated and may die. That would seem to push people toward diagnosing the condition just in case.

But the "in case" option has its own costs. Diagnosing a patient for a malignant cancer who does not have it means an uncomfortable regimen of further tests and treatments. The ultimate diagnosis can be a judgment call. What's more, part of that judgment may involve the radiologist's own confidence in their ability. If you worry that you may miss something, you may tend toward false positives rather than false negatives.

The radiologist's judgment comes from training and experience. Each individual radiologist applies their judgment to each decision that comes their way.

In other situations, judgment does not reside with many individuals but instead may be the outcome of a more centralized process, which is what happens with the credit card network. In that case, an algorithm can predict whether a transaction is fraudulent, but the judgment that guides how to treat that prediction needs to be prethought, coded, and applied at scale. The judgment is provided and resides centrally.

The radiologist and credit card network examples illustrate two broad sources of judgment. Individuals can provide judgment locally for each decision or globally to scale for a large number of decisions. Local judgment is of most value when the context of the decision to local factors is important or it is difficult to codify judgment to work across decisions. Global judgment is of most value when there is a gain to having consistent decision processes across the organization and local context is less important. The distinction between judgment that might be tailored to local contexts and judgment that is applied globally at scale is important because when AI improves predictions, it can change the best source for judgment.

This is already apparent in the credit card example. Before credit cards, the dominant payment instruments were cash and checks. Cash was, of course, reliable and hard to be conducted fraudulently. Checks were another matter, and merchants decided whether they accepted checks or not from a particular customer. They would make their own prediction of the likelihood the check would be honored, but also match that with their own judgment regarding the consequences of accepting a check or insisting on cash.

When credit card networks scaled, they came with a host of data that allowed them to predict, even before AI, whether or not to honor a card transaction. Initially, the fraud management focused on recovery after the fact. But with better prediction, they could more reliably scale the accept or reject decision without, say, asking merchants to call in suspicious actors. Thus, better prediction led to a change in where the source of judgment could come from: local context to global scale.

Radiologists still predict and so apply judgment in that context. The source of judgment continues to be local. However, as AI begins to improve, the question is whether radiologists will remain the best source for judgment that leads to diagnosis.

Radiologists do more than prediction. As noted in chapter 8, there are thirty different tasks that make up the radiologist's workflow, and just one is fundamentally about predictions that are directly affected by an image recognition AI.[14] The others involve actions like conducting physical examinations and judgments like developing treatment plans.[15] A radiologist spends years in training after medical school. Many spend those years learning how to interpret images. Once the AI does prediction, the question is who is best positioned to undertake the other tasks radiologists now do. It likely needs to be a medical professional who understands the local context. Better prediction in medical imaging might mean that more medical professionals can use judgment, changing the decision-making power from radiologists to a wider range of medical professionals.

Prediction can increase or decrease the concentration of who gets to judge.

Judgment and Control

We have discussed two aspects of judgment and control. Sometimes the decoupling of prediction and judgment means different people implement judgment, and sometimes it is the same people. Sometimes, the control over decision-making becomes more concentrated and sometimes less. (Figure 15-2 summarizes.)

When a few people hold the most efficient judgment, and the AI means that those people should be different from those currently making decisions, then there is potential for disruption. We already saw this kind of disruption in the payment industry, where the judgment of the managers of centralized networks replaced millions of merchants. It occurred in Flint, when the old ways of doing things were unsustainable in the face of data.

When different people judge, even AI point solutions will face resistance, which slows AI's diffusion, lengthening the years spent in The Between Times. It also reinforces the potential for disruption and the

FIGURE 15-2

Judgment and control

Control over decision-making

		More concentrated	Less concentrated
	Same	Customer support, hiring	Medical imaging
People implementing judgment	Different	Credit cards, lead pipes in Flint	Uber drivers, meteorology

need for AI system solutions. If the people with power in the current system won't relinquish their position, then a new system—perhaps developed by an enterprising AI systems entrepreneur—will allocate judgment to the people best positioned to provide it.

However, even with the right judges in place, as we will see in part 6, it is important to recognize that systems involve interrelated decisions. Thus, changing how one decision is implemented can have consequences for many others. This has consequences for system design.

KEY POINTS

- When the implementation of an AI results in decoupling prediction and judgment, there may be an opportunity to increase value creation, but that may require redesigning the system in a way that moves the locus of judgment from current decision-makers to others. When this happens, power is reallocated. Those who confer judgment ultimately decide and thus have power. New system design that leverages AI may reduce the power of certain individuals who therefore may resist change.

- When we design a new system, how do we allocate decision rights? We choose the person or group most likely to make the decision in the best interests of the organization at the lowest cost. That is *decision efficiency.* There are four primary factors to consider: (1) information: Who has access to or who should be given access to the information necessary to make the decision?; (2) skills: Who has the skills and expertise necessary to make the decision?; (3) incentives: Who has incentives that are most aligned with the interests of the organization with respect to this particular decision?; and (4) coordination: If the decision impacts multiple parts of the organization, then who has the necessary organization-spanning authority, information, and incentives to make the decision most aligned with the overall interests of the organization? The answer to these questions might be very different when the requirement is prediction plus judgment versus judgment only, because the AI is delivering the prediction.

- New system design may concentrate power if judgment is codifiable and thus scalable. Credit card networks and radiology departments are two examples. In the case of credit card networks, power is concentrated in a few credit card companies rather than across many merchants, as was the case in the past. In the radiology case, some speculate that the key skill of pattern recognition and anomaly detection in medical images lends itself to the concentration of prediction in an AI solution. In that case, if radiologists are no longer required for their prediction skills, are they best suited to provide judgment? If not, nurses, social workers, or other trained health-care professionals may provide judgment.

PART SIX

Envisaging
New Systems

16

Designing Reliable Systems

Thomas Schelling, decades before winning the Nobel Prize in economics, posited the following thought experiment:

> You are to meet somebody in New York City. You have not been instructed where to meet; you have no prior understanding with the person on where to meet; and you cannot communicate with each other. You are simply told that you will have to guess where to meet and that he is being told the same thing and that you will just have to try to make your guesses coincide.[1]

When we put this to students today, they can't even understand how this problem would arise. Surely, you just text them? But back in the day, it was a more familiar conundrum. And the whole point was to see what you could do without being able to communicate.

In class, before 2000 or so, if you asked students in New York, they quickly arrived at a location: Grand Central Station under the big clock. In Melbourne, it was the steps in front of Flinders Street Station. In Toronto, it might be at the big Toronto sign at Nathan Phillips Square.

These are focal points. Most cities and towns have one. You both know you are trying to achieve the same thing, and you both know that the other person knows that and so forth.

In our experience, the people who struggled were out-of-town or foreign students. They knew what they needed to know, but they just didn't have the requisite common knowledge. They may have actually found it easier to answer Schelling's follow-up question: "You were told the date but not the hour of the meeting . . . the two of you must guess the exact minute of the day for meeting. At what time will you appear at the meeting place?" Anyone can answer this: noon.[2] This time is even a stronger focal point than location.

Thomas Schelling's career was shaped by war, specifically, the Cold War. His research concerned how to avoid it and allow people to coordinate on something in their mutual best interests. The tools he used were those of game theory. When thinking about how to coordinate the decisions of many different people, even when they are all directed toward a common cause, these tools can illuminate when such coordination will be hard and when it will be straightforward.

What we are interested in here is how inserting AI to help with one decision in a system changes the nature of how to coordinate all decisions (whether done with AI or not). And the answer hinges on *reliability*.

The Schelling focal point exercise shows how useful it is to rely on others who share a similar knowledge base. Within organizations, this can matter, but often our reliance comes from expecting things done elsewhere to be somewhat clear. When other people are following rules, this task is often easy, and we can glue separate parts of the organization together. But when rules change to decisions, the challenges of building an oiled system become apparent. We often don't communicate what we are doing to others all the time because that itself has costs. Instead, we create expectations of what they might be doing, and then, when making our choices in our own domains, we align our actions with those expectations. If those expectations are not reliable, then we will have trouble aligning all the decisions.

It doesn't have to be that way. If you can design the system so that expectations remain reliable, you can reap the benefits of better prediction to enable new ways of serving customers.

The AI Bullwhip

Imagine you are running a restaurant. Diners come in and order meals. The cooks then make the meals. This seems pretty simple, because expectations are aligned. At any given time, the cooks are constrained in what meals they can make. These constraints are driven by their skill, the number of orders, and the availability of ingredients and equipment. If you allow your customers to order any dish they might fancy, there will be problems. What you do, therefore, is set a menu. You limit the choices of your customers so that you can actually make what they order. From the perspective of the kitchen, the menu itself creates reliability and prevents unexpected surprises.

Every week you need to order ingredients. The ingredients are based on the menu. If guacamole is on the menu, you need avocados. You order a hundred pounds every week. Sometimes a hundred pounds is too much, and you throw out the excess. Other times, a hundred pounds is too little, and you miss out on sales.

Then you adopt an AI for demand forecasting. It works. Now some weeks, you order as little as thirty pounds. Other weeks, you need three hundred pounds. You waste less and sell more. Profitability rises.

Your local supplier had been used to buying a hundred pounds each week for you. Now it faces more unpredictability from you. Its other customers are also using AIs for demand forecasting. Demand starts to fluctuate widely.

So, the supplier decides to adopt an AI for its own demand forecasting. It used to order 25,000 pounds per week. Now its order varies from 5,000 pounds to 50,000 pounds. Its supplier, in turn, needs to adopt an AI, and its orders begin to fluctuate. And so on, all the way to the growers that need to make crop size decisions a year or more in advance.

We call this effect—when implementing an AI improves the quality of one decision but harms others in the system by lowering reliability for other decisions—the AI bullwhip. Like a bullwhip, a small change in one place can lead to a big crack elsewhere.

AI can be used to resolve uncertainty, but unless that can translate into aligned decisions all the way down, the fundamental problem—

that demand needs to be aligned with supply—hasn't really been solved. Like the swing of a bullwhip, your own solution has reverberations down the line.

We are left with somewhat of a paradox. The value of AI comes from being able to make better decisions by matching what you do with factors that might otherwise be uncertain. But, as a consequence, your own decisions become less reliable for others. You are potentially passing the uncertainty buck, which means that it may be better not to adjust to uncertainty using AI but stick with a more reliable system.

There are two ways to build an AI system solution to handle this: increase coordination or increase modularity.

The Value of Coordination

The restaurant AI predicts demand. The restaurant manager makes several other decisions; for example, what to offer on the menu. If the AI bullwhip means that the grower can't supply enough avocados, then the restaurant needs to change the menu. It can only do this if it knows that the avocados aren't coming. That requires coordination.

Such synergies mean that it is important to consider how to achieve coordination across multiple decision-makers, managing variability and adjustment rather than a process of transformation and change.

To understand this, consider the operation of an eight-rower team. Two things determine how a team will perform in a race. First, they row in unison. Second, they adjust rowing speed as the race progresses to ensure one or more rowers does not expend all their energy before the finish. The coxswain, who sits at the back of the boat, is essential for the second but not the first function.

This might seem surprising, as the coxswain is calling out "stroke, stroke, stroke" and coordinating all the rowers to keep the same time. But that doesn't require a separate person. One of the rowers could do this, which occurs in races where a coxswain is not present. But when monitoring strategy in the race and obtaining cues about the status of individual rowers—that is, gathering information and aggregating it—the coxswain is critical. The coxswain can assess the need to change the rhythm and adjust the message sent to rowers accordingly. Again, if a single stroke rate were used for the whole race, there would be no need for that function. The coxswain is there precisely because the team wants to respond to information but needs to ensure that they adapt in a coordinated fashion.

For such synchronization problems, the organizational design is predicated on the need for synergies, so modularity cannot do the job. The same type of coordinated response to information is also needed for problems that economists Paul Milgrom and John Roberts call assignment problems.[3] These are problems where you need to assign resources to an activity, but you know that only a certain number of resources needs to be used; any more would be wasted, while any less would be insufficient. Consider the problem of ambulance dispatch. If there is a medical emergency, one ambulance is critical, but two is wasteful. To ensure that only one responds, you need a central dispatcher, whether human or software, who receives calls (i.e., information) regarding an emergency and then assigns one ambulance to respond. If, say, ambulances all received an emergency message and then chose individually whether to respond, you may end up with no responders or too many responders. In this case, having a way to coordinate is best, precisely because the stakes are high and sending one ambulance instead of another to an emergency is far less of a problem than not sending one or sending too many.

Instead of compartmentalizing decisions and protecting other parts of the organization from the decisions made by one part in response to AI prediction, you are providing resources and effort to a communication system to ensure that the bad outcomes that arise from a point solution—a lack of synchronization or poor resource assignments—do not occur. You are now more able to have key decisions respond to AI prediction precisely because potential downside costs are kept to a minimum through efficient communication and system design. The combination of prediction and coordination is the system solution. Each decision improves because it responds to predictions without compromising reliability.

The Value of Modularity

Modularity is a way of building a wall around a decision driven by AI prediction to avoid the costs associated with a lack of alignment between that decision and others in the organization. Modularity reduces the coordination costs, but it can come at the expense of synergies that might be achieved if the AI prediction that drove one decision also allowed other decisions to move in a similar vein. When coordination isn't possible, modularity enables some decisions to benefit from AI, while shielding others from the reduced reliability.

Herbert Simon, the only person to win the Nobel Prize in economics and the Turing Award in computer science, once posited a parable about organizations dealing with more complex situations.[4] In the parable, two watchmakers manufacture high-quality products. Both are in demand and are constantly peppered by inquiries from new customers. One prospers while the other is failing. Why?

Watches comprise a thousand parts. One approach is to assemble each watch in one go, which leads to a higher-quality timepiece. But if the watchmaker is interrupted during the process (say, by another customer), they have to start assembling again from scratch. The other approach is to assemble the watch in smaller elements, each with, say, ten or so parts. These then have to be fit together, which is a little more time-consuming and perhaps not as perfect an end result. But this has the advantage that, if there are interruptions to the process, all that is lost is a small element. In the end, it is a much quicker process and allows the watchmaker to make more watches. The second process, which is termed *modular*, is more resilient and more scalable, especially for more-complex products.[5]

If you do everything at once, you have to coordinate all the decisions. Some mis-specification can lead to problems. By contrast, if you can organize what you do into modules, the individual parts can do their own thing without regard to what is happening elsewhere. This does not mean that what they do doesn't matter for the final outcome—if one module doesn't do its job, then the entire product may fail. But it means that a larger problem becomes smaller and more manageable.

Another advantage comes from the resilience of the system to changes in what happens in one of the modules: the module can improve without disrupting the rest of the system. That is, modules can be innovated upon.

History is replete with examples in which modularity made innovation easier; for example, when we switched from analog to digital telephones, that involved changing the dialing device but not the network itself. But at other times, innovation has been constrained because of a lack of modularity. When airplanes were upgraded from propellers to jet engines, engineers thought that the airframes of planes could be produced as they always had been. However, the types of vibrations the new engines caused were so different that the entire structure of the plane had to be redesigned. This slowed the transition.[6]

Modularity is an opportunity for a restaurant to adopt AI without the AI bullwhip effect, but it is not something they can determine for themselves. If a restaurant wants to vary its menu, its suppliers need to have their own modular system to handle that variation in demand. In our example, the supply of avocados was constrained by variable demand across the industry. With enough restaurants across many regions being supplied, even if individual restaurant demand is highly variable, the aggregate can be more stable. Scale can provide an opportunity for modularity across the supply chain. Generally, with respect to AI adoption, modularity can help address difficulties that arise because decisions are interrelated.[7]

The Value of Design

Adopting AI for one decision will be much easier if the decisions made do not have to align with decisions elsewhere in the system. This is a matter of degree. Of course, conceptually, it would be better if the entire system could move as one. The question is whether, if that cannot occur, it will be possible to reap the benefits of AI over and above any costs that might be felt elsewhere.

To understand this, consider the operations of Amazon, which supplies millions of products worldwide. Amazon procures them, stores them in warehouses, captures customer orders, and ships to those customers. But it also involves helping the customer figure out what to purchase in the first place, that is, providing them with recommendations.

Conceptually, Amazon then faces the problem of our restaurant. It wants to supply customers with what they want when they want it, but products do not magically appear. A supply chain spans thousands of kilometers and months in time. Thus, if it recommends a product to a customer that is unavailable, then what?

It is tempting to think that the solution is: don't do that. If you don't have a product available, don't recommend it to a customer. But there is a problem with that approach: How do you learn whether there was an unavailable product that the customer really wanted? If you only recommend what you have, you miss opportunities to grow and expand.

This is why Amazon recommends products that are out of stock or may take longer to reach its customers. The decisions are coordinated in the sense that Amazon communicates the likely delay to the customer. The customer may well choose the product that is available, but occasionally they won't. Amazon then learns how much effort it needs to make in carrying inventory for those items.

Achieving this balance requires careful design. Amazon has a modular organization that has allowed it to slot better AI prediction into recommendations that minimize the impact on the rest of the organization. But taken to an extreme, that would be a step too far. Thus, the inventory and ordering choices it makes cannot be fully independent of how the recommendation AI operates, precisely because the customer choices and reactions give rise to information that the logistics department needs to communicate and act on.

The adoption of AI will often involve a system solution that finds an optimal balance of modularity and coordination. Modularity insulates decisions from the variability that comes from AI. It reduces the importance of reliability. Coordination, in contrast, creates reliability directly. Successful AI systems enable coordination where possible and modularity where necessary.

Sailing Systems

Sailboat makers and sailors have been honing their craft for five thousand years. The innovations haven't stopped, even as commercial shipping no longer relies on the wind for propulsion. The winner of the America's Cup race claims sailing's top prize and the oldest trophy in international sports. The race is about both the technology developed for the boat and the skills of the sailors.

Millions of dollars go into boat design. Since the physics of wind, water, and ship are well understood, competitors use simulators to identify the most effective designs long before construction begins. The simulators allow the sailors to test a boat without building it. The team with the best simulator gains an advantage. Team New Zealand used its simulator to win in 2017.

As the team planned for the 2021 race, it wondered if it could speed up the design process. Partnering with the global consultancy McKinsey, it identified the main bottleneck to innovation: human sailors. When humans sail in the simulator, it takes time. There is no way to speed up how quickly humans respond to conditions and how the boat reacts.

Using similar technology to the AI that beat the world's top Go players, the team taught a prediction machine to sail. They didn't have to manage around the sailors' availability. The bot didn't need to sleep or eat, and it could run hundreds of simulations in the time that human sailors would run just a handful. After eight weeks, the AI started to beat the sailors in the simulator.

This is when things started to get interesting. AI sailors started teaching the human sailors new tricks. Previously, innovation in boat design occurred at human speed. If there was a learning process to figuring out the best way to use a newly designed boat, that process occurred over hours, days, or weeks as human sailors tried different things and learned.

The AI, in contrast, could experiment with different variations of the boat. It could try different racing tactics. It sped the cycle of design iteration and enabled the development of new maneuvers specific to the new design. Then, once the AI figured out a superior solution, the human sailors could copy the AI and learn new tricks from the AI sailors for sailing the simulated boats. As one team member put it, "Accelerating the learning process is extremely valuable, both in terms of allowing the design team to explore as much of the design space as possible and the sailors to maximize performance for a given design."[8] Team New Zealand claimed the trophy, winning seven races to three.

In this example of an AI system solution, the AI led to changes in more than one decision. Specifically, race preparation involves two types of decisions. There are decisions on boat design and decisions on sailing maneuvers. Simulators had long been used for boat design. Humans had always done sailing maneuvers. The AI sailor didn't actually pilot the boat in the race—real people still pilot real boats. Instead, the AI sped up the innovation process, allowing better coordination between boat design and sailing maneuvers. The complete system of the simulated boat and AI sailor enabled improvements to both.

System Twins

The sailing simulator is an example of a "digital twin," or a virtual representation of a physical object or system.[9] Digital twins provide information as a replacement for physical resources. With the right sensors in place, they enable real-time monitoring and predictive maintenance. These virtual representations can do much more. They provide a framework for system-level simulation. Accenture calls this "a risk-free playground for innovation."[10] As Michael Grieves, executive director of the Digital Twin Institute, put it, "Systems do not burst forth fully formed. They progress through a life cycle of creation, production, operation, and disposal. With 'physical-only' systems, this was a linear progression. The Digital Twin allows for a more iterative, simultaneous development."[11]

When combined with AI, this creates the opportunity to design a new way of doing things. As Team New Zealand discovered in preparing for the 2021 America's Cup, simulated systems enable teams to figure out the best way to coordinate decisions, such as boat designs and sailing maneuvers. In this way, they can reduce trial and error.[12] When a manager develops an idea for how to change a system, it is possible to simulate the impact of that idea without the cost of building the machines or the risk of operational downtime.

The simulations can also focus on AI implementation. If a prediction machine is added to one part of a system, simulation can help identify what other decisions need to be coordinated or how a system might be made more modular.

Systems are complex because they are combinations of decisions that interact with each other. Imagine a system with only one binary decision: loosen the sail (L) or tighten the sail (T). There are only two options [L, T]. Now, imagine that a second decision impacts the first decision: stay straight (S) or lean right (R). There are now four options (LS, LR, TS, TR).

Now imagine that there is a third decision about adding another sail (A) or not (N) that depends on the first two decisions. Now there are eight options (LSA, LSN, LRA, LRN, TSA, TSN, TRA, TRN).

In the first case, we have $2^1 = 2$ options; in the second case, we have $2^2 = 4$ options; and in the third case, we have $2^3 = 8$ options. By the time we have 10 interacting decisions, we have 1,024 options, and 20 interacting decisions generate 1,048,576 options. Sail racing can involve hundreds of decisions that need coordinating, and it won't take long to have more options than there are atoms in the observable universe.

The point here is that systems with interdependent decisions can get very complex, very quickly. That key insight lays the foundation for why simulation is so powerful for system design. It leverages the same insight we discussed in chapter 3 on why AI is so successful at playing games: it is relatively easy to simulate new data. While it is very costly—in some cases, physically impossible—to experiment with all options to find the best one, we can use digital assets, including digital twins of physical environments, to simulate different options and use AI to predict the outcome from each one. So, we can explore many more options than we could in the physical world and increase our chances of finding a better combination than the one we are likely to settle on in the absence of simulation.

Virtual Singapore is a simulation of the terrain, water bodies, vegetation, transportation infrastructure, and buildings down to the building materials in the city state. This digital twin is a tool that enables managers to simulate an AI system solution and avoid several costly failures. It cost tens of millions of dollars to develop. This model allows planners to assess the impact of new parks or buildings on traffic and crowds, and to explore cellular network coverage. It can also be used to assess how adding a prediction machine will affect the life of the citizens and residents of Singapore. For example, AI might enable better optimization of public transportation. The model could assess whether that optimization requires additional changes to traffic management. In other words, it could assess whether public and private transportation systems could be treated as modular or needs to be coordinated.[13] It could then develop a better AI-enabled transportation system, either by embracing modularity or by ensuring coordination as needed.

South Korea's Doosan Heavy Industries & Construction and Microsoft developed a digital twin of a wind farm that exemplifies the various benefits of simulated systems.[14] The simulation combined physics-based models and machine learning to predict production for each turbine on the farm. Comparing the predicted and actual output of the turbines enabled operators to fine-tune the controls and optimize production. Furthermore, the twin enabled innovation in the design and development of the overall wind farm, improving reliability. Finally, it enabled the coordination of decisions. The accurate predictions of energy output enabled Doosan to increase its output commitments to the energy grid operators, while avoiding fines for failing to meet the commitments. It reduced the risk of building the system solution and sticking with a less valuable but simpler point solution. For example, better prediction enabled decisions on which turbines would operate and which needed maintenance. This in turn enabled decisions on the commitment to the energy grid.

Systems for AI

Simulation isn't the only way to build an AI-driven system, but it demonstrates the opportunity. By finding the right way for decision-makers to coordinate, Team New Zealand found a path to victory. AI can be adopted when a system is modular, but its impact can be much bigger if coordination is possible. The challenge is to figure out what kind of coordination is needed.

KEY POINTS

- Decisions don't operate in a vacuum. Often, multiple other decisions or actions are influenced by the outcome of a single decision. That's why we sometimes use predetermined decisions (rules) instead of real-time decisions because rules enhance reliability, so we accept worse localized decisions in exchange for greater reliability for the benefit of the overall system. Reliability is a key feature of systems with interdependent decisions.

- There are two main system design approaches for addressing the reduced reliability that results from introducing AI-based decision-making: (1) coordination and (2) modularity. Coordination involves specifying the overall objective and then designing information flows, incentives, and decision rights so that each decision-maker in the system has the information and the incentives to optimize for the overall goal. Modularity involves building a wall around an AI-enhanced decision to avoid the costs associated with a lack of alignment between that decision and others in the organization. Modularity reduces coordination costs, but comes at the expense of synergies.

- Systems are combinations of decisions that interact with each other. Consider a set of related binary decisions. Three decisions lead to eight different combinations. Ten interacting decisions generate 1,024 combinations, and twenty interacting decisions generate 1,048,576 combinations. Systems with interdependent decisions can get very complex very quickly. That's why simulation is so powerful for system design. We can use digital twins to simulate different combinations and use AI to predict the outcome from each combination.

17

The Blank Slate

Imagine visiting your doctor for a medical exam. At the end, your doctor says, "There is a significant chance that you will get very sick in three years. Thank you for coming in." Then your doctor walks out and begins a session with her next patient. You would be flabbergasted. Why didn't she tell you what was going to make you sick? Why didn't she explain what you could do to reduce your chances of getting sick?

While this story seems implausible, it happens in the insurance industry every day. Insurance firms charge some people higher insurance premiums than others. Why? Because they predict that certain customers are more likely than others to suffer a loss. How do insurance firms know who is at greater risk? Because they invest heavily in collecting and analyzing data in order to predict the likelihood of the customer suffering a loss and filing a claim.

It's not surprising that insurance firms are at the frontier of data science. They have to be. It's their job to make predictions. What is surprising, however, is that they don't share their insights on risk with their customers. This valuable information could help customers *reduce* their risk, rather than just insure themselves against it.

For example, home insurance companies are applying AI to generate higher fidelity predictions. Many are now able to predict risk at the peril or sub-peril level (e.g., risk of electrical fire from poor wiring, risk of flooding from a leaky pipe). So, if a home insurance company predicts that a particular homeowner has an especially high risk of electrical fire or flooding, rather than just charging them a high premium due to their high likelihood of filing a claim, the company could share this information so their customers could take action if they wanted to lower their risk. Such customers could, for example, invest in low-cost devices for early detection of heightened fire or flood risk. The insurance firm might even decide to subsidize these risk mitigation tools, because the reduction in expected losses might outweigh the cost of the devices.

Surprisingly, few insurance firms have gone down this path with any significant scale. Instead, most are focusing their efforts on building and deploying AIs that enhance their traditional underwriting predictions. They are building point solutions. Why have most insurance firms not pursued opportunities to better serve their customers by shifting from a business model predicated on pooling risk among customers and transferring risk from customers to carriers to also *mitigating* risk for their customers? Agents might not like it because lowering risk means lower premiums, which might translate into lower income. Overall, though, this seems like it would create significant value for customers.

In many cases, it appears that insurers haven't fully appreciated this opportunity because it is outside their normal business model. In addition to agent incentives, there are so many business rules, government regulations, and methods of doing things in this industry that what may seem obvious from an outsider's vantage point is hard to see from an insider's perspective. That's why we suggest the blank slate approach. To facilitate this, we introduce the *AI Systems Discovery Canvas*.

Thinking Like an Economist

One of our skills as economists is to take something exciting and impenetrable and deconstruct it into something boring and understandable. While that doesn't make us great party guests, it does allow us to sometimes see things that others miss. We've designed a framework to help you do this too. The AI Systems Discovery Canvas is helpful if you want to develop a system mindset for evaluating AI's value.

In this chapter, we provide you with a tool that you can use to build on a blank slate. The idea is to identify the minimum important decisions that you would need to make in your industry, if you had high-fidelity prediction machines, in order to achieve your mission. AI prediction, by its nature, will enter any organization at the level of a decision. But knowing how one decision or decision type impacts others is the first important step in developing a view on how AI may have systemwide impacts.

There are two reasons why this exercise is valuable when you are trying to evaluate how adopting AI prediction may lead to disruption and how to consider whether you need system-level innovation. The first is that there are likely to be many rules in an organization and the possibility that some functions have built up to hide the uncertainty associated with those rules. The blank slate requires you to go back to first principles and consider the decisions that go into fulfilling your organization's mission. In the process, some of those decisions may already exist as rules, and some may offer opportunities to adopt predictions that will turn those rules into decisions. (We will, however, defer our use of a blank slate for this type of purpose until the next chapter.)

The other reason this exercise has value is that you can use it to evaluate the impact specific AI solutions might have on systems. By using a blank slate, you can take a broader perspective on how the decision informed by AI predictions might interact with other decisions or rules of your organization. In this chapter, we will demonstrate the usefulness of starting with a blank slate to evaluate the system implications of particular AI solutions.

In insurance, for example, some entrepreneurs have developed applications whereby the user takes a picture of a car or house following damage, and the company automatically uses those pictures to calculate a claim account and instantly issue payment for repairs. The consumer doesn't have to wait for an assessor or drive around to find quotes. Just open the app, take some pictures, and you are done. Another set of applications comes in devices that monitor your driving or your house. Those applications can determine quickly if you are doing something risky—not simply to tell you to stop but warn you that if the behavior persists, your premium might be different next month or next year.

It is easy to see why entrepreneurs might target insurers with these application solutions. But the question is: Will they be useful? To get a handle on that, you need to understand an industry, like the car or home insurance industry, at its essence. That means working out what decisions the industry needs to make and whether this particular AI solution is informing one of the decisions. Then you can work out a plan of attack. Is there someone already in charge of that decision? Or is there no obvious single decision-maker? Perhaps rules are in place instead? If you want to change that rule to a decision, what else is that likely to impact? To get to those critical questions, you need a starting point. That's what we provide here.

The AI Systems Discovery Canvas

We have come to appreciate over time that people implementing real changes like to lay out their approaches on a canvas. A canvas is a blank chart where you can start anywhere, as long as by the end of your process, you have thought through the entire chart. It is not a step-by-step manual for implementation but a way of organizing your thinking.

Figure 17-1 shows a chart that allows you to map out the critical decisions in an industry. A key task is to identify the mission of your business. This need not be a precise statement but instead a broad reminder of your goals.

The idea is to identify the decisions needed to achieve that mission. Obviously, there may be many decisions (conceptually, in the millions). Identifying them all is not the purpose here. Instead, the purpose is to state the broad classes of decisions needed. If you had very powerful prediction machines to enhance your decision-making, then what is the smallest number of decisions required to achieve your mission? Identify only the most important or core decisions.

After identifying the decisions, it is time to drill down. What information do you need to gather in order to make a decision? This is not simply the information you have or could easily obtain but, instead, the

FIGURE 17-1

AI Systems Discovery Canvas

What are the fewest decisions you can reduce your business to?

1. Mission			
2. Decision			
3. Prediction			
4. Judgment			

information you can imagine being important. Most decisions are made under uncertainty. However, with a prediction, you potentially have the information you need to make a better decision. Predictions are what AI can potentially supply, so this exercise links predictions to the core decisions in your organization.

Finally, no prediction is perfect. If you have a perfect prediction, decision-making is easy and potentially automatic. But while the canvas is aspirational, its job is not to be unrealistic. Thus, for each decision, you need to articulate the key trade-offs involved. Indeed, we advocate using an "error frame." If my prediction is wrong or nonexistent, what types of mistakes can we make? This gives you a sense of the riskiness of the decision. In the umbrella choice in chapter 4, if your weather forecast is wrong, you either carry an umbrella unnecessarily or you get wet. Your judgment is how you rank those errors. For each decision on your canvas, you want to identify the consequences of errors and potentially how you would rank them—say, with an explicit calculation of costs or something more subjective.

Next, you can take any potential AI-driven prediction and associate it with a decision in order to evaluate (a) whether your organization is explicitly taking those decisions; (b) who currently owns the decision; and (c) if you used AI to make that decision, what disruption might that cause to the rest of your current organization? (We consider these last steps in chapter 18 and the epilogue.) For now, you want the starting point—the blank slate—and the system underlying your industry.

The Insurance Industry

In many ways, there isn't a more stable industry than insurance. Starting centuries ago, it has evolved into a staple of modern life. Consumer insurance products are simple. People pay annual premiums and, in return, get payouts if they have car accidents, home damage or theft, or they die. The information technology revolution brought some advances. It became easier to calculate actuarial tables, which could then be modified to supply a wider set of insurance products. But in the end, the main variation in those products came from things seemingly outside a customer's control, like their age or where they lived.

What does it take to provide insurance products? Let's consider homeowner's insurance. The mission for a business in that industry might be stated as follows: "To provide homeowners with peace of mind against catastrophic loss of what is for many the most valuable asset they own." You would place this in the top box of the canvas (see figure 17-2).

In the figure, we have identified three classes of decisions—marketing, underwriting, and claims. These are often the divisions in insurance companies, which makes this a somewhat straightforward industry to analyze.

Marketing is responsible for customer acquisition: finding those people who could use insurance and selling products to them. Marketers' decisions revolve around where to place resources in order to target customers. Underwriting creates insurance products and assesses customer risk profiles to determine premiums and also whether an acquired customer becomes an insured customer. In other words, underwriters are responsible for pricing insurance products, which means they understand the costs of insuring particular customers or groups of customers with certain characteristics. Finally, the claims department determines whether

FIGURE 17-2

AI Systems Discovery Canvas: Home insurance

What are the fewest decisions you can reduce your business to?

1. Mission	To provide homeowners with peace of mind against catastrophic loss of what is for many the most valuable asset they own		
2. Decision	**Marketing:** Decide who to target with marketing	**Underwriting:** Decide price (insurance premium)	**Claims:** Decide whether to pay a claim
3. Prediction	Predict willingness to pay for each prospective customer	Predict the likelihood a homeowner will file a claim in a range of values	Predict the likelihood a submitted claim is valid and should be paid
4. Judgment	Determine the cost of targeting someone who doesn't purchase vs. not targeting someone who would have purchased	Set strategy (growth vs. profitability): determine the cost of pricing too low (losses) vs. too high (losing customers)	Determine the cost of not paying a legitimate claim (frustrated customer, reputation) vs. paying an illegitimate claim (expense)

or not to pay a claim. In effect, it handles what in other businesses would be called customer experience: how pleasant it is to hand benefits to customers, but perhaps this is also done with an eye to not provide those benefits if possible.

Figure 17-2 also outlines the predictions critical for those decisions to be enabled, as well as the judgment in terms of the consequences of prediction—or broadly—decision errors. The business of insuring something like a house has a very simple path to profitability. You want to sell policies where the expected losses from payouts are less than the premiums you bring in. Customers care about the premiums but also about service in terms of how easy it is to sign up for policies and make claims. In this competitive business, an established insurance company cannot do much to improve premium levels, but if it can reduce expected losses, it will earn more profits.

How does an insurance company do that? It wants to find customers who have a lower expected loss and sell policies to them, while making sure it only sells policies to high-expected-loss customers at higher premiums. But absent good information on who has a lower or higher expected loss, many customers receive a similar premium. The lower-expected-loss customers pay too much, and the higher-expected-loss ones, too little. Moreover, without the right information, competition can't sort out that issue. Thus, the company wants to predict which customers have a lower likelihood of filing a claim and target them in marketing. These predictions are associated with the marketing and underwriting decisions. The company also wants to make sure to pay claims when appropriate and not otherwise—that is, it wants to avoid fraud. Making claims mistakes ends up impacting the company's ability to compete because that raises its costs. Thus, it can judge how mistakes impact the insurance business. (Examples of these are listed in figure 17-2.)

By laying out these decisions, we can also see how they are linked. As we have already noted, AI prediction represents an opportunity for insurance, particularly for underwriters, who have the job of predicting a customer's risk profile, a near-perfect application for AI. At the same time, by speeding this up, the marketers' job is made easier, as salespeople can respond to potential customers quickly. Regulatory issues in different jurisdictions constrain how companies use AI to create risk profiles, but underwriting and marketing are aligned on their value. AI can also more easily assess the validity of claims, which flows back into marketing and underwriting. But in effect, the claims department is just doing a better job within its own lane.

We can see how the AI applications mentioned earlier might fit into this system. The application that allowed assessment of claims with the click of a camera is designed to automate claims decisions. It is just another way of making that decision, neatly slotting into that department. Having better customer experiences with claims then makes the job of marketing easier, and marketers might choose to allocate their resources to customers who most value that better experience. Of course, this may cause more complicated issues for underwriting. Will customers who find it easier to make claims file more claims? Will marketing target customers who are more likely to make claims? Will the costs of the claims department rise (with more claims) or fall (with lower costs of assessments)? Thus, while the application neatly falls into the claims decisions, its adoption may impact other decisions. Interestingly, it does not fundamentally change what those decisions are doing, the judgment involved, or the predictions needed. It is likely that such applications could be adopted (or not) without systemwide change.

What about the application that allowed monitoring and feedback to customers on their risk profiles and behavior? At the heart of the insurance industry's current system is the assessment of that risk, usually at the customer acquisition stage, although in some cases, it is reassessed on insurance contract renewal. If customers are insuring a home, they might reduce their premiums by verifying that they have an alarm system that immediately calls outside help or a water-monitoring system that automatically shuts off the water if it detects a burst pipe. But the risks of adverse events are unlikely to be determined by house characteristics but by behavior. For instance, the National Fire Prevention Association reports that cooking caused 49 percent of house fires in the United States.[1] Delve into its reports, and you find that it is not just any cooking, but cooking with oils and, in particular, frying. This makes sense and is hardly news. The question then is why someone who rarely cooks at home pays the same premium as a large family that fries their food every day.

The answer is pretty straightforward; aside from ripping out a kitchen entirely, an insurance company cannot monitor whether someone is cooking, let alone whether they are cooking with oil. The best that the company can do is alter the insurance payout based on these facts, but that means that it would not be insuring people against the bad luck part of cooking as opposed to their overall risk profile.

But AI technologies may cover these gaps and monitor ongoing risk in a cost-effective way. Some are automatic intervention mechanisms like an AI monitoring water (e.g., Phyn) or electrical hazard (e.g., Ting) that work like smoke detectors. Insurers already encourage their use. For car insurance, there are driver monitoring devices that not only consider how much driving someone does but the quality of their driving. Install these, and your premiums can be reduced accordingly.

But cooking, heating, smoking, or the use of candles all have behavioral qualities that are more challenging. However, all these behaviors could be monitored, and the relevant metrics for risk assessment sent to insurance companies on an ongoing basis, with premiums adjusted in real time. Of course, this type of monitoring introduces privacy and related concerns. But just as car insurers have been able to get customers to voluntarily agree to have their driving monitored, they could do the same for house insurance. If such monitoring meant that people who found a 25 percent reduction in premiums made it worthwhile to adjust their behavior and reduce fire risk by 25 percent, that is a good deal for all concerned.[2]

However, all these behaviorally responsive insurance products haven't been supplied previously because such monitoring hasn't been available. Many would not necessarily involve consumers, but insurance for businesses whose risks are notoriously hard to assess.

Creating these new products requires coordination across current divisions. The lines between marketing and underwriting, in particular, become blurred. If marketing envisioned a new product to take advantage of some new AI prediction technology, it would require underwriting to adjust its own procedures to accommodate it. Also, which division would be responsible for monitoring and adjusting premiums? Would it be underwriting, with expertise in setting premiums, or claims, with experience in verification? As division lines become blurred, there are pressures to reallocate decision authority and change who is responsible for processing information in insurance companies.

Perhaps the reason insurance companies have not tackled the problem of reducing risk head-on, using technology to build new products, is precisely because this would be difficult or impossible to do with existing systems that take the level of risk as a fact of life. In addition, reducing risk means reducing premiums, which may face resistance from agents and everyone else in the system whose compensation is tied to premiums. But if an insurance company put mitigation of risk rather than transfer of risk at its core, then they would design an incentive system that aligns everyone's interest to focus on risk mitigation. While average premiums would be lower due to lowered risk, the company might also see higher profits and more policies. With enhanced prediction, insurance firms would know so much more about the specific sources of risk associated with a home than homeowners themselves. As a consequence, it would greatly benefit society (and be good business!) to shift the emphasis of the value proposition from risk transfer to risk management. To do this, insurance firms need a new system that will require not only new technology but also organizational change.

The Impact of Customization

One of the promises of AI prediction is the ability to offer more highly customized products that reflect customer context more precisely. We have already seen this with personalized advertising and entrepreneurial education. By matching information about products with predictions of customer needs and tastes, a company can provide a more personalized good or service. As a result, it creates value because customers are getting something that matches their own preferences.

Customization often requires an increase in the automation of processes. If you go from offering a few hundred or thousand distinct products to offering millions and matching them with fewer consumers, humans have difficulty managing the process. Thus, you want a system that can automate both the prediction and also the delivery of the products to customers. That automation process is a challenge to design and also necessarily impacts people who are already working in established organizations. It creates conflicts over the allocation of power that can stifle the design of a new system.

Using the AI Systems Discovery Canvas, we can analyze the potential impact of customization on insurance. Insurance companies have long tried to acquire information to help underwrite policies and set appropriate premiums. Where a house is situated (which speaks to flood and fire risk), whether it has smoke detection systems, and what materials it is built with can all play a role in underwriting. But AI prediction offers the potential for more.[3] By gathering more data across claims, the company can dramatically improve its estimate of the expected loss of a particular house. This is precisely what "insurtech" companies like Lemonade are trying to do.[4] But we still don't know whether AI can impact underwriting in a meaningful way.

But suppose that an insurtech company can examine a house and provide a more precise expected loss and tailor a premium appropriately. Suppose also that this allows the insurance company to more clearly price policies based on house characteristics, signaling to owners whether it is worthwhile to make changes to optimize their insurance premiums. This has two broad effects: one competitive and one organizational.

The competitive effect is that if the insurtech company identifies lower-risk customers, it can discount premiums to attract them, while other companies that cannot similarly identify those customers cannot. This is complicated because if the insurtech company makes a big enough splash, established insurers may imitate the premiums offered by the insurtech, safely learning which customers to target by observing the insurtech. Still, this process likely will give the insurtech company a competitive advantage.

Existing insurers may be spurred to respond. Unlike the insurtech company, they are not startups, so they would have to change to adopt more precise underwriting. The traditional process of selling a policy involves gathering some basic information from the customer, having a human underwriter assess that information, and then returning a premium. The process is part of marketing to the customer. The insurtech company automates this process, without a human signing off before offering a premium to a customer. This has a speed advantage, but it does not have the human element. Many insurtech companies tout this as a key advantage and advertise their ability to deliver insurance with fewer people.[5] In 2018, for example, Lemonade claimed it could write 2,500 policies per employee, compared with 1,200 for Allstate and 650 for GEICO. The consequence of AI adoption in insurance will be fewer underwriters, salespeople, and their immediate supervisors.

Many people will resist change. We can imagine the objections they would raise if they are taken out of the loop. Existing insurers have expressed skepticism. An insurance industry trade publication called Lemonade's IPO "a unicorn vomiting a rainbow."[6] We can argue that setting premiums and selling policies aren't purely objective, and there are subjective elements that a skilled underwriter can identify. The insurance companies would claim that Lemonade will not be able to reduce expected losses by ignoring this. And what of the existing customers whose expected losses increase, thus incurring higher premiums? Will an existing insurer be able to do that without damaging its own brand? All these objections have a ring of truth precisely because of the uncertainty that a new AI-driven organization will work. The paradox is that if an established insurer does not want to bet its existing organization on the uncertainty if resolved in AI's favor, change may come too late. Existing organizations face this dilemma when adopting innovations that may require new systems. To the extent that new systems give their innovators power, they take power away from those running older systems.

KEY POINTS

- Most companies have created systems comprising so many inter-dependent rules, along with so much associated scaffolding to manage uncertainty, that it's difficult to think about how to undo parts of it and contemplate the new system design possibilities AI predictions afford. So, rather than thinking through the implications of changing some rules or scaffolding and how those changes will impact other parts of the system, we instead suggest starting from scratch: the blank slate. The AI Systems Discovery Canvas involves three steps: (1) *articulate* the mission; (2) *reduce* the business to the fewest possible decisions required to achieve the mission if you had super-powerful, high-fidelity AIs; and (3) *specify* the prediction and judgment associated with each of the primary decisions.

- With home insurance, the business could be reduced to three primary decisions: (1) marketing: decide how to allocate marketing resources for customer acquisition to optimize either profitability or growth; (2) underwriting: decide premiums for any given home-owner policy to maximize profitability or growth (could be not offered at all if the prediction is that the risk is too high for the policy to be profitable, given regulatory restrictions on price); and (3) claims: decide whether any given claim is legitimate and, if so, pay it. If three super-powerful, high-fidelity AIs could predict: (1) the lifetime value of a potential client multiplied by probability of converting, (2) the likelihood of filing a claim multiplied by claim magnitude, and (3) the legitimacy of claims, then you could redesign a much improved fast, efficient, low-cost, and highly profitable home insurance business that would outperform competitors in both price and convenience. That is precisely the objective of some of the new insurtech firms.

- The AI Systems Discovery Canvas can also provide insight into new business opportunities. For example, if an AI that predicts the likelihood of filing a claim multiplied by the magnitude of the claim becomes good enough such that it can generate its predictions at the peril level or the sub-peril level (e.g., a sensor to provide early detection of a heightened electrical fire risk or an increased risk of flooding from a leaky pipe), then the company could predict which risk mitigation solutions will have a high enough return on investment to warrant the cost of implementation. Then, the insurance firm could subsidize the risk mitigation device and reduce the premium, providing a whole new value proposition to the customer: risk mitigation. Not only does the insurance company transfer risk from the homeowner to the carrier, but it also reduces the risk—a valuable service the insurance industry has historically not offered except in a minority of cases. To fully exploit this opportunity requires designing a *new system* that is optimized for risk mitigation.

18

Anticipating System Change

A patient arrives at the emergency department with chest pain. Is it a heart attack? A doctor can find out by conducting a test. A positive test will allow the doctor to treat the patient quickly, with clear benefits. But the tests are expensive and also invasive. Imaging tests use radiation, which can increase the long-term risk of cancer. A treadmill session poses a small but defined risk of cardiac arrest. Cardiac catheterization involves radiation as well as a risk of arterial damage.[1] It isn't an easy decision.

The physician needs to weigh these benefits and costs. How likely is it that the patient is really having a heart attack? This is a prediction. If the prediction is that the likelihood is high, that pushes the physician toward testing and treating. If it is low, the bigger the chance that the test is wasted, risking the patient for little reason.

In deciding whether to conduct a test or not, the benefits are the revelation of information about further interventions (such as putting in a stent). If the patient is having a heart attack, then she will benefit from treatments for heart attack; if not, then she will have no benefit. So, the value of testing is purely derived from the decision value it creates, in targeting interventions to patients who will benefit the most.

Testing isn't a free lunch. Stress tests can cost thousands of dollars. Catheterization can cost tens of thousands of dollars. You'd happily pay for a stress test to avoid a cost ten times as high.

This is just the monetary cost. Some tests require overnight monitoring and observation. Then the tests themselves create their own risks: Of all imaging tests, stress tests carry the single highest dose of ionizing radiation, which is thought to substantially raise long-term cancer risks. Exercise on a treadmill in the setting of a heart attack poses a small but definite risk of cardiac arrest. Sending the patient directly to catheterization has the benefit that the treatment (typically inserting a stent) can be completed as part of the same procedure as the diagnosis.

Then again you don't necessarily want to avoid a stress test and its associated risks because the catheterization procedure is also risky. An invasive procedure involves a large dose of ionizing radiation as well as injection of intravenous contrast material that can cause kidney failure and carries a risk of arterial damage and debilitating stroke. So before the decision of whether to treat a patient for a heart attack come the decisions of whether to test someone for a heart attack, and whether to first conduct a stress test or to send the patient directly to catheterization.

The testing decisions lie with the doctor. Tests tend to be a precursor to the procedure. But doctors apply plenty of judgment in deciding what to do. What is the age of the patient? Do people require more care (say, in a nursing home)? What other conditions (e.g., cancer) does the patient have? All these weigh into those decisions.

Now suppose the doctor had help—superhuman help—with the prediction part of the equation: that is, suppose an AI that could assess whether a patient needed that test or not and do it quickly. It's not hard to see the potential benefits here. This isn't hypothetical. Economists Sendhil Mullainathan and Ziad Obermeyer built an AI based on the same information that doctors had in the emergency department when diagnosing a patient.[2] They showed that their AI was more accurate than doctors at predicting heart attacks. Doctors' decisions showed plenty of overtesting. Patients were getting tests they didn't need. Given some of the incentives in the US health-care system, perhaps this result was easy to anticipate. No one wants to face the liability associated with not testing, especially when you get paid more to test more.

Surprisingly, they also found a significant amount of undertesting. Thousands of patients that the AI predicts to be at high risk never receive tests. The patients that the AI algorithm predicted to be high risk ended up having worse outcomes, in terms of returning to the hospital or dying.

The AI algorithm appeared to be great on all fronts. It was cheap, fast, and seemingly less error-prone in both directions. You could take the same volume of tests and reallocate them from low- to high-risk patients and achieve better outcomes all around, helping patients and likely reducing liability exposure. Alternatively, you could reduce testing and keep the same quality of health care.

Point and Application Solutions

This looks like a no-brainer for AI adoption. AI diagnosis in emergency departments provides an excellent and effective point solution. The AI supports the doctor, who is then able to make better decisions and incrementally improve patient health at somewhat lower cost. The workflow doesn't change and no one's job is threatened. The doctor isn't spending much time on the diagnosis step, as decoupled from judgment.

The question is whether these benefits are worth the cost of implementing a new tool. Health-care administrators are faced with many promising new technologies. Each one requires training and tweaks to processes. Each also has risks. In practice, technologies are rarely as good as they seem in testing. The administrators might decide that the incremental benefit of the AI point solution for heart attack diagnosis isn't worth the costs.

The administrators might, however, find an AI application solution compelling. Instead of an AI that provides a prediction to the doctor, they implement an AI that determines whether to test. The doctor is removed from the decision for the patient. Instead, when the patient arrives at the emergency department, the machine predicts the likelihood that the patient is having a heart attack. If the prediction is below some threshold, the patient is sent home. If the prediction is in some intermediate range, the patient is sent for a stress test. If the AI predicts that the patient is very likely having a heart attack, then the patient is sent directly to catheterization. The thresholds between the send-home, stress-test, and catheterize decisions are judgment. In this case, that judgment might come from the hospital's leaders or from a committee of physicians and other medical specialists.

Can the System Handle It?

Hospitals are typically organized into two overarching divisions, each with its own responsibilities.[3] The *administration* is responsible for the money side, obtaining payments (or reimbursements from government or other insurance), hiring staff, and procuring resources. *Medicine* is responsible for the diagnosis and treatment of patients. Within hospitals, there are subdivisions within each, but in the allocation of decision authority, one division has the money and resources while the other division has the medical. The conflicts between the two are ongoing. But most functioning hospitals have settled into terms of engagement between divisions that allow each to make their own decisions, subject to constraints imposed by the other.

For a diagnosis AI in the emergency department, one can imagine potential sources of resistance. Physicians receive some private benefit from doing more tests, in the form of protection from malpractice risk or perhaps extra revenue. If AIs are making better predictions than the doctors, then the doctors' training and experience become less important. Their value is reduced relative to those who build those AIs. Administrators might worry about the costs of implementation. In the application solution, physicians are removed from the decision, and their training and experience might become irrelevant. Physicians who have made many past decisions may be skeptical that the AI can do better than they can.

The potential of an AI may be even larger, but that requires some system change. In most hospital emergency departments, when a patient arrives, the doctors decide whether to send the patient home, give a stress test, or catheterize. Long before that decision is made, the administration decides which tests to make available. Currently, the incentives appear to be aligned. Mullainathan and Obermeyer estimate that 15 percent of the patients that doctors send for a test are actually having a heart attack. At that accuracy, both doctors and administrators seem to agree that sending the patient for a stress test first is best.[4]

An AI that incrementally improved this prediction would improve patient outcomes with little change in incentives. At 20 percent accuracy, whether AI is implemented as a point solution or an application solution, both doctors and administration would likely want to send patients for a stress test first. Such improvements might be incremental enough that neither the doctors nor the administration think it is worthwhile to adopt.

If it were possible to build an AI that was near perfect, then there is an opportunity to improve patient care and redesign the system. If the AI predicts that a patient is having a heart attack with 99 percent accuracy, then both doctors and administration would recognize that it is best to go straight to catheterization and skip the stress test. Once the AI is good enough across all patients, everyone will agree that stress tests are unnecessary. The administration will stop offering the stress test as an option, and doctors will never want to use one.

Between today's accuracy and a near-perfect AI, there is an intermediate range where doctors' and administrators' incentives can change and conflict. Administrators might perceive a bigger cost to unnecessary stress testing than doctors, either because the administrators don't want to spend the resources or because they are less worried about the liability risk. In that case, at 50 percent accuracy, doctors might still want to stress test, but administrators want to send the patient to catheterization.

The solution, given the divisions described, seems easy. It suggests a relatively straightforward system change in which the administration takes a decision away from the doctors. The administration would refuse to provide stress tests. Doctors then can choose only between sending the patient directly to catheterization or sending the patient home. In that case, patients go straight to catheterization, the administrators get what they want, and doctors grumble but accept the hand they are dealt.

To us, that seems unlikely. Doctors will push back. A regulatory body might be called in. Patients' rights will be discussed. When the decision-makers are no longer aligned, the ways decisions are allocated in the existing system might no longer be acceptable. This change in decision alignment might, in turn, mean that the AI tool is never adopted. Given that AIs improve with feedback data, the intermediate-term misalignment might prevent the long-term, highly beneficial AI from being possible.

To overcome this, the doctors and administrators would need to jointly set up a new decision structure. This means a bigger system change than skipping a testing decision. For AI tools like the one we've described for heart attacks, that bigger system change might not be worth it.

On the other hand, once you recognize the possibility for system change, an opportunity arises to use the AI Systems Discovery Canvas to reimagine what emergency medicine might look like.

Canvassing Emergency Medicine

Building a canvas is necessarily a speculative exercise. It involves taking a complicated industry and describing it in its most basic form. As we outlined in the previous chapter, it starts with the mission. An emergency department's mission might be "to improve the outcomes of acutely ill and injured patients through high-quality, cost-efficient care."[5]

To provide that care, administrators and doctors make thousands of decisions. The exercise with the canvas is to summarize these decisions into their essential categories. For emergency medicine, one way to divide it is into just two core decisions (see figure 18-1). There is the treatment decision when a medical professional decides what medical services to offer the patient, and there is the resourcing decision when the administration decides what equipment and staffing to make available in the department. Treatments depend on diagnoses and an understanding of the medical evidence supporting different treatments given a diagnosis. The diagnosis, as we have discussed, is a prediction problem. Resourcing also depends on diagnoses, but not patient by patient. Instead, resourcing depends on a prediction of the distribution of diagnoses over time.

Let's take this speculative exercise to the limit, where AIs for diagnosis become useful across a range of settings. Eric Topol, a cardiologist we introduced in chapter 8, believes better AI predictions will herald a golden age of medicine, where doctors can focus on the human aspects of health care and leave the mechanical processes to machines.[6] Heart attack prediction is just one example where AI is starting to outperform doctors at diagnosis.[7]

FIGURE 18-1

AI Systems Discovery Canvas: Emergency

What are the fewest decisions you can reduce your business to?

1. Mission	Improve the outcomes of acutely ill and injured patients through high-quality, cost-efficient care	
2. Decision	**Treatment:** Decide which treatment to prescribe	**Resourcing:** Decide how much of each type of equipment and staffing should be deployed
3. Prediction	**Diagnosis:** Predict the reason for the patient's symptoms	**Number and type of patients:** Predict the quantity of patients and the distribution of diagnoses
4. Judgment	What are the consequences of overtreating, undertreating, and incorrectly treating patients?	What are the consequences of having too little equipment and staff on hand relative to having too much?

As the predictions underlying decision number one get better and faster, patients increasingly receive appropriate treatments. With enough data, it might be possible to move those predictions out of the triage space in a hospital's emergency department altogether and back into a patient's home. Thus, before the ambulance is called, it is possible to imagine high-quality predictions that provide a diagnosis.

Such a diagnosis might enable a variety of system-level changes. Patients might skip the emergency department entirely and get sent straight to the relevant medical department, be it cardiology or orthopedics. Many patients will never need to go to the hospital, after being diagnosed with something that a pharmacist or a primary care physician can help treat. Paramedics could take patients to different hospitals, based on where the relevant expertise—and slack in the system—might be.

The role of the paramedic could also change. Paramedics could train to specialize in particular medical conditions. Then, when a patient has an emergency that requires cardiology expertise, the appropriately trained paramedic could be sent, along with an ambulance filled with cardiology-focused equipment. The patient would not have to wait to arrive at the hospital to receive treatment. In many emergencies, those minutes matter.

We know what you're thinking. That's impossible. Even if the predictions are good enough, paramedics can't be so specialized. They need to be generalists because they need to handle whatever might come their way. If we needed specialists, every ambulance station would need far more paramedics than we could possibly train and pay for.

That's where the second decision comes in: resourcing. If the prediction on the distribution of needs is good enough (and population density is high enough), it becomes possible to put the necessary equipment and the necessary well-trained personnel in the right place at the right time. The AI prediction for patient diagnosis becomes a complement to the AI prediction on the distribution of needs over time.

At the limit, this version of emergency medicine has most patients treated at home with specialized equipment brought by a paramedic trained in specifically relevant skills. Those patients who are sent to the hospital are those who require extensive stays or large teams of medical personnel to treat them. Patient outcomes are better. Hospitals become smaller. Medical training and personnel change. The mission to improve outcomes through high-quality cost-efficient care might be achieved in a spectacular fashion.

This isn't imminent. It probably isn't even possible. The AIs are not good enough yet and might never be. The costs to overhaul the system would be significant, although the long-term savings might be, too. The resistance of medical professionals and administrators to such dramatic change would be extraordinary. Still, it might happen on a smaller scale. Many jurisdictions already dispatch physicians alongside paramedics.[8] Prediction machines could help identify when a physician is needed.[9] An entrepreneurial organization taking the first step to a new system, integrating the AI into dispatch to identify which physician (and which equipment), is needed.

System Choices

We are surely disingenuous to claim that systemic change is complicated and then offer a highly simplistic view of what choices define a system and how their change comes with the adoption of new technology. However, sometimes to illustrate the complexity, there is value in oversimplification. The idea is to strip away a mess to find key parts of its essence. That's what the AI Systems Discovery Canvas does, and what our thought experiment on AI in emergency medicine accomplished.

There are two broad classes of choices that define what we call a "system." The first is who sees what. The second is who decides what. This provides another framework for understanding the system changes we've described. For who sees what, an organization's job is to filter information. A vast amount of information can be brought into the organization, but the key task is to bring in the information that is relevant to current decision-making. Thus, an organization sets about allocating roles in observing and processing information to particular areas—divisions like administration and medicine. In some cases, divisions collect information and keep it within the division. In others, divisions filter and communicate information to other divisions. Medicine sees a predicted diagnosis for each patient when they arrive at the emergency department. Administration only sees the distribution after the fact. The point is that there will be information that is not brought into the organization at all, and there is even less information that is commonly used across the entire organization.

For who decides what, the allocation of decision authority is a combination of who has the skills to best use information, who has the information, and who has the right incentives to make a decision aligned with the organization's interests. In principle, if there were a superindividual, one person could just make all the decisions. But no such individual exists. Thus, in allocating decision authority, the organization makes trade-offs all over the place.

The divisions take advantage of specialization and minimize the need for coordination between them, so everyone can get on with their jobs. But that also means that there is no one who can see everything. Good organizational design makes sure that divisions can recognize when a situation is outside their lane and refer it to someone else. But there is no perfect way of doing this. Thus, organizations allocate decisions and information to something that works well. The larger the organization, the more necessary or likely that this settling down has occurred. Smaller organizations have fewer divisions, but that limits their size.[10]

Existing systems as defined by divisional responsibilities will be very good at adopting new technologies whose benefits are confined within a division. In these cases, there is adoption of AI point solutions and AI application solutions. Hospital administrations have adopted AI for scheduling maintenance staff and screening résumés, both clearly related to resource allocation. The technologies serve the division's mission and do not require a change in who decides what, which can lead to resistance internally as changes in responsibility often track changes in power.

By contrast, for new technologies whose benefits are distributed across divisions or, perhaps worse, involve costs for one division and benefits in another, adoption is much harder. Even if those opportunities can be recognized, achieving coordination requires reallocating who decides what. That underlies the challenges in adopting the AI for diagnosis in emergency departments. Thus, carefully negotiated and robust trade-offs need to be confronted and recalibrated. Such change is, to put it mildly, disruptive and therefore might be easier to achieve when starting from scratch.[11]

When it comes to AI prediction, new innovations can come in many forms. Many are point solutions or application solutions that divisions can adopt without ensuing conflict or difficulties in coordination. For others, that is not possible. Their adoption involves disruption and change. The question here is how business leaders can tell whether they are missing these latter opportunities precisely because their organization has been designed to not see them, let alone evaluate their potential favorably when they arise.

Given this, to conduct thought experiments on whether you can adopt a current or potential AI innovation in your organization, we offer a two-step procedure.

STEP 1: Identify the information the prediction provides or the uncertainty it resolves and which decision or decisions it will improve.

STEP 2: Is that information or are those decisions contained within a single division or across more than one division?

Now let's return to AI adoption in emergency departments, specifically, the AI that predicts whether a patient is having a heart attack. In step 1, the

AI predicts a diagnosis. The AI was set up to use information only available in hospital systems to physicians at the time a patient comes into the emergency room. The main decision this diagnosis informs is which tests and treatments to provide. For step 2, clearly this information and this decision are all firmly in the purview of the doctors in the medical division. The choice over whether to adopt such algorithms to assist with this type of triage seems like an easy one, seemingly making it more likely to be adopted as a point solution.

We then explored the question whether the emergency department should offer a stress test. This adds a new decision to step 1: the resources that should be available. Looking at step 2, this is no longer constrained to one division, and as noted earlier, system-level challenges might prevent adoption. There might also be ways to improve the AI that require coordinating information across divisions. AI diagnosis before the patient arrives at the hospital might require access to patient data for weeks and perhaps years before the event. That requires the administration to approve data collection outside the bounds of the hospital. Regulations would need to be adjusted. Patients would need to be convinced. And therein lies the potential conflict. The current organizational structures of hospitals cannot easily adopt AI prediction technologies and their resulting changes to operations. It requires a new system.

It's Hard to Make Predictions about Systems

By 1880, it was clear that electricity had great potential to improve how factories operate. But it required another forty years to understand how to design a factory system that took advantage of electric power. To the best of our knowledge, no one envisaged the ultimate systems that were built of electricity. The process of discovery took time, as people evolved in their understanding of what electricity could do.

With AI, we are closer to 1880 than 1920. It seems likely that AI will lead to entirely new systems in many industries. We believe that precisely because of AI prediction's role in decision-making and the fact that when it generates new decisions, the actions are taken and outcomes from those decisions reflect rather than insulate or hide underlying uncertainty. Because decisions often interact with other decisions, there are likely to be systemwide effects. The very fact that without prediction, existing ways of doing things can be reliable—even if they are technically wasteful—tells us that, without system innovation, AI adoption will be muted.

In these last few chapters, we provided guideposts and methods that help unpack the systems that AI may enter. Insurance and health care are the types of industries that may be ripe for change. But we are in the early days of The Between Times. Even if you use these methods to understand how a system might change, there are many more steps before you can work out if such change is worthwhile and what AI prediction advances are required to make restructuring worthwhile. Even then, system innovation requires disruption, which carries with it changes in the distribution of power with winners and losers. The balance between those pulling for change and those pushing against it will determine whether and how quickly it occurs.

Thus, we emphasize the caveat that the history of technology tells us much about whether a general purpose technology, as AI appears to be, will be disruptive and take time. A clear and objective analysis of precisely what AI is doing, namely, prediction, and where it enters systems—in augmenting decisions—provides a compass to guide our direction rather than a map that shows our destination. Ultimately, even when studying prediction machines, the old adage applies: "It's hard to make predictions, especially about the future."

KEY POINTS

- Two economists built an AI that was superhuman in its ability to predict when someone was having a heart attack. It was cheaper, faster, and seemingly less error-prone than the average doctor in terms of both false positives and false negatives. This prediction machine could be deployed as a point solution, impacting only a single decision: whether to administer a test. The point solution application of this AI would enhance the productivity of the hospital by better allocating heart attack detection tests.

- While the point solution could have a meaningful impact on improving health care via a better allocation of testing, a highly accurate heart attack prediction AI could potentially underpin a system-level solution that would have a much greater impact. Using the AI System Discovery Canvas, we see that one of the key decisions is whether to test, and it's based on the prediction of a person having a heart attack. If that prediction becomes good enough and can be generated with easily collected data—by a smartwatch, for example—then it might be possible to move those predictions out of the triage space in a hospital's emergency department to a patient's home. Many patients will never need to go to the hospital, after being diagnosed with something that a pharmacist or a primary care physician can help treat at home.

- A key attribute of the AI System Discovery Canvas is that it abstracts the organization to its core decisions. By doing so, it unshackles the mission of the organization, which remains fixed, from the plethora of rules and decisions associated with the status quo, which are dispensable. Designers then have freedom to imagine a multitude of different system-level solutions that could be enabled by powerful prediction machines that underpin the primary decisions. The single heart attack prediction AI could enable not one but several alternative system-level solutions. The thought process begins with identifying the key decisions, speculating on what is possible if the predictions become highly accurate, and then reimagining the types of systems that can exploit those predictions in a manner optimized for mission success.

EPILOGUE

AI Bias and Systems

In retrospect, it was unlikely to turn out well. But in 2016, Microsoft researchers released an AI algorithm called Tay to learn how to interact on Twitter. Within hours, it learned and began to spew out offensive tweets. Tay was not alone in becoming the worst of us. Stories like this abound and make many, including businesses, reluctant to adopt AI, not because AI prediction performs worse than people. Instead, AI may be too good at behaving like them.

This shouldn't be a surprise. AI prediction requires data, and especially for data that involves predicting something about people, the training data comes from people. This can have merit, such as when training to play a game against people, but people are imperfect, and AI inherits those imperfections.

What many do not recognize is that this is a current problem because of how we have been thinking about AI solutions. When you are interested in, say, allowing your human resources department to screen hundreds of applicants, a first potential use for AI is to employ an algorithm rather than people for that job. It is, after all, a predictive task—what is the likelihood that this person with these credentials will succeed in this business? But this way of using AI is a point solution, which can work, but as we have stressed throughout this book, often will take a full system-level redesign. When removing the adverse consequences of bias, a system mindset is required.

Our starting point is our perspective on bias in AI, which is different and, dare we say, a contrarian view regarding whether AI will perpetuate discrimination. When viewed using a system mindset, the opportunities for AI with respect to bias are promising. They offer a solution to many aspects of discrimination. And precisely because they offer this, they face resistance. The uncomfortable truth about discrimination is that eliminating it generates winners and losers as power shifts. Thus, resistance to adopting AIs is likely to be higher precisely when AIs have the potential to engender new systems that eliminate many aspects of discrimination.

The Antidiscrimination Opportunity

Because AIs lay bare an opportunity to understand the sources of bias and with this knowledge can be used appropriately in decision-making, they offer the opportunity to reduce discrimination.[1]

Consider a simple example. People of color report much higher knee pain than white people. There are two distinct explanations for this. First, people of color might have more severe osteoarthritis within the knee. Alternatively, other factors external to the knee, such as life stress or social isolation, may lead people of color to report higher levels of knee pain.

These explanations imply different treatments. If the issue is more severe osteoarthritis, then physiotherapy, medication, and surgery could help. If the issue is external to the knee, then the most effective treatments might focus on improving mental health.

Many doctors suspected that factors external to the knee were more important in explaining the racial disparities. Studies have compared the pain reported by patients with radiologists' assessment of knee osteoarthritis based on medical imaging. The radiologists base their assessments on methods such as the Kellgren-Lawrence (KL) classification, through which doctors examine images of a patient's knee and assign a score based on the presence of bone spurs, bone deformities, and other factors.[2] Even after adjusting for these assessments, people of color report higher levels of pain.[3]

Computer scientist Emma Pierson and her coauthors suspected the issue might be in the classification system. The methods for measuring osteoarthritis, including KL classification, were developed decades ago in white populations.[4] They might miss the physical causes of pain in nonwhite populations. Radiologists may also be biased in their assessment of nonwhite patients, downplaying their pain in developing a diagnosis.

AI can help. Pierson and her coauthors took thousands of images of knees. For each image, they had the patient's self-reported level of pain. When radiologists scored the images, only 9 percent of the racial disparities in pain appeared to be explained by factors internal to the knee.

The authors then assessed whether an AI could use the images to predict the reported pain. Their AI predicted 43 percent of the racial disparities in pain. The AI identified factors within the knee that the humans missed, and these factors explained nearly five times as much of the difference in reported pain between people of color and white people.

This racial disparity in treatment suggests that many nonwhite patients would receive treatment external to the knee when there is clearly something in the knee causing the pain. Here, AI helped identify systemic discrimination in health care and provides a path for fixing it.

To address discrimination, both of these are necessary. You need to detect the discrimination and you need to fix it. This is true of both human and machine predictions. In other words, eliminating discrimination requires a system.

Detecting Discrimination

Detecting discrimination is hard. Despite plenty of legal claims decrying discrimination in technology and other industries, few are decided in favor of the plaintiffs. Many of the most prominent cases where employees sued for discrimination ended up decided in favor of the employer or dropped.[5]

Many of these cases focus on whether the firms discriminated in salary or promotions. Suppose a tech firm is accused of gender discrimination in promotions. There is no question that the firm has promoted several men instead of the plaintiff who has been at the firm longer, but the question at the heart of the litigation would be *why*.

The plaintiff will claim that the firm intentionally discriminated against her. The firm will respond that the particular plaintiff "is less a victim of discrimination than a difficult and conniving employee who rejected advice to improve," as the *New York Times* described one defendant's approach.[6] Managers will be asked if they discriminated in their recommendations for promotions. Of course, they will say no. The plaintiff's lawyer might ask, bluntly, "Would my client have been promoted if she were a man?" "No." The plaintiff's lawyer would try to compare the performance of those who were promoted to the plaintiff's performance, but performance is hard to measure and there is too much ambiguity in the comparison.[7]

Even when there is discrimination, it is hard to prove. No two people are exactly alike. Managers consider a variety of factors when making promotion and hiring decisions. Without an explicit statement of intent to discriminate, it is difficult for a judge or jury to be confident that a human's decision was discriminatory. It is impossible to know what is truly in someone's mind.

No Two People Are Exactly Alike. Unless They Are

Sendhil Mullainathan is an expert on detecting discrimination. In 2001, just three years after he got his PhD, Mullainathan and coauthor Marianne Bertrand set out to measure discrimination in the US labor market.[8] They sent fictitious résumés to help wanted ads in Boston and Chicago newspapers. For each ad, they sent four résumés. Two were high quality, and two were low quality. They randomly assigned one of the high-quality résumés an African American–sounding name (Lakisha Washington or Jamal Jones), and the other a white-sounding name (Emily Walsh or Greg Baker). Similarly, they randomly assigned one of the low-quality résumés an African American name and the other a white-sounding name.

Then they waited to see if their fictitious applicants were called for interviews. White names received 50 percent more callbacks. The gap between high-quality résumés with white-sounding names and high-quality résumés with African American–sounding names was even larger. There was clearly discrimination in the labor market.

Fifteen years later, Mullainathan did it again. Now a University of Chicago professor and recipient of a MacArthur "Genius Grant," he and his coauthors discovered that a widely used algorithm employed to identify patients with complex health needs was racially biased. At a given risk score, African American patients were actually considerably sicker than white patients. Remedying the disparity would nearly triple the fraction of African American patients receiving additional resources to manage their care.[9]

The bias arose because the machine was designed to predict health-care costs as a proxy for illness, rather than the illness itself. Unequal access to care means that the US health-care system spends less money caring for African American patients than for white patients. So a prediction machine that uses health-care spending as a proxy for illness will underestimate the severity of illness in African Americans and other patient groups with less access to care.

In the aftermath of this study, Mullainathan reflected on the two projects.

> Both studies documented racial injustice: In the first, the applicant with a Black-sounding name got fewer job interviews. In the second, the Black patient received worse care.
>
> But they differed in one crucial respect. In the first, hiring managers made biased decisions. In the second, the culprit was a computer program.
>
> As a co-author of both studies, I see them as a lesson in contrasts. Side by side, they show the stark differences between two types of bias: human and algorithmic.[10]

The earlier study required an extraordinary amount of creativity and effort to detect discrimination. He describes it as a "complex covert operation" that went on for months.

In contrast, the later study was more straightforward. Mullainathan described it as "a statistical exercise—the equivalent of asking the algorithm 'what would you do with this patient?' hundreds of thousands of times and mapping out the racial differences. The work was technical and rote, requiring neither stealth nor resourcefulness."

Measuring discrimination in people is hard, requiring careful control over the circumstances. Measuring discrimination by machines is more straightforward. Feed the machines the right data and see what comes out. The researcher can go to the AI and say, What if the person is like this? What if the person is like that? It is possible to try thousands of what-ifs. That's not possible with humans. "Humans are inscrutable in a way that algorithms are not," Mullainathan noted.

Fixing Discrimination

Detecting discrimination is just the first step. Once discrimination is detected, you want to fix it. Humans are hard to fix. Thus, you need a system that doesn't rely on that.

In the résumé study, even if you could get over the challenge of figuring out which companies were at fault, "changing people's hearts and minds is no simple matter."[11] The evidence on tools like implicit bias training is mixed. We don't know of a fix available that can reduce discrimination by thousands or even millions of humans every day. Two decades after that initial study, Emily and Greg remain more employable than Lakisha and Jamal.

Contrast that with an AI. Even before they published the study on algorithmic discrimination, Mullainathan and his coauthors were already working with the company to fix the problem. They started by contacting the company, which was able to replicate the study's result with its own simulations. As a first step, it showed that including health prediction with the existing cost prediction would reduce bias by 84 percent.[12] The authors offered their services, for free, to a number of health-care systems using these types of algorithms. Many took them up on the offer.

Obermeyer and colleagues' academic paper concludes that "label biases are fixable. . . . Because labels are the key determinant of both predictive quality and predictive bias, careful choice can allow us to enjoy the benefits of algorithmic predictions while minimizing their risk."[13] As Mullainathan put it, "[C]hanging algorithms is easier than changing people: software on computers can be updated; the 'wetware' in our brains has so far proven much less pliable."[14]

Inside the AI Box

AIs are susceptible to bias. This could mean that disadvantaged groups receive worse treatment than others. In other words, AIs can be a source of discrimination.

AIs can also reduce discrimination. They can detect discriminatory practices in humans, as in the detection of knee pain. They are also scrutable. It is much easier to detect discrimination by an algorithm than discrimination by humans.

AI discrimination is also fixable. The software can be adjusted, and the identified sources of bias can be eliminated.

Fixing such discrimination is not easy. First, it requires humans who want to fix the bias. If the humans who manage the AI want to deploy an AI that discriminates, they will have little difficulty doing so. And because the AI is software, its discrimination can happen at scale. However, it is easier to catch a deliberately discriminatory AI than a deliberately discriminatory human. The AI leaves an audit trail. A well-funded regulator with well-trained auditors who can access the AI can run simulations to look for discrimination, just as Mullainathan and his coauthors did. Unfortunately, our current legal and regulatory systems struggle with these challenges, as they were designed for a world of human decision-makers, unaided by algorithms.[15]

Second, even when deployed by well-intentioned humans who want to reduce biases, details matter. And focusing on details is time-consuming and expensive. There are many ways bias can seep into the AI's predictions. Fixing bias requires understanding its source.[16] This requires investments in storing data about past decisions. It requires investments in simulating potential sources of bias to see how the AI holds up. And the first attempt might not work. New data might need to be collected. New processes might be required.[17]

Third, an AI that reduces bias can change who holds decision-making power in an organization. Without AI, it might be individual managers who make decisions on who to hire. These managers, even with the best intentions, might hire through their social connections in a way that leads to unintended bias. With an AI designed to reduce bias, hiring through social connections will be harder. A more senior executive would set the threshold for which résumés to consider. That executive might recognize that if all managers across the company were hired through their social connections, a diverse workforce would be impossible. The AI reduces discrimination, but it also reduces the discretion that individual managers have in hiring relative to the objectives set by the executive suite. So, those managers might resist a system-level change that will reduce their power.

Not everyone will celebrate a reduction in bias. In 2003, Major League Baseball used a new tool for identifying the location of pitches over the plate called the QuesTec Umpire Information System. QuesTec evaluated the balls and strikes called by umpires. Unsurprisingly, the umpires resisted the tool. So did some of the star players. Sandy Alderson, then vice president of operations, described one motivation for the tool, claiming that some veteran players would get the benefit of the doubt and have balls and strikes called in their favor. Many of the game's biggest stars complained, including award-winning pitcher Tom Glavine and multiple MVP winner Barry Bonds. Then–Arizona Diamondbacks ace pitcher Curt Schilling became a modern-day Luddite, smashing a camera after a loss.[18] An automated tool in which a computer predicted balls and strikes might have decreased bias, but those who benefit from the bias might not like that.

It Takes a System

Amazon hires a lot of people. One of every 153 workers in the United States is an Amazon employee.[19] Thus, it should not surprise you that it was very interested in developing an AI to assist with its recruiting. In 2014, it did just that. Just a year later, it scrapped the system and never put in the field. Why? Because it was not evaluating candidates for software and other technical jobs in a gender-neutral way.[20] The reason was a familiar one. Amazon's AI was trained on past data overwhelmingly of male candidates. The AI was explicitly down-weighting references to women, including women's colleges. Simple tweaks could not restore neutrality.

You read stories like this and think that AI is hopelessly biased. But the other way you can read this story is that the AI was biased, was judged to be, and so was not deployed. Can the same be said for human recruiters?

We actually know the answer: the AI was trained on those recruiters in the first place.

At the same time, this experience has taught AI developers that training on past data can often not be good enough. They need new sources of data, which will take time to develop. But in the end, the resulting AI can be evaluated. What's more, it can be continually monitored for performance.

This is a potentially profound improvement over how we deal with discrimination now. Today's interventions to alleviate discrimination are primarily outcome based: Is there a difference between the outcomes of different groups? And the interventions are often direct rules to try and redress a balance and achieve outcome parity. The problem is that those interventions can be divisive.

By contrast, what people often want is to remove the source of the bias—in particular, the motivations of people who are making decisions. They don't want to fix equal outcomes per se (although achieving that is not a problem), but instead they want equal treatment. However, when people are making the decisions and we can't see their motivations, how can we have confidence that there is equal treatment?

If AI prediction can be at the heart of such decisions, we can achieve an objective benchmark. We can see how the AI treats people, and because we know the AI does not have explicit motivations to treat otherwise similar people differently, we can work on ensuring the AI actually does that.

Automated predictions make it easier to create standards. Just as all baseball players can face the same strike zone, all drivers can face the same traffic enforcement standards. There are well-documented biases in traffic enforcement; for example, Black drivers get pulled over more than whites. An easy point solution is to automate speeding tickets. We have the technology for this. Detect speed, take pictures, and then punish the drivers. An automated system is fairer and safer, reducing the chance of a violent encounter between police and the public.

But the benefits of doing that go well beyond the point solution. Having confidence that people are being treated equally changes how people interact with the system and how safe they feel acting within it. It also removes the need for interventions that simply try to look good on the books, like having outcomes be part of fixed buckets or even quotas.

But moving to eliminate disparate treatment will not be seamless; this is precisely because it will change outcomes in the system. Not everyone will welcome an automated system. Just like the star baseball players, the drivers that receive the benefit of officer discretion might resent the cameras. Some people will struggle to pay the fines. Furthermore, an automated system is not lenient if someone is speeding for good reasons like a medical emergency. Police can't use stops to detect crimes other than speeding.

Still, speed kills. Having drivers stay below the speed limit will save lives. But enforcement is uneven, and often discriminatory. Automated enforcement will catch more drivers and reduce discrimination.[21]

When AIs are implemented as point solutions, they can amplify existing biases and increase discrimination. This has led to the negative headlines on AI and discrimination that we see in the press. When AI is seen as a point solution, AI bias is a problem and may create appropriate resistance to adopting prediction machines.

When bias is viewed from a system mindset, AIs can lead to change that reduces discrimination. While the people who benefit from the existing biases will resist, there is a reason for optimism. Like Mullainathan, we see the potential for AIs to reduce bias in all sorts of decisions. This optimism about AI does disguise a broader pessimism about human decision-making. Both humans and AIs will be biased. As MIT computer scientist Marzyeh Ghassemi put it after a lecture on biases in machine learning in health care, when it comes to bias, "Humans are awful."[22] AI bias can be detected and then addressed. New AI system solutions across all domains, from education to health care and from banking to policing, can be designed and implemented to reduce discrimination. AI systems can be monitored continuously and retroactively to ensure continued success in removing discrimination. If only it were that easy to fix in humans.

KEY POINTS

- The popular narrative around AIs is that they learn human bias and amplify it. We agree and advocate for constant vigilance. Another narrative is that AI systems should not be introduced in important decisions like hiring, bank loans, insurance claims, legal rulings, and university admissions because they are opaque—we can't see inside the black box—and they perpetuate discrimination. We disagree. We think they should be introduced in important decisions precisely because they are scrutable in a way that humans are not. We cannot effectively interrogate a human hiring manager we suspect of discrimination with thousands of questions like "Would you have hired this person if they were exactly the same, except white?" and expect an honest response. However, we can ask precisely that question, and thousands more, of an AI system and receive rapid and accurate answers.

- University of Chicago professor Sendhil Mullainathan contrasted two of his studies on bias. In one, he measured human discrimination in hiring. In the other, he measured AI discrimination in health care. Comparing the two, he noted how much easier it was to both detect and fix discrimination in AI systems compared to human systems: "[C]hanging algorithms is easier than changing people: software on computers can be updated; the 'wetware' in our brains has so far proven much less pliable."

- Today, the individuals who most resist adopting AI systems are those who are most concerned about discrimination. We anticipate that will exactly reverse. Once people realize that discrimination is easier to detect and fix in AI systems than in humans, the greatest resistance to adopting AI systems will come not from those who want to reduce discrimination but rather from those who benefit from it most.

NOTES

Preface

1. Here is the prime minister's fireside chat at our conference with Shivon Zilis, director of operations and special projects at Neuralink, Elon Musk's company that is building a brain-machine interface: "Justin Trudeau in Conversation with Shivon Zilis," YouTube, November 9, 2017, https://www.youtube.com/watch?v=zm7A1KXUaS8&t=853s.

2. "About Canada's Innovation Superclusters," Government of Canada, n.d., https://www.ic.gc.ca/eic/site/093.nsf/eng/00016.html.

3. "04: Human vs. Machine," *Spotify: A Product Story*, podcast, March 2021, https://open.spotify.com/episode/0T3nb0PcpvqA4o1BbbQWpp.

4. Money laundering is a big problem. The United Nations estimates that up to US$2 trillion is laundered through the financial system every year. The market for automation and vendor solutions to this problem is US$13 billion, according to Oliver Wyman, an international management consulting company. Nasdaq, "Nasdaq to Acquire Verafin, Creating a Global Leader in the Fight Against Financial Crime," press release, November 19, 2020, https://www.nasdaq.com/press-release/nasdaq-to-acquire-verafin-creating-a-global-leader-in-the-fight-against-financial.

5. Erica Vella, "Tech in T.O.: Why Geoffrey Hinton, the 'Godfather of A.I.,' Decided to Live in Toronto," Global News, October 8, 2019, https://globalnews.ca/news/5929564/geoffrey-hinton-artificial-intelligence-toronto/.

6. Geoff Hinton, "On Radiology," Creative Destruction Lab: Machine Learning and the Market for Intelligence, YouTube, November 24, 2016, https://www.youtube.com/watch?v=2HMPRXstSvQ.

Chapter 1

1. Richard B. Du Boff, "The Introduction of Electric Power in American Manufacturing," *Economic History Review* 20, no. 3 (1967): 509–518, https://doi.org/10.2307/2593069.

2. Du Boff, "The Introduction of Electric Power in American Manufacturing."

3. Warren D. Devine Jr., "From Shafts to Wires: Historical Perspective on Electrification," *Journal of Economic History* 43, no. 2 (1983): 347–372.

4. Nathan Rosenberg, *Inside the Black Box: Technology and Economics* (New York: Cambridge University Press, 1982), 78.

5. Nathan Rosenberg, "Technological Change in the Machine Tool Industry, 1840–1910," *Journal of Economic History* 23, no. 4 (1963): 414–443.

6. Paul A. David, "The Dynamo and the Computer: An Historical Perspective on the Modern Productivity Paradox," *American Economic Review* 80, no. 2 (1990): 355–361.

7. The framework regarding the different choices faced by entrepreneurs in exploiting new technological opportunities is derived from Joshua Gans, Erin L. Scott, and Scott Stern, "Strategy for Start-Ups," *Harvard Business Review,* May–June 2018, 44–51. Point solutions are entrepreneurs pursuing what they term a value chain strategy that is oriented toward execution and toward slotting into existing value chains. Application solutions are mainly what they call a disruption strategy that is also oriented toward execution and toward providing new value chains. These can also be examples of intellectual property strategies that involve using formal intellectual property to protect device designs. Finally, system solutions are architectural strategies that involve new value chains as well as an investment in control to make those systems defensible.

Chapter 2

1. For the proceedings from this conference, see Ajay Agrawal, Joshua Gans, and Avi Goldfarb, eds., *The Economics of Artificial Intelligence: An Agenda* (Chicago: University of Chicago Press, 2019).

2. Paul Milgrom, personal email, January 17, 2017.

3. See Colin F. Camerer, "Artificial Intelligence and Behavioral Economics," comment by Daniel Kahneman, in Agrawal et al., *The Economics of Artificial Intelligence*, chapter 24, page 610.

4. See Betsey Stevenson, "Artificial Intelligence, Income, Employment, and Meaning," in Agrawal et al., *The Economics of Artificial Intelligence*, chapter 7, page 190.

5. Erik Brynjolfsson, Daniel Rock, and Chad Syverson, "Artificial Intelligence and the Modern Productivity Paradox: A Clash of Expectations and Statistics," in Agrawal et al., *The Economics of Artificial Intelligence*, chapter 1.

6. Timothy F. Bresnahan and Manuel Trajtenberg, "General Purpose Technologies 'Engines of Growth'?" *Journal of Econometrics* 65, no. 1 (1995): 83–108; T. Bresnahan and S. Greenstein, "Technical Progress and Co-invention in Computing and in the Uses of Computers," *Brookings Papers on Economic Activity, Microeconomics* (1996): 1–83.

7. Alanna Petroff, "Google CEO: AI is 'More Profound Than Electricity or Fire,'" CNN Business, January 24, 2018, https://money.cnn.com/2018/01/24 /technology/sundar-pichai-google-ai-artificial-intelligence/index.html.

8. S. Ransbotham et al., "Expanding AI's Impact with Organizational Learning," *MIT Sloan Management Review,* October 2020.

9. Catherine Jewell, "Artificial Intelligence: The New Electricity," *WIPO Magazine,* June 2019, https://www.wipo.int/wipo_magazine/en/2019/03/article _0001.html.

10. Ransbotham et al., "Expanding AI's Impact with Organizational Learning."

11. See figure 1 comparing panels A and B, in Daron Acemoglu et al., "Automation and the Workforce: A Firm-Level View from the 2019 Annual Business

Survey," conference paper, National Bureau of Economic Research, Cambridge, MA, February 2022, https://conference.nber.org/conf_papers/f159272.pdf.

12. Nathan Rosenberg, *Inside the Black Box: Technology and Economics* (New York: Cambridge University Press, 1982), 59.

13. Michael Specter, "Climate by Numbers," *New Yorker*, November 4, 2013, https://www.newyorker.com/magazine/2013/11/11/climate-by-numbers.

14. Michael Lewis, *The Fifth Risk* (New York: W. W. Norton & Company, 2018), 185, Kindle.

15. Lewis, *The Fifth Risk,* 186, Kindle.

16. Lewis, *The Fifth Risk,* 186, Kindle.

17. Lewis, *The Fifth Risk,* 186, Kindle.

Chapter 3

1. The challenges of determining whether advertising causes sales are even harder because advertisers target their ads to people they expect to purchase. For a discussion of causality in advertising, see T. Blake, C. Nosko, and S. Tadelis, "Consumer Heterogeneity and Paid Search Effectiveness: A Large-Scale Field Experiment," *Econometrica* 83 (2015): 155–174, https://doi.org/10.3982/ECTA12423; and Brett R. Gordon et al., "A Comparison of Approaches to Advertising Measurement: Evidence from Big Field Experiments at Facebook," *Marketing Science* 38, no. 2 (2019), https://pubsonline.informs.org/doi/10.1287/mksc.2018.1135. More generally, two recent books focus on explaining causal inference to a nonacademic audience. Judea Pearl and Dana Mackenzie's *The Book of Why* (New York: Basic Books, 2018) provides a computer science perspective. John List's *The Voltage Effect* (New York: Random House, 2022) provides an economics perspective that emphasizes that even when experiments are conducted, the results of those experiments may not apply when a solution is deployed at scale.

2. Larry Hardesty, "Two Amazon-Affiliated Economists Awarded Nobel Prize," Amazon Science, October 13, 2021, https://www.amazon.science/latest-news/two-amazon-affiliated-economists-awarded-nobel-prize.

3. Satinder Singh, Andy Oku, and Andrew Jackson, "Learning to Play Go from Scratch," *Nature*, October 19, 2017, https://www.nature.com/articles/550336a.

4. Avi Goldfarb and Jon R. Lindsay, "Prediction and Judgment: Why Artificial Intelligence Increases the Importance of Humans in War," *International Security* 46, no. 3 (2022): 7–50, doi: https://doi.org/10.1162/isec_a_00425.

5. Bonnie G. Buchanan and Danika Wright, "The Impact of Machine Learning on UK Financial Services," *Oxford Review of Economic Policy* 37, no. 3 (2021): 537–563, https://doi.org/10.1093/oxrep/grab016.

6. Kwame Opam, "Amazon Plans to Ship Your Packages Before You Even Buy Them," *Verge*, January 18, 2014, https://www.theverge.com/2014/1/18/5320636/amazon-plans-to-ship-your-packages-before-you-even-buy-them.

7. Anu Singh, Tyana Grundig, and David Common, "Hidden Cameras and Secret Trackers Reveal Where Amazon Returns End Up," CBC News, October 10, 2020, https://www.cbc.ca/news/canada/marketplace-amazon-returns-1.5753714.

8. You might wonder, if Amazon is just throwing out returns anyway, why even bother to pick up those products under ship-then-shop. The problem is, how

would Amazon know then that a consumer is disposing of a product rather than just using it?

Chapter 4

1. Michael Lewis, "Obama's Way," *Vanity Fair*, October 2012, https://www.vanityfair.com/news/2012/10/michael-lewis-profile-barack-obama.
2. H. Simon, "Administration of Public Recreational Facilities in Milwaukee," unpublished manuscript, Herbert A. Simon papers, Carnegie Mellon University Library.
3. L. Lamport, "Buridan's Principle," *Foundations of Physics* 42, no. 8 (2012): 1056–1066, http://lamport.azurewebsites.net/pubs/buridan.pdf.
4. For the exception that literally proves this rule, consider what happened the day Obama wore a tan suit: "Obama Tan Suit Controversy," Wikipedia, https://en.wikipedia.org/wiki/Obama_tan_suit_controversy.
5. This is just to make the math easier. For those algebraically inclined, suppose that the probability that it rains is p and that the cost of getting wet is w and the cost of carrying an umbrella if it doesn't rain is c. Then you'll be indifferent between carrying and not if $pw = (1-p)c$. Our example in the text assumes $p = 0.5$ and $w = c = \$10$.
6. Natalia Emanuel and Emma Harrington, "'Working' Remotely? Selection, Treatment and the Market Selection of Remote Work," mimeo, Harvard, 2021, https://scholar.harvard.edu/files/eharrington/files/trim_paper.pdf.
7. S. Larcom, F. Rauch, and T. Willems, "The Benefits of Forced Experimentation: Striking Evidence from the London Underground Network," *Quarterly Journal of Economics* 132, no. 4 (2017): 2019–2055.
8. D. P. Byrne and N. de Roos, "Startup Search Costs," *American Economic Journal: Microeconomics* 14, no. 2 (May 2022): 81–112.
9. Atul Gawande, *The Checklist Manifesto: How to Get Things Right* (New York: Henry Holt and Co., 2009), 61–62, Kindle.

Chapter 5

1. Economists feel a special affinity for this statement. We referenced the same quote in *Prediction Machines* when talking about airport lounges.
2. SF Staff, "Airports Are Becoming More Like Tourist Destinations," *Simple Flying*, January 5, 2020, https://simpleflying.com/airports-tourist-destinations/.
3. "Destination Airports," Gensler, n.d., https://www.gensler.com/blog/destination-airports.
4. Paul Brady, "The Top 10 International Airports," *Travel and Leisure*, September 8, 2021, https://www.travelandleisure.com/airlines-airports/coolest-new-airport-terminals.
5. Elliott Heath, "The Golf Course Inside an Airport," *Golf Monthly*, June 6, 2018, https://www.golfmonthly.com/features/the-game/golf-course-inside-an-airport-157780.
6. Incheon International Airport Corporation, 2016 Annual Report, https://www.airport.kr/co_file/en/file01/2016_annualReport(eng).pdf.
7. Airports Council International, "ACI Report Shows the Importance of the Airport Industry to the Global Economy," press release, April 22, 2020,

https://aci.aero/2020/04/22/aci-report-shows-the-importance-of-the-airport
-industry-to-the-global-economy/.

8. "Putting the AI in Air Traffic Control," Alan Turing Institute, January 17,
2020, https://www.turing.ac.uk/research/impact-stories/putting-ai-air-traffic
-control.

9. Arnoud Cornelissen, "AI System for Baggage Handling at Eindhoven Airport
Proves Successful," Innovation Origins, January 28, 2021, https://innovation
origins.com/en/ai-system-for-baggage-handling-at-eindhoven-airport-proves
-successful/.

10. Tower Fasteners, "The Future of AI in Aviation," press release, n.d., https://
www.towerfast.com/press-room/the-future-of-ai-in-aviation.

11. Xinyu Hu et al., "DeepETA: How Uber Predicts Arrival Times Using Deep
Learning," Uber Engineering, February 10, 2022, https://eng.uber.com/deepeta
-how-uber-predicts-arrival-times/.

12. From William Booth, "Maintaining a Competitive Hedge," *Washington Post*,
January 11, 2019, https://www.washingtonpost.com/graphics/2019/world/british
-hedgerows/; and the BBC documentary *Prince, Son and Heir: Charles at 70*,
December 31, 2018.

13. Steven D. Levitt and Stephen J. Dubner, *Freakonomics: A Rogue Economist
Explores the Hidden Side of Everything,* revised and expanded ed. (New York:
William Morrow, 2006), xiv.

14. Massachusetts Department of Agricultural Resources, "Greenhouse BMPs,"
n.d., https://ag.umass.edu/sites/ag.umass.edu/files/book/pdf/greenhousebmpfb.pdf.

15. Ric Bessin, Lee H. Townsend, and Robert G. Anderson, "Greenhouse Insect
Management," University of Kentucky, n.d., https://entomology.ca.uky.edu/ent60.

16. Massachusetts Department of Agricultural Resources, "Greenhouse BMPs."

17. Ecoation, "Human + Machine," n.d., https://www.ecoation.com/; Ecoation,
"Integrated Pest Management," n.d., https://7c94d4b4-da17-40b9-86cd
-fc64ec50f83b.filesusr.com/ugd/0a894f_a83293fa199c4f60a71254187a0b7f4c.pdf.

18. Ecoation, "Integrated Pest Management," Case 4.

Chapter 6

1. Atul Gawande, "The Checklist," *New Yorker*, December 2, 2007, https://www
.newyorker.com/magazine/2007/12/10/the-checklist.

2. A. Kwok and M-L McLaws, "How to Get Doctors to Hand Hygiene: Nudge
Nudge," *Antimicrobial Resistance and Infection Control* 4, supplement 1 (2015): O51,
https://www.ncbi.nlm.nih.gov/pmc/articles/PMC4474702/.

3. Ali Goli, David H. Reiley, and Hongkai Zhang, "Personalized Versioning:
Product Strategies Constructed from Experiments on Pandora," working paper,
presented at Quantitative Marketing and Economics Conference, UCLA, October 8,
2021. As we discussed in chapter 3, sometimes AI requires an experiment in order
to collect the data necessary for making the predictions. Here the AI complements
the experiment.

4. For the first analysis of this problem, see Susan Athey, Emilio Calvano, and
Joshua S. Gans, "The Impact of Consumer Multi-homing on Advertising Markets
and Media Competition," *Management Science* 64, no. 4 (2018): 1574–1590.

5. "Without Rules, There Is Chaos," YouTube, https://www.youtube.com
/watch?v=qoHU57KtUws.

6. John Stuart Mill, *On Liberty*, ed. David Spitz (New York: W. W. Norton and Company, 1975, based on 1859 edition), 98.

7. New York State Education Department, "The New York State Kindergarten Learning Standards," n.d., http://www.p12.nysed.gov/earlylearning/standards /documents/KindergartenLearningStandards2019-20.pdf.

8. "The State of the Global Education Crisis: A Path to Recovery," World Bank, n.d., https://www.worldbank.org/en/topic/education; "Overview," World Bank, n.d., https://www.worldbank.org/en/topic/education/overview#1; "Digital Technologies in Education," World Bank, n.d., https://www.worldbank.org/en/topic/edutech#1.

9. "Training Entrepreneurs," *VoxDevLit* 1, no. 2 (August 9, 2021), https:// voxdev.org/sites/default/files/Training_Entrepreneurs_Issue_2.pdf.

10. We discussed why such trials are useful in chapter 3.

11. Ken Robinson, *The Element: How Finding Your Passion Changes Everything* (New York: Penguin, 2009), 230.

Chapter 7

1. Worldometer, "Coronavirus Cases," https://www.worldometers.info/corona virus/country/us/, accessed November 25, 2021.

2. For a complete treatment of this, see Joshua Gans, *The Pandemic Information Gap: The Brutal Economics of COVID-19* (Cambridge, MA: MIT Press, 2020).

3. June-Ho Kim et al., "Emerging COVID-19 Success Story: South Korea Learned the Lessons of MERS," *Our World in Data*, March 5, 2021, https://our worldindata.org/covid-exemplar-south-korea.

4. Jennifer Chu, "Artificial Intelligence Model Detects Asymptomatic Covid-19 Infections through Cellphone-Recorded Coughs," *MIT News*, October 29, 2020, https://news.mit.edu/2020/covid-19-cough-cellphone-detection-1029.

5. Some AI solutions have begun to emerge. For instance, a study at the Greek border showed that a suitably developed reinforcement learning algorithm (taking into account, for example, mode of travel, departure points, and demographic information), updated weekly, could detect 1.85 times as many asymptomatic people as random surveillance. H. Bastani et al., "Efficient and Targeted COVID-19 Border Testing via Reinforcement Learning," *Nature* 599 (2021): 108–113, https:// doi.org/10.1038/s41586-021-04014-z.

6. Hannah Beech, "On the Covid Front Lines, When Not Getting Belly Rubs," *New York Times*, May 31, 2021, https://www.nytimes.com/2021/05/31/world/asia /dogs-coronavirus.html.

7. Michael J. Mina and Kristian G. Andersen, "COVID-19 Testing: One Size Does Not Fit All," *Science* 371, no. 6525 (2020): 126–127; Daniel B. Larremore et al., "Test Sensitivity Is Secondary to Frequency and Turnaround Time for COVID-19 Screening," *Science Advances* 7, no. 1 (2021), https://www.science.org/doi/10.1126 /sciadv.abd5393.

8. Joshua S. Gans, Avi Goldfarb, Ajay K. Agrawal, Sonia Sennik, Janice Stein, and Laura Rosella, "False-Positive Results in Rapid Antigen Tests for SARS-CoV-2," *JAMA* 327, no. 5 (2022): 485–486, https://jamanetwork.com/journals/jama/fullarticle /2788067.

9. Laura C. Rosella, Ajay K. Agrawal, Joshua S. Gans, Avi Goldfarb, Sonia Sennik, and Janice Stein, "Large-Scale Implementation of Rapid Antigen Testing for COVID-19 in Workplaces," *Science Advances* 8, no. 8 (2022), https://www

.science.org/doi/10.1126/sciadv.abm3608; "CDL Rapid Screening: Supporting the Launch of Workplace Rapid Screening across Canada," Creative Destruction Lab Rapid Screening Consortium, https://www.cdlrapidscreeningconsortium.com/.

10. The launch of the program was reported in "Like Wartime: Canadian Companies Unite to Start Mass Virus Testing," *New York Times*, February 18, 2021, https://www.nytimes.com/2021/01/30/world/americas/canada-coronavirus-rapid-test.html.

11. Laura C. Rosella et al., "Large-Scale Implementation of Rapid Antigen Testing for COVID-19 in Workplaces."

12. Joshua published the first book on the economics of Covid-19, focused on this precise point: Joshua Gans, *The Pandemic Information Gap: The Brutal Economics of COVID-19* (Cambridge, MA: MIT Press, 2020).

Chapter 8

1. Brian Christian, *The Most Human Human: What Artificial Intelligence Teaches Us About Being Alive* (New York: Anchor, 2011).

2. Ajay Agrawal, Joshua Gans, and Avi Goldfarb, "Artificial Intelligence: The Ambiguous Labor Market Impact of Automating Prediction," *Journal of Economic Perspectives* 33, no. 2 (2019): 31–50, https://pubs.aeaweb.org/doi/pdfplus/10.1257/jep.33.2.31.

3. Carl Benedikt Frey and Michael A. Osborne, "The Future of Employment: How Susceptible Are Jobs to Computerisation?" *Technological Forecasting and Social Change* 114 (January 2017): 254–280, https://www.sciencedirect.com/science/article/abs/pii/S0040162516302244; "A Study Finds Nearly Half of Jobs Are Vulnerable to Automation," *Economist*, April 24, 2018, https://www.economist.com/graphic-detail/2018/04/24/a-study-finds-nearly-half-of-jobs-are-vulnerable-to-automation; Aviva Hope Rutkin, "Report Suggests Nearly Half of US Jobs Are Vulnerable to Computerization," *MIT Technology Review*, September 12, 2013, https://www.technologyreview.com/2013/09/12/176475/report-suggests-nearly-half-of-us-jobs-are-vulnerable-to-computerization/.

4. Daron Acemoglu, "Harms of AI," working paper 29247, National Bureau of Economic Research, Cambridge, MA, September 2021, https://www.nber.org/papers/w29247; Daron Acemoglu and Pascual Restrepo, "Automation and New Tasks: How Technology Displaces and Reinstates Labor," *Journal of Economic Perspectives* 33 no. 2 (2019): 3–30; Jeffrey D. Sachs, "R&D, Structural Transformation, and the Distribution of Income," in *The Economics of Artificial Intelligence: An Agenda*, eds. Ajay Agrawal et al. (Chicago: University of Chicago Press, 2019), chapter 13. For an overall assessment, see Joshua Gans and Andrew Leigh, *Innovation + Equality: Creating a Future That Is More Star Trek than Terminator* (Cambridge, MA: MIT Press, 2019).

5. Tim Bresnahan, "Artificial Intelligence Technologies and Aggregate Growth Prospects," working paper, Stanford University, May 2019, https://web.stanford.edu/~tbres/AI_Technologies_in_use.pdf.

6. Our conclusion here is similar to Erik Brynjolfsson's in his discussion of the Turing Trap. Our argument, however, is different. We emphasize that it is in the AI developer's interest to focus on value and augmentation. Erik Brynjolfsson, "The Turing Trap: The Promise and Peril of Human-Like Artificial Intelligence," Stanford Digital Economy Lab, January 12, 2022, https://digitaleconomy.stanford.edu/news/the-turing-trap-the-promise-peril-of-human-like-artificial-intelligence/.

7. See, for example, Alvin Rajkomar, Jeffrey Dean, and Isaac Kohane, "Machine Learning in Medicine," *New England Journal of Medicine* 380 (2019): 1347–1358, https://www.nejm.org/doi/full/10.1056/NEJMra1814259; Sandeep Redd, John Fox, and Maulik P. Purchit, "Artificial Intelligence-Enabled Healthcare Delivery," *Journal of the Royal Society of Medicine* 112, no. 1 (2019), https://journals.sagepub .com/doi/full/10.1177/0141076818815510; Kun-Hsing Yu, Andrew L. Beam, and Isaac S. Kohane, "Artificial Intelligence in Healthcare," *Nature Biomedical Engineering* 2 (2018): 719–731, https://www.nature.com/articles/s41551-018-0305-z.

8. James Shaw et al., "Artificial Intelligence and the Implementation Challenge," *Journal of Medical Internet Research* 21, no. 7 (2019): e13659, doi: 10.2196 /13659; Yu et al., "Artificial Intelligence in Healthcare."

9. Siddhartha Mukherjee, "A.I. versus M.D.," *New Yorker*, March 27, 2017; and Cade Matz and Craig Smith, "Warnings of a Dark Side to AI in Health Care," *New York Times*, March 21, 2019.

10. Although we have never met Topol, we are fans of his work. We benefited greatly from his clear, timely, and insightful Twitter feed and other writings during our work creating a national program for rapid antigen testing during Covid-19. "CDL Rapid Screening Consortium," Creative Destruction Lab, https://www .cdlrapidscreeningconsortium.com/.

11. Avi Goldfarb, Bledi Taska, and Florenta Teodoridis, "Artificial Intelligence in Health Care? Evidence from Online Job Postings," *AEA Papers and Proceedings* 110 (2020): 400–404.

12. Steven Adelman and Harris A. Berman, "Why Are Doctors Burned Out? Our Health Care System Is a Complicated Mess," *STAT*, December 15, 2016, https://www.statnews.com/2016/12/15/burnout-doctors-medicine/.

13. Eric Topol, *Deep Medicine* (New York: Basic Books, 2019).

14. World Bank, "Leveling the Playing Field," *World Development Report 2021*, https://wdr2021.worldbank.org/stories/leveling-the-playing-field/, 104.

15. Morgane le Cam, "The Day Bluetooth Brought a Cardiologist to Every Village in Cameroon," *Geneva Solutions*, n.d., https://genevasolutions.news /explorations/11-african-solutions-for-the-future-world/the-day-bluetooth -brought-a-cardiologist-to-every-village-in-cameroon.

16. Steve Lohr, "What Ever Happened to IBM's Watson?" *New York Times*, July 16, 2021, https://www.nytimes.com/2021/07/16/technology/what-happened -ibm-watson.html?smid=tw-share.

17. A process we recommended using *Prediction Machine*'s AI Canvas.

Chapter 9

1. Rob Toews, "AlphaFold Is the Most Important Achievement in AI—Ever," *Forbes*, October 3, 2021, https://www.forbes.com/sites/robtoews/2021/10/03/alphafold-is -the-most-important-achievement-in-ai-ever/; Ewen Callaway, "'It Will Change Everything': DeepMind's AI Make Gigantic Leap in Solving Protein Structures," *Nature*, November 30, 2020, https://www.nature.com/articles/d41586-020-03348-4.

2. Will Douglas Heaven, "DeepMind's Protein-Folding AI Has Solved a 50-Year-Old Grand Challenge of Biology," *MIT Technology Review*, November 30, 2020, https://www.technologyreview.com/2020/11/30/1012712/deepmind -protein-folding-ai-solved-biology-science-drugs-disease/.

3. Toews, "AlphaFold Is the Most Important Achievement in AI—Ever."

4. Callaway, "'It Will Change Everything.'"

5. Iain M. Cockburn, Rebecca Henderson, and Scott Stern, "The Impact of Artificial Intelligence on Innovation: An Exploratory Analysis," in *The Economics of Artificial Intelligence: An Agenda*, eds. Agrawal et al. (Chicago: University of Chicago Press, 2019), 120. Stern delivered an excellent and highly accessible presentation of the ideas in this paper at our Machine Learning and the Market for Intelligence conference in 2018: Scott Stern, "AI, Innovation, and Economic Growth," YouTube, November 1, 2018, https://www.youtube.com/watch?v=zPeme4murCk&t=8s.

6. We see many AI-based research tools at our Creative Destruction Lab. Three examples of CDL graduates that are building research tools and have raised significant financing as of this writing: (1) Atomwise has raised $175 million to design an AI tool to predict the binding affinity of molecules to proteins to discover new small molecule medicines. Atomwise, "Behind the AI: Boosting Binding Affinity Predictions with Point-Based Networks," August 4, 2021, https://blog.atomwise.com/behind-the-ai-boosting-binding-affinity-predictions-with-point-based-networks; (2) Deep Genomics has raised $240 million to design an AI tool to predict the consequences of genetic mutations to discover new genetic medicines. Deep Genomics, "Deep Genomics Raises $180M in Series C Financing," July 28, 2021, https://www.deepgenomics.com/news/deep-genomics-raises-180m-series-c-financing/; (3) BenchSci has raised $100 million to design an AI to predict the optimal reagent for experiments to enhance therapeutic discovery. BenchSci, "BenchSci AI-Assisted Reagent Selection, n.d., https://www.benchsci.com/platform/ai-assisted-reagent-selection.

7. As extolled by Oliver Wendell Holmes; see H. J. Lane, N. Blum, and E. Fee, "Oliver Wendell Holmes (1809–1894) and Ignaz Philipp Semmelweis (1818–1865): Preventing the Transmission of Puerperal Fever," *American Journal of Public Health* 100, no. 6 (2010), 1008–1009, https://doi.org/10.2105/AJPH.2009.185363.

8. Dokyun Lee and Kartik Hosanagar, "How Do Recommender Systems Affect Sales Diversity? A Cross-Category Investigation via Randomized Field Experiment," *Information Systems Research* 30, no. 1 (2019): iii–viii, https://pubsonline.informs.org/doi/abs/10.1287/isre.2018.0800; email correspondence with Dokyun Lee, November 16, 2021.

9. Ajay Agrawal, John McHale, and Alex Oettl, "Superhuman Science: How Artificial Intelligence May Impact Innovation," working paper, Brookings, 2022.

10. Ewen Callaway, "'It Will Change Everything': DeepMind's AI Makes Gigantic Leap in Solving Protein Structures," *Nature* 588 (2020): 203–204, https://www.nature.com/articles/d41586-020-03348-4.

11. "AI for Discovery and Self-Driving Labs," Matter Lab, n.d., https://www.matter.toronto.edu/basic-content-page/ai-for-discovery-and-self-driving-labs.

Chapter 10

1. Severin Borenstein and James Bushnell, "Electricity Restructuring: Deregulation or Reregulation?" *Regulation* 23, no. 2 (2000), http://faculty.haas.berkeley.edu/borenste/download/Regulation00ElecRestruc.pdf.

2. Clayton M. Christensen, *The Innovator's Dilemma: When New Technologies Cause Great Firms to Fail* (Boston: Harvard Business Review Press, 1997). Prior work, such as Richard Foster's *Innovation: The Attacker's Advantage* (New York: Summit Books, 1986) explored similar ideas, although did not emphasize the term "disruption."

3. However, history has taught us that businesses faced with the kind of disruption that comes from the bottom up are often able to respond and co-opt the technology regardless. They can acquire entrants or double down in their investments and catch up. This allows them to leverage their other assets, and while waters might be stormy for a time, they can survive the process. For a broader discussion of these responses, see Joshua S. Gans, *The Disruption Dilemma* (Cambridge, MA: MIT Press, 2016).

4. Jill Lepore, "The Disruption Machine," *New Yorker*, June 16, 2014.

5. Tim Harford, "Why Big Companies Squander Good Ideas," *Financial Times*, September 6, 2018, https://www.ft.com/content/3c1ab748-b09b-11e8-8d14 -6f049d06439c.

6. Rebecca M. Henderson, and Kim B. Clark, "Architectural Innovation: The Reconfiguration of Existing Product Technologies and the Failure of Established Firms," *Administrative Science Quarterly* (1990): 9–30.

7. For more discussion of these differences, see Gans, *The Disruption Dilemma*.

8. A formal economic model of this is provided in Joshua Gans, "Internal Conflict and Disruptive Technologies," mimeo, Toronto, 2022.

9. For a detailed account of all of the machinations in the ebb and flow of Blockbuster's demise, see Gina Keating, *Netflixed: The Epic Battle for America's Eyeballs* (New York: Penguin, 2012). For a reminiscent account of the rise and fall of Blockbuster, watch the documentary *The Last Blockbuster* that explains how the business worked and provides a heartwarming account of the last remaining Blockbuster store, in Bend, Oregon.

Chapter 11

1. Joan Baum, *The Calculating Passion of Ada Byron* (Hamden, CT: Archon Books, 1986).

2. Ada is a graduate of our CDL program, and as of this writing has raised approximately $200 million to finance its growth.

3. Ada, "Zoom, the World's Fastest Growing Company, Delivers on Customer Experience with Ada," case study, n.d., https://www.ada.cx/case-study/zoom ?hsCtaTracking=bbb3dca6-ad19-42b2-97e3-8bcd92813842%7C754f3b30-ab8b -418d-b36c-d0ab3be3514f.

4. David Zax, "'I'm Feeling Lucky': Google Employee No. 59 Tells All," *Fast Company*, July 12, 2011, https://www.fastcompany.com/1766361/im-feeling-lucky -google-employee-no-59-tells-all; Nicholas Carlson, "Google Just Kills the 'I'm Feeling Lucky Button,'" *Business Insider*, September 8, 2010, https://www .businessinsider.com/google-just-effectively-killed-the-im-feeling-lucky-button -2010-9. Marissa Meyer claimed: "I think what's delightful about 'I'm Feeling Lucky' is that it reminds you there are real people here."

A philosopher thought it was all about Google's God complex—we kid you not. John Durham Peters, "Google Wants to Be God's Mind: The Secret Theology of 'I'm Feeling Lucky,'" *Salon*, July 19, 2015, https://www.salon.com/2015/07/19/google _wants_to_be_gods_mind_the_secret_theology_of_im_feeling_lucky/. We have to quote this:

> The home page's two options for scouting the web—"Google search" and "I'm feeling lucky"—are an essential touch. "I'm feeling lucky" is a subjective mode of address. This is not Google addressing its user with "You're feeling

lucky"; this is me, the first person, entering the web, and also the cry of the gambler, muttering incantations over something he can't control. The Google search page is the portal of desire, the throne to which people bring their petitions. (Its servers house the Archive of Wants.) "I'm feeling lucky" also invokes religious practices of casting lots. The frequent effectiveness of the "I'm feeling lucky" button gives Google a reason to brag. (Of late it usually takes you to a Wikipedia page, but earlier its results could be more surprising.)" It goes on: Even though Google makes no money on the 1 percent or so of searches that are done on the "lucky" button (which delivers only a single result, and thus none of the advertising peripherals), the company's leaders have been remarkably firm in keeping it in the face of criticism from the guardians of the bottom line. They know what they are doing. The lucky button amply repays the lost income by maintaining the oracular aura and geeky charm. Its loss would be incalculable. At the Google search page, you stand on the threshold and knock. Two alternatives await you side by side: the ancient one of divination and the modern one of Google. The cultural resonance of the company comes in pairing its computerized claim to trawl the totality with *I Ching*-like mystery. Ancient, modern; God, Google—the continuities are clear. Its search page is perhaps most religious in the simple structure of the search or quest. What do people seek? A signal amid the static. True love. A fugitive from justice. A lost key ring. Google can help find some of these things.

5. Janelle Shane, *You Look Like a Thing and I Love You* (New York: Little Brown, 2019), 144.

6. Lewis Mumford. *Technics and Civilization* (New York: Harcourt, Brace, 1934), 27.

Chapter 12

1. This chapter is based on Ajay Agrawal, Joshua Gans, and Avi Goldfarb, "How to Win with Machine Learning," *Harvard Business Review*, September–October 2020.

2. Marco Iansiti and Karim Lakhani, *Competing in the Age of AI* (Cambridge, MA: Harvard Business Review Press, 2020).

3. Joseph White, "GM Buys Cruise Automation to Speed Self-Driving Car Strategy," Reuters, March 11, 2016, https://www.reuters.com/article/us-gm -cruiseautomation-idUSKCN0WD1ND.

4. Clara Curiel-Lewandrowski et al., "Artificial Intelligence Approach in Melanoma," *Melanoma*, ed. D. Fisher and B. Bastian (New York: Springer, 2019), https://doi.org/10.1007/978-1-4614-7147-9_43; Adewole S. Adamson and Avery Smith, "Machine Learning and Health Care Disparities in Dermatology," *JAMA Dermatology* 154, no. 11 (2018): 1247–1248, https://jamanetwork.com/journals /jamadermatology/article-abstract/2688587.

Chapter 13

1. David J. Deming, "The Growing Importance of Decision-Making on the Job," working paper 28733, National Bureau of Economic Research, Cambridge, MA, 2021.

2. Chris Bengel, "Michael Jordan Shares Hilarious Response to Risking Injuries in Sneak Peek of 'The Last Dance' Documentary," CBS, April 19, 2020, https://www.cbssports.com/nba/news/michael-jordan-shares-hilarious-response-to-risking-injuries-in-sneak-peek-of-the-last-dance-documentary/.

3. Michael Jordan, "Depends How F—ing Bad the Headache Is!" YouTube, April 20, 2020, https://www.youtube.com/watch?v=2WWspa-mFZY; Bengel, "Michael Jordan Shares Hilarious Response."

4. Jordan, "Depends How F—ing Bad the Headache Is!"; Bengel, "Michael Jordan Shares Hilarious Response."

5. Ramnath Balasubramanian, Ari Libarikian, and Doug McElhaney, "Insurance 2030—The Impact of AI on the Future of Insurance," McKinsey, March 12, 2021, https://www.mckinsey.com/industries/financial-services/our-insights/insurance-2030-the-impact-of-ai-on-the-future-of-insurance#.

6. Fred Lambert, "Tesla Officially Launches Its Insurance Using 'Real-Time Driving Behavior,' Starting in Texas," Elektrek, October 14, 2021, https://electrek.co/2021/10/14/tesla-officially-launches-insurance-using-real-time-driving-behavior-texas/.

7. Miremad Soleymanian, Charles B. Weinberg, and Ting Zhu, "Sensor Data and Behavioral Tracking: Does Usage-Based Auto Insurance Benefit Drivers?," *Marketing Science* 38, no. 1 (2019).

8. Paul Green and Vithala Rao, "Conjoint Measurement for Qualifying Judgmental Data," *Journal of Marketing Research* 8, 355–363, p. 355. https://journals.sagepub.com/doi/pdf/10.1177/002224377100800312

9. Robert Zeithammer and Ryan P. Kellogg, "The Hesitant *Hai Gui*: Return-Migration Preferences of U.S.-Educated Chinese Scientists and Engineers," *Journal of Marketing Research* 50, no. 5 (2013), https://journals.sagepub.com/doi/abs/10.1509/jmr.11.0394?journalCode=mrja.

10. Of course, Bajari would say he wasn't the one who did it and that it was a little more complicated. He'd emphasize that he was part of a team that built the economics and data science groups at Amazon.

11. Katrina Lake, "Stitch Fix's CEO on Selling Personal Style to the Mass Market," *Harvard Business Review*, May–June 2018.

Chapter 14

1. Tom Krisher, "Feds: Uber Self-Driving SUV Saw Pedestrian, Did Not Brake," AP News, May 24, 2018, https://apnews.com/article/north-america-ap-top-news-mi-state-wire-az-state-wire-ca-state-wire-63ff0b97fe1c44f98e4ee02c70a6397e; T.S, "Why Uber's Self-Driving Car Killed a Pedestrian," *Economist*, May 29, 2018, https://www.economist.com/the-economist-explains/2018/05/29/why-ubers-self-driving-car-killed-a-pedestrian.

2. Uriel J. Garcia and Karina Bland, "Tempe Police Chief: Fatal Uber Crash Likely 'Unavoidable' for Any Kind of Driver," *AZCentral*, March 2018, https://www.azcentral.com/story/news/local/tempe/2018/03/20/tempe-police-chief-fatal-uber-crash-pedestrian-likely-unavoidable/442829002/.

3. National Transportation Safety Board, "Collison between Vehicle Controlled by Developmental Automated Driving System and Pedestrian, Accident Report (Washington, DC: NTSB, March 18, 2018), https://www.ntsb.gov/investigations/AccidentReports/Reports/HAR1903.pdf.

4. Hilary Evans Cameron, Avi Goldfarb, and Leah Morris, "Artificial Intelligence for a Reduction of False Denials in Refugee Claims," *Journal of Refugee Studies* 35, no. 1 (2022), https://doi.org/10.1093/jrs/feab054.

5. Hilary Evans Cameron, *Refugee Law's Fact-Finding Crisis: Truth, Risk, and the Wrong Mistake* (Cambridge, UK: Cambridge University Press, 2018).

6. For an analysis of such thinking ahead, see P. Bolton and A. Faure-Grimaud, "Thinking Ahead: The Decision Problem," *Review of Economic Studies* 76, no. 4 (2009): 1205–1238. For its application to prediction machines, see Ajay Agrawal, Joshua Gans, and Avi Goldfarb, "Prediction, Judgment, and Complexity: A Theory of Decision-Making and Artificial Intelligence," in *The Economics of Artificial Intelligence: An Agenda* (Chicago: University of Chicago Press, 2018), 89–110.

7. A model of judgment acquired by experience is contained in Ajay Agrawal, Joshua S. Gans, and Avi Goldfarb, "Human Judgment and AI Pricing," *AEA Papers and Proceedings* 108 (2018): 58–63.

8. This draws on ideas about changes in medical regulation discussed in Ariel Dora Stern and W. Nicholson Price II, "Regulatory Oversight, Causal Inference, and Safe and Effective Health Care Machine Learning," *Biostatistics* 21, no. 2 (2020): 363–367, https://academic.oup.com/biostatistics/article/21/2/363/5631849.

Chapter 15

1. Peter Baghurst et al., "Environmental Exposure to Lead and Children's Intelligence at the Age of Seven Years: The Port Pirie Cohort Study," *New England Journal of Medicine* 327, no. 18 (1992): 1279–1284.

2. This 80% number is based on a list they provided. More formally, the area under the receiver operating characteristic (AUROC) is 0.95. In other words, given a choice between a lead pipe and a nonlead pipe, their model will correctly pick the lead one 95% of the time, where pure chance would be 50%.

3. Alexis C. Madrigal, "How a Feel-Good Story Went Wrong in Flint," *Atlantic*, January 3, 2019, https://www.theatlantic.com/technology/archive/2019/01/how-machine-learning-found-flints-lead-pipes/578692/.

4. "The Lead-Pipe Finder," The Best Inventions of 2021, *Time*, November 10, 2021, https://time.com/collection/best-inventions-2021/6113124/blueconduit/; Zahra Ahmad, "Flint Replaces More Lead Pipes Using Predictive Model, Researches Say," MLive, June 27, 2019, https://www.mlive.com/news/flint/2019/06/flint-replaces-more-lead-pipes-using-predictive-model-researchers-say.html; Adele Peters, "We Don't Know Where All the Lead Pipes Are. This Tool Helps Find Them," *Fast Company*, October 4, 2021, https://www.fastcompany.com/90682174/this-tool-figures-out-which-houses-are-most-likely-to-have-lead-pipes; Sidney Fussell, "An Algorithm Is Helping a Community Detect Lead Pipes," *Wired*, January 14, 2021, https://www.wired.com/story/algorithm-helping-community-detect-lead-pipes/; Madrigal, "How a Feel-Good Story Went Wrong in Flint."

5. National Weather Association, "About NWA," n.d., https://nwas.org/about-nwa/; Ben Alonzo, "Types of Meteorology," *Sciencing*, April 24, 2017, https://sciencing.com/types-meteorology-8031.html; much of this section draws on an interview with former National Weather Association president Todd Lericos on November 17, 2021.

6. Author interview with Todd Lericos, November 17, 2021.

7. Michael Lewis, *The Fifth Risk* (New York: W. W. Norton & Company, 2018), 131, Kindle.

8. Author interview with Todd Lericos.

9. Andrew Blum, *The Weather Machine* (New York: Ecco, 2019), 159, Kindle.

10. Blum, *The Weather Machine,* 160.

11. Author interview with Todd Lericos.

12. Author interview with Todd Lericos.

13. It is also possible that a more senior manager may rely on an AI to make direct recommendations that they are likely to follow rather than people who work for them. An AI has the advantage of having its objectives aligned with the senior manager compared with people who have their own interests. Nonetheless, when prediction machines are imperfect, the manager might want people to expend effort in coming up with recommendations that drive decisions. This will have an impact on whether the manager follows the AI or instead gives subordinates some degree of decision authority. For more, see Susan C. Athey, Kevin A. Bryan, and Joshua S. Gans, "The Allocation of Decision Authority to Human and Artificial Intelligence," *AEA Papers and Proceedings* 110 (2020): 80–84.

14. Ajay Agrawal, Joshua S. Gans, and Avi Goldfarb, "Artificial Intelligence: The Ambiguous Labor Market Impact of Automating Prediction," *Journal of Economic Perspectives* 33, no. 2 (2019): 31–50, https://pubs.aeaweb.org/doi/pdfplus/10.1257/jep.33.2.31.

15. Agrawal et al., "Artificial Intelligence."

Chapter 16

1. Thomas C. Schelling, *The Strategy of Conflict* (Cambridge, MA: Harvard University Press, 1960), 80.

2. If you answered 4:20 p.m., you have another reason why you miss lots of meetings.

3. J. Roberts and P. Milgrom, *Economics, Organization and Management* (Englewood Cliffs, NJ: Prentice-Hall, 1992), 126–311.

4. H. A. Simon, *The Sciences of the Artificial,* 3rd ed. (Cambridge, MA: MIT Press, 2019).

5. For a mathematical treatment, see J. Sobel, "How to Count to One Thousand," *Economic Journal* 102, no. 410 (1992): 1–8.

6. R. M. Henderson and K. B. Clark, "Architectural Innovation: The Reconfiguration of Existing Product Technologies and the Failure of Established Firms," *Administrative Science Quarterly* 35, no. 1 (1990): 9–30.

7. Ajay K. Agrawal, Joshua S. Gans, and Avi Goldfarb, "AI Adoption and System-Wide Change," working paper w28811, National Bureau of Economic Research, Cambridge, MA, 2021.

8. https://www.mckinsey.com/business-functions/mckinsey-digital/how-we-help-clients/flying-across-the-sea-propelled-by-ai.

9. Maggie Mae Armstrong, "Cheat Sheet: What Is Digital Twin?," *IBM Business Operations* blog, December 4, 2020, https://www.ibm.com/blogs/internet-of-things/iot-cheat-sheet-digital-twin/.

10. "The Power of Massive, Intelligent, Digital Twins," Accenture, June 7, 2021, https://www.accenture.com/ca-en/insights/health/digital-mirrored-world.

11. Michael Grieves and John Vickers, "Digital Twin: Mitigating Unpredictable, Undesirable Emergent Behavior in Complex Systems," *Transdisciplinary Perspectives*

on Complex Systems (New York: Springer, 2016), 85–113, https://link.springer.com /chapter/10.1007/978-3-319-38756-7_4.

12. Grieves and Vickers, "Digital Twin: Mitigating Unpredictable, Undesirable Emergent Behavior in Complex Systems."

13. "Virtual Singapore," Prime Minister's Office, National Research Foundation, Singapore, https://www.nrf.gov.sg/programmes/virtual-singapore; DXC Technology, "Why Cities Are Creating Digital Twins," GovInsider, March 18, 2020, https://govinsider.asia/innovation/dxc-why-cities-are-creating-digital-twins/.

14. "Pushing the Boundaries of Renewable Energy Production with Azure Digital Twins," Microsoft Customer Stories, November 30, 2020, https://customers .microsoft.com/en-in/story/848311-doosan-manufacturing-azure-digital-twins.

Chapter 17

1. "Cooking," National Fire Protection Association, n.d., https://www.nfpa.org /Public-Education/Fire-causes-and-risks/Top-fire-causes/Cooking.

2. Isaac Ehrlich and Gary S. Becker, "Market Insurance, Self-Insurance, and Self-Protection," *Journal of Political Economy* 80, no. 4 (1972): 623–648; and John M. Marshall, "Moral Hazard," *American Economic Review* 66, no. 5 (1976): 880–890.

3. Daniel Schreiber, "Precision Underwriting," *Lemonade* blog, n.d., https:// www.lemonade.com/blog/precision-underwriting/.

4. Daniel Schreiber, "AI Eats Insurance," *Lemonade* blog, n.d., https://www .lemonade.com/blog/ai-eats-insurance/.

5. Daniel Schreiber, "Two Years of Lemonade: A Super Transparency Chronicle," *Lemonade* blog, n.d., https://www.lemonade.com/blog/two-years-transparency/.

6. IPC Research, "Lemonade IPO: A Unicorn Vomiting a Rainbow," *Insurance Insider*, June 9, 2020, https://www.insidepandc.com/article/2876fsvzg2scz9uy1iww0 /lemonade-ipo-a-unicorn-vomiting-a-rainbow.

Chapter 18

1. Sendhil Mullainathan and Ziad Obermeyer, "Diagnosing Physician Error: A Machine Learning Approach to Low-Value Health Care," *Quarterly Journal of Economics* 137, no. 2 (2022): 679–727, online appendix 3, https://academic.oup.com /qje/advance-article-abstract/doi/10.1093/qje/qjab046/6449024.

2. Mullainathan and Obermeyer, "Diagnosing Physician Error."

3. See the classic treatment by Jeffrey E. Harris, "The Internal Organization of Hospitals: Some Economic Implications," *Bell Journal of Economics* (1977): 467–482. Or the textbook discussion in Jay Bhattacharya, Timothy Hyde, and Peter Tu, *Health Economics* (London: Red Globe Press, 2014).

4. This discussion is based on Ajay Agrawal, Joshua Gans, and Avi Goldfarb, "Similarities and Differences in the Adoption of General Purpose Technologies," working paper, University of Toronto, 2022, https://conference.nber.org/conf _papers/f158748.pdf, which in turn draws on Mullainathan and Obermeyer's appendix 3. Of course, this discussion abstracts from a variety of other considerations that are covered by Mullainathan and Obermeyer, such as physician private information and patients at high risk that the doctors don't send for a test.

5. See, e.g., Department of Emergency Medicine, "Mission," University of Pittsburgh website, https://www.emergencymedicine.pitt.edu/about/mission.

6. Eric Topol, *Deep Medicine* (New York: Basic Books, 2019).

7. Alvin Rajkomar, Jeffrey Dean, and Isaac Kohane, "Machine Learning in Medicine," *New England Journal of Medicine* 380 (2019): 1347–1358, https://www.nejm.org/doi/pdf/10.1056/NEJMra1814259?articleTools=true.

8. Jürgen Knapp et al., "Influence of Prehospital Physician Presence on Survival after Severe Trauma: Systematic Review and Meta-analysis," *Journal of Trauma and Acute Care Surgery* 87, no. 4 (2019): 978–989, https://journals.lww.com/jtrauma/Abstract/2019/10000/Influence_of_prehospital_physician_presence_on.43.aspx.

9. Victor Nathan Chappuis et al., "Emergency Physician's Dispatch by a Paramedic-Staffed Emergency Medical Communication Centre: Sensitivity, Specificity and Search for a Reference Standard," *Scandinavian Journal of Trauma, Resuscitation and Emergency Medicine* 29, no. 31 (2012), https://sjtrem.biomedcentral.com/articles/10.1186/s13049-021-00844-y.

10. The classic treatments of this issue are Edith Penrose, *The Theory of the Growth of the Firm* (Oxford, UK: Oxford University Press, 2009); and Kenneth J. Arrow, *The Limits of Organization* (New York: Norton, 1974). A formal treatment is from Oliver Hart and Bengt Holmstrom, "A Theory of Firm Scope," *Quarterly Journal of Economics* 125, no. 2 (2010): 483–513.

11. Rebecca Henderson and Kim B. Clark referred to these innovations as modular and architectural innovations respectively. Rebecca M. Henderson and Kim B. Clark, "Architectural Innovation: The Reconfiguration of Existing Product Technologies and the Failure of Established Firms," *Administrative Science Quarterly* (1990): 9–30. See also Joshua Gans, *The Disruption Dilemma* (Cambridge, MA: MIT Press, 2016).

Epilogue

1. E. Pierson et al., "An Algorithmic Approach to Reducing Unexplained Pain Disparities in Underserved Populations," *Nature Medicine* 27, no. 1 (2012): 136–140, https://doi.org/10.1038/s41591-020-01192-7.

2. J. H. Kellgren and J. S. Lawrence, "Radiological Assessment of Osteo-Arthrosis," *Annals of the Rheumatic Diseases* 16, no. 4 (1957): 494, https://ard.bmj.com/content/16/4/494; Mark D. Kohn, Adam A. Sassoon, and Navin D. Fernando, "Classification in Brief: Kellgren-Lawrence Classification of Osteoarthritis," *Clinical Orthopaedics and Related Research* 474, no. 8 (2016) 1886–1893, https://www.ncbi.nlm.nih.gov/pmc/articles/PMC4925407/.

3. For example, see J. E. Collins et al., "Trajectories and Risk Profiles of Pain in Persons with Radiographic, Symptomatic Knee Osteoarthritis: Data from the Osteoarthritis Initiative," *Osteoarthritis and Cartilage* 22 (2014): 622–630.

4. E. Pierson et al., "An Algorithmic Approach to Reducing Unexplained Pain Disparities in Underserved Populations."

5. April Glaser and Rani Molla, "A (Not-So) Brief History of Gender Discrimination Lawsuits in Silicon Valley," Vox, April 10, 2017, https://www.vox.com/2017/4/10/15246444/history-gender-timeline-discrimination-lawsuits-legal-silicon-valley-google-oracle--note; Sheelah Kolhatkar, "The Tech Industry Gender-Discrimination Problem, *New Yorker*, November 13, 2017, https://www.newyorker.com/magazine/2017/11/20/the-tech-industrys-gender-discrimination-problem; David Streitfeld, "Ellen Pao Loses Silicon Valley Bias Case Against Kleiner Perkins," *New York Times*, March 27, 2015, https://www.nytimes.com/2015/03/28/technology/ellen-pao-kleiner-perkins-case-decision.html.

6. David Streitfeld, "Kleiner Perkins Portrays Ellen Pao as Combative and Resentful in Sex Bias Trial," *New York Times*, March 11, 2015, https://www.nytimes.com/2015/03/12/technology/kleiner-perkins-portrays-ellen-pao-as-combative-and-resentful-in-sex-bias-trial.html.

7. This structure builds on J. Kleinberg et al., "Algorithms as Discrimination Detectors," *Proceedings of the National Academy of Sciences* 117, no. 48 (2020): 30096-30100, https://www.pnas.org/content/pnas/117/48/30096.full.pdf.

8. Marianne Bertrand and Sendhil Mullainathan, "Are Emily and Greg More Employable Than Lakisha and Jamal? A Field Experiment on Labor Market Discrimination," *American Economic Review* 94, no. 4 (2004): 991–1013, http://www.jstor.org/stable/3592802.

9. Ziad Obermeyer et al., "Dissecting Racial Bias in an Algorithm Used to Manage the Health of Populations," *Science* 366, no. 6464 (2019): 447–453, https://www.science.org/doi/10.1126/science.aax2342.

10. Sendhil Mullainathan, "Biased Algorithms Are Easier to Fix Than Biased People," *New York Times*, December 6, 2019, https://www.nytimes.com/2019/12/06/business/algorithm-bias-fix.html.

11. Mullainathan, "Biased Algorithms Are Easier to Fix Than Biased People."

12. Obermeyer et al., "Dissecting Racial Bias."

13. Obermeyer et al., "Dissecting Racial Bias."

14. Mullainathan, "Biased Algorithms Are Easier to Fix Than Biased People."

15. Carmina Ravanera and Sarah Kaplan, "An Equity Lens on Artificial Intelligence," Institute for Gender and the Economy, Rotman School of Management, University of Toronto, August 15, 2021, https://cdn.gendereconomy.org/wp-content/uploads/2021/09/An-Equity-Lens-on-Artificial-Intelligence-Public-Version-English-1.pdf.

16. Kleinberg et al., "Algorithms as Discrimination Detectors."

17. Algorithmic bias can be decomposed completely into three components: (1) bias in the choice of input variables; (2) bias in the choice of outcome measure, and (3) bias in the construction of the training procedure. After accounting for these three forms of bias, any remaining disparity corresponds to the structural disadvantage of one group relative to another. Source: Kleinberg et al., "Algorithms as Discrimination Detectors."

18. Bernie Wilson, "Schilling Fined for Smashing Ump Camera," AP News, June 2, 2003, https://apnews.com/article/774eb21353c94032b8b175d3f55d3e7d; Katie Dean, "Umpires to Tech: You're Out!" *Wired*, June 18, 2003, https://www.wired.com/2003/06/umpires-to-tech-youre-out/.

19. Dominick Reuter, "1 Out of Every 153 American Workers Is an Amazon Employee," *Business Insider*, July 30, 2021, https://www.businessinsider.com/amazon-employees-number-1-of-153-us-workers-head-count-2021-7.

20. Jeffrey Dastin, "Amazon Scraps Secret AI Recruiting Tool That Showed Bias Against Women," Reuters, October 10, 2018, https://www.reuters.com/article/us-amazon-com-jobs-automation-insight-idUSKCN1MK08G.

21. Matthew Yglesias, "Automate as Much Traffic Enforcement as Possible," Slow Boring, November 4, 2021, www.slowboring.com/p/traffic-enforcement.

22. Marzyeh Ghassemi, lecture, NBER AI 2021, Cambridge, MA, September 23, 2021, https://www.youtube.com/watch?v=lfDu5337quU.

INDEX

ACKNOWLEDGMENTS

We express our thanks to the people who contributed to this book with their time, ideas, and patience. In particular, we thank Liran Belenzon of BenchSci, Jackie French Curran of Family Care Midwives, Ali Goli of the University of Washington, Kartik Hosanagar of the University of Pennsylvania, DK Lee of Boston University, Todd Lericos of the National Weather Service, Michael Murchison of Ada, Ziad Obermeyer of UC Berkeley, David Reiley of Pandora, and Eric Schwartz of BlueConduit for the time they spent with us in interviews. Also, we thank our colleagues for discussions and feedback, including Pieter Abbeel, Daron Acemoglu, Anousheh Ansari, Susan Athey, Joscha Bach, Laleh Behjat, James Bergstra, Dror Berman, Scott Bonham, Francesco Bova, Timothy Bresnahan, Kevin Bryan, Erik Brynjolfsson, Elizabeth Caley, Emilio Calvano, Hilary Evans Cameron, Christian Catalini, James Cham, Brian Christian, Iain Cockburn, Sally Daub, Helene Desmarais, Pedro Domingos, Mark Evans, Haig Farris, Chen Fong, Ash Fontana, Chris Forman, John Francis, Marzyeh Ghassemi, Anindya Ghose, Suzanne Gildert, Inmar Givoni, Ben Goertzel, Alexandra Greenhill, Shane Greenstein, Daniel Gross, Shane Gu, Chris Hadfield, Gillian Hadfield, Avery Haviv, Abraham Heifets, Rebecca Henderson, Geoff Hinton, Tim Hodgson, Marco Iansiti, Trevor Jamieson, Steve Jurvetson. Daniel Kahneman, Aidan Kehoe, John Kelleher, Vinod Khosla, Karin Klein, Anton Korinek, Katya Kudashkina, Michael Kuhlmann, Karim Lakhani, Allen Lau, Eva Lau, Yann LeCun, Mara Lederman, Andrew Leigh, Jon Lindsay, Shannon Liu, Hamidreza Mahyar, Jeff Marowits, Kory Mathewson, Kristina McElheran, John McHale, Roger Melko, Paul Milgrom, Timo Minssen, Matt Mitchell, Sendhil Mullainathan, Kashyap Murali, Ken Nickerson, Olivia Norton, Saman Nouranian, Alex Oettl, Barney Pell, Patrick Pichette, Ingmar

Posner, Jim Poterba, Tomi Poutanen, Andrea Prat, Nicholson Price, Samantha Price, Jennifer Redmond, Pascual Restrepo, Geordie Rose, Laura Rosella, Frank Rudzicz, Stuart Russell, Russ Salakhutdinov, Bahram Sameti, Sampsa Samila, Amir Sariri, Reza Satchu, Jay Shaw, Jiwoong Shin, Ashmeet Sidana, Brian Silverman, Bruce Simpson, Avery Slater, Dilip Soman, John Stackhouse, Janice Stein, Ariel Dora Stern, Scott Stern, Joseph Stiglitz, Scott Stornetta, K. Sudhir, Minjee Sun, Rich Sutton, Shahram Tafazoli, Isaac Tamblyn, Bledi Taska, Graham Taylor, Florenta Teodoridis, Patricia Thaine, Andrew Thompson, Tony Tjan, Rich Tong, Manuel Trajtenberg, Dan Trefler, Catherine Tucker, William Tunstall-Pedoe, Tiger Tyagarajan, Raquel Urtasun, Eric Van den Steen, Hal Varian, Ryan Webb, Dan Wilson, Nathan Yang, and Shivon Zilis. Excellent research assistance was provided by Alex Burnett, Lee Goldfarb, Leah Morris, Verina Que, Sergio Santana, Wenqi Zhang, and Yan Zhou. The Creative Destruction Lab and Rotman School staffs have been fantastic, including Carol Deneka, Rachel Harris, Jennifer Hildebrandt, Malaika Kapur, Amarpreet Kaur, Khalid Kurji, Lisa Mah, Ken McGuffin, Sonia Sennik, Kristjan Sigurdson, and many others. We thank our current and former deans for their support of this project, including Susan Christoffersen, Ken Corts, and Tiff Macklem. We also thank Jeff Kehoe for stellar editing, as well as our agent, Jim Levine. Many of the ideas in the book build on research supported by the Social Sciences and Humanities Research Council of Canada and by the Sloan Foundation with David Michel and Danny Goroff's support under the NBER Economics of Artificial Intelligence grant. We are grateful for their support. Finally, we thank our families for their patience and contributions during this process: Gina, Amelia, Andreas, Natalie, Belanna, Ariel, Annika, Rachel, Anna, Sam, and Ben.

ABOUT THE AUTHORS

AJAY AGRAWAL is a professor of strategic management and the Geoffrey Taber Chair in Entrepreneurship and Innovation at the University of Toronto's Rotman School of Management. He is the founder of the Creative Destruction Lab and cofounder of NEXT Canada, both not-for-profit programs that support the commercialization of science via entrepreneurship. He is a research associate at the National Bureau of Economic Research, in Cambridge, Massachusetts; an academic advisory council member at the Center on Regulation and Markets at Brookings, in Washington, DC; an advisory board member at Carnegie Mellon University's Block Center for Technology and Society, in Pittsburgh; and a faculty affiliate at the Vector Institute for Artificial Intelligence, in Toronto. Ajay conducts research on the economics of innovation and serves on the editorial board of *Management Science*. He is a cofounder of the AI/robotics company Sanctuary. The company's mission is to create the world's first humanlike intelligence in general-purpose humanoid robots. Ajay holds a PhD in applied economics from the University of British Columbia. He was appointed a Member of the Order of Canada in 2022.

JOSHUA GANS is a professor of strategic management and the holder of the Jeffrey S. Skoll Chair of Technical Innovation and Entrepreneurship at the Rotman School of Management, University of Toronto. Joshua is also the chief economist at the University of Toronto's Creative Destruction Lab. Joshua has over 150 peer-reviewed academic publications and is the editor (strategy) of *Management Science*. He is a research associate at the National Bureau of Economic Research and holds fellowships at MIT, e61 Institute, Luohan Academy, the International Centre for Economic Analysis, Melbourne Business School, the Acceleration Consortium, and the Academy of Social Sciences, Australia. He has authored two successful textbooks and written ten popular books, including *Parentonomics* (2009), *Information Wants to Be Shared* (2012), *The Disruption Dilemma* (2016), *Scholarly Publishing and Its Discontents* (2017), *Innovation + Equality* (2019), *The Pandemic Information Gap* (2020), and *The Pandemic Information Solution* (2021). Joshua holds a PhD in economics from Stanford University and, in 2008, was awarded the Economic Society of Australia's Young Economist Award (the Australian equivalent of the John Bates Clark medal).

AVI GOLDFARB is the Rotman Chair in Artificial Intelligence and Healthcare and a professor of marketing at the Rotman School of Management, University of Toronto. Avi is also the chief data scientist at the Creative Destruction Lab, a faculty affiliate at the Vector Institute and at the Schwartz Reisman Institute for Technology and Society, a scientific advisory board member of HiParis!, a research associate at the National Bureau of Economic Research, and a former senior editor at *Marketing Science*. Avi's research focuses on the opportunities and challenges of the digital economy. He has published academic articles in marketing, computing, law, management, medicine, physics, political science, public health, statistics, and economics. His work on online advertising won the INFORMS Society of Marketing Science Long-Term Impact Award. Avi testified before the US Senate Judiciary Committee on competition and privacy in digital advertising. He holds a PhD in economics from Northwestern University.